MW01154517

Get the eBooks FREE!

(PDF, ePub, Kindle, and liveBook all included)

We believe that once you buy a book from us, you should be able to read it in any format we have available. To get electronic versions of this book at no additional cost to you, purchase and then register this book at the Manning website.

Go to https://www.manning.com/freebook and follow the instructions to complete your pBook registration.

That's it!
Thanks from Manning!

Classic Computer Science Problems
in Python

Classic Computer Science Problems in Python

DAVID KOPEC

MANNING
SHELTER ISLAND

Manning Publications Co.
20 Baldwin Road
PO Box 761
Shelter Island, NY 11964

Development editor:	Jennifer Stout
Technical development editor:	Frances Buontemp
Review editor:	Aleksandar Dragosavljević
Production editor:	Deirdre Hiam
Copy editor:	Andy Carroll
Proofreader:	Katie Tennant
Technical proofreader:	Juan Rufes
Typesetter:	Dottie Marsico
Cover designer:	Marija Tudor

ISBN 9781617295980
Printed in the United States of America
1 2 3 4 5 6 7 8 9 10 – SP – 24 23 22 21 20 19

Dedicated to my grandmother, Erminia Antos,
a lifelong teacher and learner.

contents

acknowledgments

Thank you, everyone at Manning who helped in the production of this book: Cheryl Weisman, Deirdre Hiam, Katie Tennant, Dottie Marsico, Janet Vail, Barbara Mirecki, Aleksandar Dragosavljević, Mary Piergies, and Marija Tudor.

I thank acquisitions editor Brian Sawyer, who wisely steered us toward attacking Python after I finished Swift. Thank you, development editor Jennifer Stout, for always having a positive attitude. Thanks go to technical editor Frances Buontempo, who provided careful consideration of each chapter and gave detailed, useful feedback at every turn. I thank copyeditor Andy Carroll, whose superb attention to detail on both the Swift book and this one caught several of my mistakes, and also my technical proofreader, Juan Rufes.

The following people also reviewed the book: Al Krinker, Al Pezewski, Alan Bogusiewicz, Brian Canada, Craig Henderson, Daniel Kenney-Jung, Edmond Sesay, Ewa Baranowska, Gary Barnhart, Geoff Clark, James Watson, Jeffrey Lim, Jens Christian, Bredahl Madsen, Juan Jimenez, Juan Rufes, Matt Lemke, Mayur Patil, Michael Bright, Roberto Casadei, Sam Zaydel, Thorsten Weber, Tom Jeffries, and Will Lopez. Thanks go to all who provided constructive and specific criticism during the book's development. Your feedback was incorporated.

I thank my family, friends, and colleagues who encouraged me to take on this book project immediately following the publication of *Classic Computer Science Problems in Swift*. I thank my online friends on Twitter and elsewhere who have provided encouraging words and helped promote the book in ways small and large. And I thank my wife, Rebecca Kopec, and my mom, Sylvia Kopec, who are always supportive of my projects.

We developed this book in a fairly short period of time. The vast majority of the manuscript was written over the summer of 2018, based on the earlier Swift version. I appreciate that Manning was willing to compress its (usually much longer) process to enable me to work during a schedule that was convenient to me. I know this put pressure on the entire team as we went through three rounds of reviews at multiple different levels amongst many different people in just a few months. Most readers would be amazed at how many different kinds of reviews a technical book by a traditional publisher goes through and how many people have their part in critiquing and revising it. From the technical proofer to the copy editor, the review editor, all of the official reviewers, and everyone in between, I thank you!

Finally, most importantly, I thank my readers for purchasing this book. In a world full of halfhearted online tutorials, I think it is important to support the development of books that provide the same author's voice throughout an extended volume. Online tutorials can be superb resources, but your purchase enables full-length, vetted, and carefully developed books to still have a place in computer science education.

about this book

Trademarks

Trademarked names appear in this book. Rather than use a trademark symbol with every occurrence of a trademarked name, the names are only used in an editorial fashion and to the benefit of the trademark owner, with no intention of infringement of the trademark. "Python" is a registered trademark of the Python Software Foundation. "Connect Four" is a trademark of Hasbro, Inc.

Book forum

Purchase of *Classic Computer Science Problems in Python* includes free access to a private web forum run by Manning Publications where you can make comments about the book, ask technical questions, and receive help from the author and from other users. To access the forum, go to https://www.manning.com/books/classic-computer-science-problems-in-python. You can also learn more about Manning's forums and the rules of conduct at https://forums.manning.com/forums/about.

Manning's commitment to our readers is to provide a venue where a meaningful dialogue between individual readers and between readers and the author can take place. It is not a commitment to any specific amount of participation on the part of the author, whose contribution to the forum remains voluntary (and unpaid). We suggest you try asking him some challenging questions lest his interest stray! The forum and the archives of previous discussions will be accessible from the publisher's website as long as the book is in print.

about the author

David Kopec is an assistant professor of Computer Science & Innovation at Champlain College in Burlington, Vermont. He is an experienced software developer and the author of *Classic Computer Science Problems in Swift* (Manning, 2018), and *Dart for Absolute Beginners* (Apress, 2014). David holds a bachelor's degree in economics and a master's in computer science, both from Dartmouth College. You can reach David on Twitter @davekopec.

about the cover illustration

The figure on the cover of *Classic Computer Science Problems in Python* is captioned "Habit of a Bonza or Priest in China." The illustration is taken from Thomas Jefferys' *A Collection of the Dresses of Different Nations, Ancient and Modern* (four volumes), London, published between 1757 and 1772. The title page states that these are hand-colored copperplate engravings, heightened with gum arabic.

Thomas Jefferys (1719–1771) was called "Geographer to King George III." He was an English cartographer who was the leading map supplier of his day. He engraved and printed maps for government and other official bodies and produced a wide range of commercial maps and atlases, especially of North America. His work as a map maker sparked an interest in local dress customs of the lands he surveyed and mapped, which are brilliantly displayed in this collection. Fascination with faraway lands and travel for pleasure were relatively new phenomena in the late eighteenth century, and collections such as this one were popular, introducing both the tourist as well as the armchair traveler to the inhabitants of other countries.

The diversity of the drawings in Jefferys' volumes speaks vividly of the uniqueness and individuality of the world's nations some 200 years ago. Dress codes have changed since then, and the diversity by region and country, so rich at the time, has faded away. It's now often hard to tell the inhabitants of one continent from another. Perhaps, trying to view it optimistically, we've traded a cultural and visual diversity for a more varied personal life—or a more varied and interesting intellectual and technical life.

At a time when it's difficult to tell one computer book from another, Manning celebrates the inventiveness and initiative of the computer business with book covers based on the rich diversity of regional life of two centuries ago, brought back to life by Jefferys' pictures.

Introduction

Thank you for purchasing *Classic Computer Science Problems in Python*. Python is one of the most popular programming languages in the world, and people become Python programmers from a variety of backgrounds. Some have a formal computer science education. Others learn Python as a hobby. Still others use Python in a professional setting, but their primary job is not to be a software developer. The problems in this intermediate book will help seasoned programmers refresh themselves on ideas from their CS education while learning some advanced features of the language. Self-taught programmers will accelerate their CS education by learning classic problems in the language of their choice: Python. This book covers such a diversity of problem-solving techniques that there is truly something for everyone.

This book is not an introduction to Python. There are numerous excellent books from Manning and other publishers in that vein.[1] Instead, this book assumes that you are already an intermediate or advanced Python programmer. Although this book requires Python 3.7, mastery of every facet of the latest version of Python is not assumed. In fact, the book's content was created with the assumption that it would serve as learning material to help readers achieve such mastery. On the other hand, this book is not appropriate for readers completely new to Python.

Why Python?

Python is used in pursuits as diverse as data science, film-making, computer science education, IT management, and much more. There really is no computing field that

---

[1] If you are just starting your Python journey, you may want to first check out *The Quick Python Book*, 3rd edition, by Naomi Ceder (Manning, 2018) before beginning this book.

Python has not touched (except maybe kernel development). Python is loved for its flexibility, beautiful and succinct syntax, object-oriented purity, and bustling community. The strong community is important because it means Python is welcoming to newcomers and has a large ecosystem of available libraries for developers to build upon.

For the preceding reasons, Python is sometimes thought of as a beginner-friendly language, and that characterization is probably true. Most people would agree that Python is easier to learn than C++, for example, and its community is almost certainly friendlier to newcomers. As a result, many people learn Python because it is approachable, and they start writing the programs they want to write fairly quickly. But they may never have received an education in computer science that teaches them all of the powerful problem-solving techniques available to them. If you are one of those programmers who knows Python but does not know CS, this book is for you.

Other people learn Python as a second, third, fourth, or fifth language after a long time working in software development. For them, seeing old problems they've already seen in another language will help them accelerate their learning of Python. For them, this book may be a good refresher before a job interview, or it might expose them to some problem-solving techniques they had not previously thought of exploiting in their work. I would encourage them to skim the table of contents to see if there are topics in this book that excite them.

What is a classic computer science problem?

Some say that computers are to computer science as telescopes are to astronomy. If that's the case, then perhaps a programming language is like a telescope lens. In any event, the term "classic computer science problems" is used here to mean "programming problems typically taught in an undergraduate computer science curriculum."

There are certain programming problems that are given to new programmers to solve and that have become commonplace enough to be deemed classic, whether in a classroom setting during the pursuit of a bachelor's degree (in computer science, software engineering, and the like) or within the confines of an intermediate programming textbook (for example, a first book on artificial intelligence or algorithms). A selection of such problems is what you will find in this book.

The problems range from the trivial, which can be solved in a few lines of code, to the complex, which require the buildup of systems over multiple chapters. Some problems touch on artificial intelligence, and others simply require common sense. Some problems are practical, and other problems are fanciful.

What kinds of problems are in this book?

Chapter 1 introduces problem-solving techniques that will likely look familiar to most readers. Things like recursion, memoization, and bit manipulation are essential building blocks of other techniques explored in later chapters.

This gentle introduction is followed by chapter 2, which focuses on search problems. Search is such a large topic that you could arguably place most problems in the book under its banner. Chapter 2 introduces the most essential search algorithms, including binary search, depth-first search, breadth-first search, and A*. These algorithms are reused throughout the rest of the book.

In chapter 3, you will build a framework for solving a broad range of problems that can be abstractly defined by variables of limited domains that have constraints between them. This includes such classics as the eight queens problem, the Australian map-coloring problem, and the cryptarithmetic SEND+MORE=MONEY.

Chapter 4 explores the world of graph algorithms, which to the uninitiated are surprisingly broad in their applicability. In this chapter, you will build a graph data structure and then use it to solve several classic optimization problems.

Chapter 5 explores genetic algorithms, a technique that is less deterministic than most covered in the book but that sometimes can solve problems traditional algorithms cannot solve in a reasonable amount of time.

Chapter 6 covers k-means clustering and is perhaps the most algorithmically specific chapter in the book. This clustering technique is simple to implement, easy to understand, and broadly applicable.

Chapter 7 aims to explain what a neural network is and to give the reader a taste of what a very simple neural network looks like. It does not aim to provide comprehensive coverage of this exciting and evolving field. In this chapter, you will build a neural network from first principles, using no external libraries, so you can really see how a neural network works.

Chapter 8 is on adversarial search in two-player perfect information games. You will learn a search algorithm known as minimax, which can be used to develop an artificial opponent that can play games like chess, checkers, and Connect Four well.

Finally, chapter 9 covers interesting (and fun) problems that did not quite fit anywhere else in the book.

Who is this book for?

This book is for both intermediate and experienced programmers. Experienced programmers who want to deepen their knowledge of Python will find comfortably familiar problems from their computer science or programming education. Intermediate programmers will be introduced to these classic problems in the language of their choice: Python. Developers getting ready for coding interviews will likely find this book to be valuable preparation material.

In addition to professional programmers, students enrolled in undergraduate computer science programs who have an interest in Python will likely find this book helpful. It makes no attempt to be a rigorous introduction to data structures and algorithms. *This is not a data structures and algorithms textbook.* You will not find proofs or extensive use of big-O notation within its pages. Instead, it is positioned as an approachable, hands-on tutorial to the problem-solving techniques that should be the end product of taking data structure, algorithm, and artificial intelligence classes.

Once again, knowledge of Python's syntax and semantics is assumed. A reader with zero programming experience will get little out of this book, and a programmer with zero Python experience will almost certainly struggle. In other words, *Classic Computer Science Problems in Python* is a book for working Python programmers and computer science students.

Python versioning, source code repository, and type hints

The source code in this book was written to adhere to version 3.7 of the Python language. It utilizes features of Python that only became available in Python 3.7, so some of the code will not run on earlier versions of Python. Instead of struggling and trying to make the examples run in an earlier version, please just download the latest version of Python before starting the book.

This book only makes use of the Python standard library (with a slight exception in chapter 2, where the `typing_extensions` module is installed), so all of the code in this book should run on any platform where Python is supported (macOS, Windows, GNU/Linux, and so on). The code in this book was only tested against CPython (the main Python interpreter available from python.org), although it is likely that most of it will run in a Python 3.7–compatible version of another Python interpreter.

This book does not explain how to use Python tools like editors, IDEs, debuggers, and the Python REPL. The book's source code is available online from the GitHub repository: https://github.com/davecom/ClassicComputerScienceProblems InPython. The source code is organized into folders by chapter. As you read each chapter, you will see the name of a source file in the header of each code listing. You can find that source file in its respective folder in the repository. You should be able to run the problem by just entering `python3 filename.py` or `python filename.py` depending on your computer's setup with regards to the name of the Python 3 interpreter.

Every code listing in this book makes use of Python type hints, also known as type annotations. These annotations are a relatively new feature for the Python language, and they may look intimidating to Python programmers who have never seen them before. They are used for three reasons:

1 They provide clarity about the types of variables, function parameters, and function returns.

2 They self-document the code in a sense, as a result of reason 1. Instead of having to search through a comment or docstring to find the return type of a function, you can just look at its signature.

3 They allow the code to be type-checked for correctness. One popular Python type checker is mypy.

Not everyone is a fan of type hints, and choosing to use them throughout the book was frankly a gamble. I hope they will be a help instead of a hindrance. It takes a little more time to write Python with type hints, but it provides more clarity when read back. An interesting note is that type hints have no effect on the actual running of the code in the Python interpreter. You can remove the type hints from any of the code in this book, and it should still run. If you have never seen type hints before and feel you need a more comprehensive introduction to them before diving into the book, please see appendix C, which provides a crash course in type hints.

No graphics, no UI code, just the standard library

There are no examples in this book that produce graphical output or that make use of a graphical user interface (GUI). Why? The goal is to solve the posed problems with solutions that are as concise and readable as possible. Often, doing graphics gets in the way or makes solutions significantly more complex than they need to be to illustrate the technique or algorithm in question.

Further, by not making use of any GUI framework, all of the code in the book is eminently portable. It can as easily run on an embedded distribution of Python running on Linux as it can on a desktop running Windows. Also, a conscious decision was made to only use packages from the Python standard library instead of any external libraries, as most advanced Python books do. Why? The goal is to teach problem-solving techniques from first principles, not to "pip install a solution." By having to work through every problem from scratch, you will hopefully gain an understanding about how popular libraries work behind the scenes. At a minimum, only using the standard library makes the code in this book more portable and easier to run.

This is not to say that graphical solutions are not sometimes more illustrative of an algorithm than text-based solutions. It simply was not the focus of this book. It would add another layer of unnecessary complexity.

Part of a series

This is the second book in a series titled *Classic Computer Science Problems* published by Manning. The first book was *Classic Computer Science Problems in Swift*, published in 2018. In each book in the series, we aim to provide language-specific insight while teaching through the lens of the same (mostly) computer science problems.

If you enjoy this book and plan to learn another language covered by the series, you may find going from one book to another an easy way to improve your mastery of that language. For now, the series covers just Swift and Python. I wrote the first two books myself, because I have significant experience in both of those languages, but we are already discussing plans for future books in the series co-authored by people who are experts in other languages. I encourage you to look out for them if you enjoy this book. For more information about the series, visit https://classicproblems.com/.

Small problems

To get started, we will explore some simple problems that can be solved with no more than a few relatively short functions. Although these problems are small, they will still allow us to explore some interesting problem-solving techniques. Think of them as a good warm-up.

1.1 The Fibonacci sequence

The Fibonacci sequence is a sequence of numbers such that any number, except for the first and second, is the sum of the previous two:

```
0, 1, 1, 2, 3, 5, 8, 13, 21...
```

The value of the first Fibonacci number in the sequence is 0. The value of the fourth Fibonacci number is 2. It follows that to get the value of any Fibonacci number, n, in the sequence, one can use the formula

```
fib(n) = fib(n - 1) + fib(n - 2)
```

1.1.1 A first recursive attempt

The preceding formula for computing a number in the Fibonacci sequence (illustrated in figure 1.1) is a form of pseudocode that can be trivially translated into a *recursive* Python function. (A recursive function is a function that calls itself.) This mechanical translation will serve as our first attempt at writing a function to return a given value of the Fibonacci sequence.

Listing 1.1 fib1.py

```python
def fib1(n: int) -> int:
    return fib1(n - 1) + fib1(n - 2)
```

6

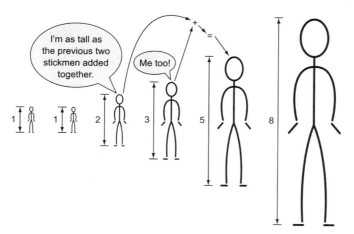

Figure 1.1   The height of each stickman is the previous two stickmen's heights added together.

Let's try to run this function by calling it with a value.

Listing 1.2   fib1.py continued

```
if __name__ == "__main__":
    print(fib1(5))
```

Uh-oh! If we try to run fib1.py, we generate an error:

```
RecursionError: maximum recursion depth exceeded
```

The issue is that `fib1()` will run forever without returning a final result. Every call to `fib1()` results in another two calls of `fib1()` with no end in sight. We call such a circumstance *infinite recursion* (see figure 1.2), and it is analogous to an *infinite loop.*

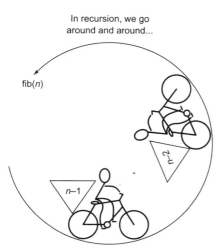

Figure 1.2   The recursive function `fib(n)` calls itself with the arguments `n-2` and `n-1`.

1.1.2   *Utilizing base cases*

Notice that until you run `fib1()`, there is no indication from your Python environment that there is anything wrong with it. It is the duty of the programmer to avoid infinite recursion, not the compiler or the interpreter. The reason for the infinite recursion is that we never specified a base case. In a recursive function, a base case serves as a stopping point.

In the case of the Fibonacci function, we have natural base cases in the form of the special first two sequence values, 0 and 1. Neither 0 nor 1 is the sum of the previous two numbers in the sequence. Instead, they are the special first two values. Let's try specifying them as base cases.

Listing 1.3   fib2.py

```
def fib2(n: int) -> int:
    if n < 2:  # base case
        return n
    return fib2(n - 2) + fib2(n - 1)   # recursive case
```

NOTE   The `fib2()` version of the Fibonacci function returns 0 as the zeroth number (`fib2(0)`), rather than the first number, as in our original proposition. In a programming context, this kind of makes sense because we are used to sequences starting with a zeroth element.

`fib2()` can be called successfully and will return correct results. Try calling it with some small values.

Listing 1.4   fib2.py continued

```
if __name__ == "__main__":
    print(fib2(5))
    print(fib2(10))
```

Do not try calling `fib2(50)`. It will never finish executing! Why? Every call to `fib2()` results in two more calls to `fib2()` by way of the recursive calls `fib2(n - 1)` and `fib2(n - 2)` (see figure 1.3). In other words, the call tree grows exponentially. For example, a call of `fib2(4)` results in this entire set of calls:

```
fib2(4) -> fib2(3), fib2(2)
fib2(3) -> fib2(2), fib2(1)
fib2(2) -> fib2(1), fib2(0)
fib2(2) -> fib2(1), fib2(0)
fib2(1) -> 1
fib2(1) -> 1
fib2(1) -> 1
fib2(0) -> 0
fib2(0) -> 0
```

If you count them (and as you will see if you add some print calls), there are 9 calls to `fib2()` just to compute the 4th element! It gets worse. There are 15 calls required to

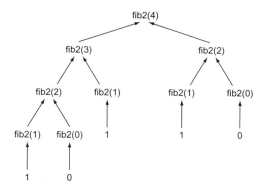

Figure 1.3 Every non-base-case call of `fib2()` results in two more calls of `fib2()`.

compute element 5, 177 calls to compute element 10, and 21,891 calls to compute element 20. We can do better.

1.1.3 Memoization to the rescue

Memoization is a technique in which you store the results of computational tasks when they are completed so that when you need them again, you can look them up instead of needing to compute them a second (or millionth) time (see figure 1.4).[1]

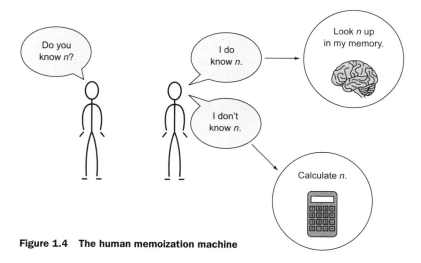

Figure 1.4 The human memoization machine

Let's create a new version of the Fibonacci function that utilizes a Python dictionary for memoization purposes.

---

[1] Donald Michie, a famous British computer scientist, coined the term *memoization*. Donald Michie, *Memo functions: a language feature with "rote-learning" properties* (Edinburgh University, Department of Machine Intelligence and Perception, 1967).

Listing 1.5   fib3.py

```
from typing import Dict
memo: Dict[int, int] = {0: 0, 1: 1}   # our base cases


def fib3(n: int) -> int:
    if n not in memo:
        memo[n] = fib3(n - 1) + fib3(n - 2)   # memoization
    return memo[n]
```

You can now safely call `fib3(50)`.

Listing 1.6   fib3.py continued

```
if __name__ == "__main__":
    print(fib3(5))
    print(fib3(50))
```

A call to `fib3(20)` will result in just 39 calls of `fib3()` as opposed to the 21,891 of `fib2()` resulting from the call `fib2(20)`. memo is prefilled with the earlier base cases of 0 and 1, saving `fib3()` from the complexity of another `if` statement.

1.1.4   *Automatic memoization*

`fib3()` can be further simplified. Python has a built-in decorator for memoizing any function automagically. In `fib4()`, the decorator `@functools.lru_cache()` is used with the same exact code as we used in `fib2()`. Each time `fib4()` is executed with a novel argument, the decorator causes the return value to be cached. Upon future calls of `fib4()` with the same argument, the previous return value of `fib4()` for that argument is retrieved from the cache and returned.

Listing 1.7   fib4.py

```
from functools import lru_cache


@lru_cache(maxsize=None)
def fib4(n: int) -> int:   # same definition as fib2()
    if n < 2:   # base case
        return n
    return fib4(n - 2) + fib4(n - 1)   # recursive case


if __name__ == "__main__":
    print(fib4(5))
    print(fib4(50))
```

Note that we are able to calculate `fib4(50)` instantly, even though the body of the Fibonacci function is the same as that in `fib2()`. `@lru_cache`'s maxsize property indicates how many of the most recent calls of the function it is decorating should be cached. Setting it to None indicates that there is no limit.

1.1.5 Keep it simple, Fibonacci

There is an even more performant option. We can solve Fibonacci with an old-fashioned iterative approach.

> **Listing 1.8 fib5.py**

```python
def fib5(n: int) -> int:
    if n == 0: return n  # special case
    last: int = 0  # initially set to fib(0)
    next: int = 1  # initially set to fib(1)
    for _ in range(1, n):
        last, next = next, last + next
    return next

if __name__ == "__main__":
    print(fib5(5))
    print(fib5(50))
```

> **WARNING** The body of the for loop in fib5() uses tuple unpacking in perhaps a bit of an overly clever way. Some may feel that it sacrifices readability for conciseness. Others may find the conciseness in and of itself more readable. The gist is, last is being set to the previous value of next, and next is being set to the previous value of last plus the previous value of next. This avoids the creation of a temporary variable to hold the old value of next after last is updated but before next is updated. Using tuple unpacking in this fashion for some kind of variable swap is common in Python.

With this approach, the body of the for loop will run a maximum of n - 1 times. In other words, this is the most efficient version yet. Compare 19 runs of the for loop body to 21,891 recursive calls of fib2() for the 20th Fibonacci number. That could make a serious difference in a real-world application!

In the recursive solutions, we worked backward. In this iterative solution, we work forward. Sometimes recursion is the most intuitive way to solve a problem. For example, the meat of fib1() and fib2() is pretty much a mechanical translation of the original Fibonacci formula. However, naive recursive solutions can also come with significant performance costs. Remember, any problem that can be solved recursively can also be solved iteratively.

1.1.6 Generating Fibonacci numbers with a generator

So far, we have written functions that output a single value in the Fibonacci sequence. What if we want to output the entire sequence up to some value instead? It is easy to convert fib5() into a Python generator using the yield statement. When the generator is iterated, each iteration will spew a value from the Fibonacci sequence using a yield statement.

Listing 1.9   fib6.py

```
from typing import Generator

def fib6(n: int) -> Generator[int, None, None]:
    yield 0  # special case
    if n > 0: yield 1  # special case
    last: int = 0  # initially set to fib(0)
    next: int = 1  # initially set to fib(1)
    for _ in range(1, n):
        last, next = next, last + next
        yield next  # main generation step

if __name__ == "__main__":
    for i in fib6(50):
        print(i)
```

If you run fib6.py, you will see 51 numbers in the Fibonacci sequence printed. For each iteration of the for loop `for i in fib6(50):`, fib6() runs through to a yield statement. If the end of the function is reached and there are no more yield statements, the loop finishes iterating.

1.2   *Trivial compression*

Saving space (virtual or real) is often important. It is more efficient to use less space, and it can save money. If you are renting an apartment that is bigger than you need for your things and family, you could "downsize" to a smaller place that is less expensive. If you are paying by the byte to store your data on a server, you may want to compress it so that its storage costs you less. *Compression* is the act of taking data and encoding it (changing its form) in such a way that it takes up less space. *Decompression* is reversing the process, returning the data to its original form.

If it is more storage-efficient to compress data, then why is all data not compressed? There is a tradeoff between time and space. It takes time to compress a piece of data and to decompress it back into its original form. Therefore, data compression only makes sense in situations where small size is prioritized over fast execution. Think of large files being transmitted over the internet. Compressing them makes sense because it will take longer to transfer the files than it will to decompress them once received. Further, the time taken to compress the files for their storage on the original server only needs to be accounted for once.

The easiest data compression wins come about when you realize that data storage types use more bits than are strictly required for their contents. For instance, thinking low-level, if an unsigned integer that will never exceed 65,535 is being stored as a 64-bit unsigned integer in memory, it is being stored inefficiently. It could instead be stored as a 16-bit unsigned integer. This would reduce the space consumption for the actual number by 75% (16 bits instead of 64 bits). If millions of such numbers are being stored inefficiently, it can add up to megabytes of wasted space.

In Python, sometimes for the sake of simplicity (which is a legitimate goal, of course), the developer is shielded from thinking in bits. There is no 64-bit unsigned integer type, and there is no 16-bit unsigned integer type. There is just a single `int` type that can store numbers of arbitrary precision. The function `sys.getsizeof()` can help you find out how many bytes of memory your Python objects are consuming. But due to the inherent overhead of the Python object system, there is no way to create an `int` that takes up less than 28 bytes (224 bits) in Python 3.7. A single `int` can be extended one bit at a time (as we will do in this example), but it consumes a minimum of 28 bytes.

> **NOTE** If you are a little rusty regarding binary, recall that a bit is a single value that is either a 1 or a 0. A sequence of 1s and 0s is read in base 2 to represent a number. For the purposes of this section, you do not need to do any math in base 2, but you do need to understand that the number of bits that a type stores determines how many different values it can represent. For example, 1 bit can represent 2 values (0 or 1), 2 bits can represent 4 values (00, 01, 10, 11), 3 bits can represent 8 values, and so on.

If the number of possible different values that a type is meant to represent is less than the number of values that the bits being used to store it can represent, it can likely be more efficiently stored. Consider the nucleotides that form a gene in DNA.[2] Each nucleotide can only be one of four values: A, C, G, or T. (There will be more about this in chapter 2.) Yet if the gene is stored as a `str`, which can be thought of as a collection of Unicode characters, each nucleotide will be represented by a character, which generally requires 8 bits of storage. In binary, just 2 bits are needed to store a type with four possible values: 00, 01, 10, and 11 are the four different values that can be represented by 2 bits. If A is assigned 00, C is assigned 01, G is assigned 10, and T is assigned 11, the storage required for a string of nucleotides can be reduced by 75% (from 8 bits to 2 bits per nucleotide).

Instead of storing our nucleotides as a `str`, they can be stored as a *bit string* (see figure 1.5). A bit string is exactly what it sounds like: an arbitrary-length sequence of 1s and 0s. Unfortunately,

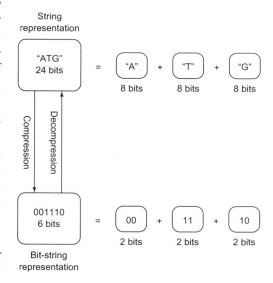

Figure 1.5 Compressing a `str` representing a gene into a 2-bit-per-nucleotide bit string

---

[2] This example is inspired by *Algorithms*, 4th Edition, by Robert Sedgewick and Kevin Wayne (Addison-Wesley Professional, 2011), page 819.

the Python standard library contains no off-the-shelf construct for working with bit strings of arbitrary length. The following code converts a str composed of As, Cs, Gs, and Ts into a string of bits and back again. The string of bits is stored within an int. Because the int type in Python can be of any length, it can be used as a bit string of any length. To convert back into a str, we will implement the Python __str__() special method.

Listing 1.10   trivial_compression.py

```python
class CompressedGene:
    def __init__(self, gene: str) -> None:
        self._compress(gene)
```

A CompressedGene is provided a str of characters representing the nucleotides in a gene, and it internally stores the sequence of nucleotides as a bit string. The __init__() method's main responsibility is to initialize the bit-string construct with the appropriate data. __init__() calls _compress() to do the dirty work of actually converting the provided str of nucleotides into a bit string.

Note that _compress() starts with an underscore. Python has no concept of truly private methods or variables. (All variables and methods can be accessed through reflection; there's no strict enforcement of privacy.) A leading underscore is used as a convention to indicate that the implementation of a method should not be relied on by actors outside of the class. (It is subject to change and should be treated as private.)

TIP If you start a method or instance variable name in a class with two leading underscores, Python will "name mangle" it, changing its implementation name with a salt and not making it easily discoverable by other classes. We use one underscore in this book to indicate a "private" variable or method, but you may wish to use two if you really want to emphasize that something is private. For more on naming in Python, check out the section "Descriptive Naming Styles" from PEP 8: http://mng.bz/NA52.

Next, let's look at how we can actually perform the compression.

Listing 1.11   trivial_compression.py continued

```python
def _compress(self, gene: str) -> None:
    self.bit_string: int = 1  # start with sentinel
    for nucleotide in gene.upper():
        self.bit_string <<= 2  # shift left two bits
        if nucleotide == "A":  # change last two bits to 00
            self.bit_string |= 0b00
        elif nucleotide == "C":  # change last two bits to 01
            self.bit_string |= 0b01
        elif nucleotide == "G":  # change last two bits to 10
            self.bit_string |= 0b10
        elif nucleotide == "T":  # change last two bits to 11
            self.bit_string |= 0b11
        else:
            raise ValueError("Invalid Nucleotide:{}".format(nucleotide))
```

The _compress()method looks at each character in the str of nucleotides sequentially. When it sees an A, it adds 00 to the bit string. When it sees a C, it adds 01, and so on. Remember that two bits are needed for each nucleotide. As a result, before we add each new nucleotide, we shift the bit string two bits to the left (self.bit_string <<= 2).

Every nucleotide is added using an "or" operation (|). After the left shift, two 0s are added to the right side of the bit string. In bitwise operations, "ORing" (for example, self.bit_string |= 0b10) 0s with any other value results in the other value replacing the 0s. In other words, we continually add two new bits to the right side of the bit string. The two bits that are added are determined by the type of the nucleotide.

Finally, we will implement decompression and the special __str__() method that uses it.

Listing 1.12 trivial_compression.py continued

```python
def decompress(self) -> str:
    gene: str = ""
    for i in range(0, self.bit_string.bit_length() - 1, 2):  # - 1 to exclude
    sentinel
        bits: int = self.bit_string >> i & 0b11  # get just 2 relevant bits
        if bits == 0b00:  # A
            gene += "A"
        elif bits == 0b01:  # C
            gene += "C"
        elif bits == 0b10:  # G
            gene += "G"
        elif bits == 0b11:  # T
            gene += "T"
        else:
            raise ValueError("Invalid bits:{}".format(bits))
    return gene[::-1]  # [::-1] reverses string by slicing backward

def __str__(self) -> str:  # string representation for pretty printing
    return self.decompress()
```

decompress() reads two bits from the bit string at a time, and it uses those two bits to determine which character to add to the end of the str representation of the gene. Because the bits are being read backward, compared to the order they were compressed in (right to left instead of left to right), the str representation is ultimately reversed (using the slicing notation for reversal [::-1]). Finally, note how the convenient int method bit_length() aided in the development of decompress(). Let's test it out.

Listing 1.13 trivial_compression.py continued

```python
if __name__ == "__main__":
    from sys import getsizeof
    original: str =
        "TAGGGATTAACCGTTATATATATATAGCCATGGATCGATTATATAGGGATTAACCGTTATATATATATAGC
        CATGGATCGATTATA" * 100
```

```
print("original is {} bytes".format(getsizeof(original)))
compressed: CompressedGene = CompressedGene(original)  # compress
print("compressed is {} bytes".format(getsizeof(compressed.bit_string)))
print(compressed)  # decompress
print("original and decompressed are the same: {}".format(original ==
  compressed.decompress()))
```

Using the sys.getsizeof() method, we can indicate in the output whether we did indeed save almost 75% of the memory cost of storing the gene through this compression scheme.

Listing 1.14   trivial_compression.py output

```
original is 8649 bytes
compressed is 2320 bytes
TAGGGATTAACC...
original and decompressed are the same: True
```

> **NOTE** In the CompressedGene class, we used if statements extensively to decide between a series of cases in both the compression and the decompression methods. Because Python has no switch statement, this is somewhat typical. What you will also see in Python sometimes is a high reliance on dictionaries in place of extensive if statements to deal with a set of cases. Imagine, for instance, a dictionary in which we could look up each nucleotide's respective bits. This can sometimes be more readable, but it can come with a performance cost. Even though a dictionary lookup is technically O(1), the cost of running a hash function will sometimes mean a dictionary is less performant than a series of ifs. Whether this holds will depend on what a particular program's if statements must evaluate to make their decision. You may want to run performance tests on both methods if you need to make a decision between ifs and dictionary lookup in a critical section of code.

1.3   *Unbreakable encryption*

A one-time pad is a way of encrypting a piece of data by combining it with meaningless random dummy data in such a way that the original cannot be reconstituted without access to both the product and the dummy data. In essence, this leaves the encrypter with a key pair. One key is the product, and the other is the random dummy data. One key on its own is useless; only the combination of both keys can unlock the original data. When performed correctly, a one-time pad is a form of unbreakable encryption. Figure 1.6 shows the process.

1.3.1   *Getting the data in order*

In this example, we will encrypt a str using a one-time pad. One way of thinking about a Python 3 str is as a sequence of UTF-8 bytes (with UTF-8 being a Unicode character encoding). A str can be converted into a sequence of UTF-8 bytes (represented as the bytes type) through the encode() method. Likewise, a sequence of UTF-8 bytes can be converted back into a str using the decode() method on the bytes type.

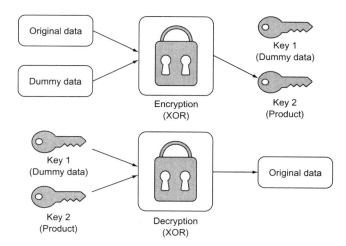

Figure 1.6 A one-time pad results in two keys that can be separated and then recombined to re-create the original data.

There are three criteria that the dummy data used in a one-time pad encryption operation must meet for the resulting product to be unbreakable. The dummy data must be the same length as the original data, truly random, and completely secret. The first and third criteria are common sense. If the dummy data repeats because it is too short, there could be an observed pattern. If one of the keys is not truly secret (perhaps it is reused elsewhere or partially revealed), then an attacker has a clue. The second criteria poses a question all its own: can we produce truly random data? The answer for most computers is no.

In this example we will use the pseudo-random data generating function `token_bytes()` from the `secrets` module (first included in the standard library in Python 3.6). Our data will not be truly random, in the sense that the `secrets` package still is using a pseudo-random number generator behind the scenes, but it will be close enough for our purposes. Let's generate a random key for use as dummy data.

Listing 1.15 unbreakable_encryption.py

```python
from secrets import token_bytes
from typing import Tuple


def random_key(length: int) -> int:
    # generate length random bytes
    tb: bytes = token_bytes(length)
    # convert those bytes into a bit string and return it
    return int.from_bytes(tb, "big")
```

This function creates an `int` filled with `length` random bytes. The method `int.from_bytes()` is used to convert from `bytes` to `int`. How can multiple bytes be converted to a single integer? The answer lies in section 1.2. In that section, you learned that the `int` type can be of arbitrary size, and you saw how it can be used as a generic bit string. `int` is being used in the same way here. For example, the `from_bytes()` method will take 7 bytes (7 bytes * 8 bits = 56 bits) and convert them into a 56-bit integer. Why is this useful? Bitwise operations can be executed more easily and performantly on a single int (read "long bit string") than on many individual bytes in a sequence. And we are about to use the bitwise operation XOR.

1.3.2   *Encrypting and decrypting*

How will the dummy data be combined with the original data that we want to encrypt? The *XOR* operation will serve this purpose. XOR is a logical bitwise (operates at the bit level) operation that returns true when one of its operands is true but returns false when both are true or neither is true. As you may have guessed, XOR stands for *exclusive or.*

In Python, the XOR operator is ^. In the context of the bits of binary numbers, XOR returns 1 for 0 ^ 1 and 1 ^ 0, but 0 for 0 ^ 0 and 1 ^ 1. If the bits of two numbers are combined using XOR, a helpful property is that the product can be recombined with either of the operands to produce the other operand:

```
A ^ B = C
C ^ B = A
C ^ A = B
```

This key insight forms the basis of one-time pad encryption. To form our product, we will simply XOR an int representing the bytes in our original str with a randomly generated int of the same bit length (as produced by random_key()). Our returned key pair will be the dummy data and the product.

Listing 1.16   unbreakable_encryption.py continued

```
def encrypt(original: str) -> Tuple[int, int]:
    original_bytes: bytes = original.encode()
    dummy: int = random_key(len(original_bytes))
    original_key: int = int.from_bytes(original_bytes, "big")
    encrypted: int = original_key ^ dummy  # XOR
    return dummy, encrypted
```

> **NOTE** int.from_bytes() is being passed two arguments. The first is the bytes that we want to convert into an int. The second is the *endianness* of those bytes ("big"). Endianness refers to the byte-ordering used to store data. Does the most significant byte come first, or does the least significant byte come first? In our case, it does not matter as long as we use the same ordering both when we encrypt and decrypt, because we are actually only manipulating the data at the individual bit level. In other situations, when you are not controlling both ends of the encoding process, the ordering can absolutely matter, so be careful!

Decryption is simply a matter of recombining the key pair we generated with encrypt(). This is achieved once again by doing an XOR operation between each and every bit in the two keys. The ultimate output must be converted back to a str. First, the int is converted to bytes using int.to_bytes(). This method requires the number of bytes to be converted from the int. To get this number, we divide the bit length by eight (the number of bits in a byte). Finally, the `bytes` method `decode()` gives us back a `str`.

Listing 1.17 unbreakable_encryption.py continued

```python
def decrypt(key1: int, key2: int) -> str:
    decrypted: int = key1 ^ key2  # XOR
    temp: bytes = decrypted.to_bytes((decrypted.bit_length()+ 7) // 8, "big")
    return temp.decode()
```

It was necessary to add 7 to the length of the decrypted data before using integer-division (`//`) to divide by 8 to ensure that we "round up," to avoid an off-by-one error. If our one-time pad encryption truly works, we should be able to encrypt and decrypt the same Unicode string without issue.

Listing 1.18 unbreakable_encryption.py continued

```python
if __name__ == "__main__":
    key1, key2 = encrypt("One Time Pad!")
    result: str = decrypt(key1, key2)
    print(result)
```

If your console outputs `One Time Pad!` then everything worked.

1.4 *Calculating pi*

The mathematically significant number pi (π or 3.14159...) can be derived using many formulas. One of the simplest is the Leibniz formula. It posits that the convergence of the following infinite series is equal to pi:

π = 4/1 - 4/3 + 4/5 - 4/7 + 4/9 - 4/11...

You will notice that the infinite series' numerator remains 4 while the denominator increases by 2, and the operation on the terms alternates between addition and subtraction.

We can model the series in a straightforward way by translating pieces of the formula into variables in a function. The numerator can be a constant 4. The denominator can be a variable that begins at 1 and is incremented by 2. The operation can be represented as either -1 or 1 based on whether we are adding or subtracting. Finally, the variable `pi` is used in listing 1.19 to collect the sum of the series as the `for` loop proceeds.

Listing 1.19 calculating_pi.py

```python
def calculate_pi(n_terms: int) -> float:
    numerator: float = 4.0
    denominator: float = 1.0
    operation: float = 1.0
    pi: float = 0.0
    for _ in range(n_terms):
        pi += operation * (numerator / denominator)
```

```
        denominator += 2.0
        operation *= -1.0
    return pi

if __name__ == "__main__":
    print(calculate_pi(1000000))
```

TIP On most platforms, Python `floats` are 64-bit floating-point numbers (or `double` in C).

This function is an example of how rote conversion between formula and programmatic code can be both simple and effective in modeling or simulating an interesting concept. Rote conversion is a useful tool, but we must keep in mind that it is not necessarily the most efficient solution. Certainly, the Leibniz formula for pi can be implemented with more efficient or compact code.

NOTE The more terms in the infinite series (the higher the value of n_terms when `calculate_pi()` is called), the more accurate the ultimate calculation of pi will be.

1.5   *The Towers of Hanoi*

Three vertical pegs (henceforth "towers") stand tall. We will label them A, B, and C. Doughnut-shaped discs are around tower A. The widest disc is at the bottom, and we will call it disc 1. The rest of the discs above disc 1 are labeled with increasing numerals and get progressively narrower. For instance, if we were to work with three discs, the widest disc, the one on the bottom, would be 1. The next widest disc, disc 2, would sit on top of disc 1. And finally, the narrowest disc, disc 3, would sit on top of disc 2. Our goal is to move all of the discs from tower A to tower C given the following constraints:

- Only one disc can be moved at a time.
- The topmost disc of any tower is the only one available for moving.
- A wider disc can never be atop a narrower disc.

Figure 1.7 summarizes the problem.

1.5.1   *Modeling the towers*

A stack is a data structure that is modeled on the concept of Last-In-First-Out (LIFO). The last thing put into it is the first thing that comes out of it. The two most basic operations on a stack are push and pop. A *push* puts a new item into a stack, whereas a *pop* removes and returns the last item put in. We can easily model a stack in Python using a `list` as a backing store.

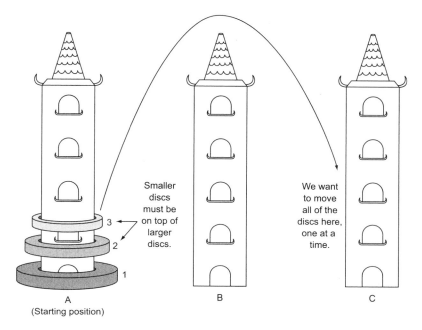

Figure 1.7   The challenge is to move the three discs, one at a time, from tower A to tower C. A larger disc may never be on top of a smaller disc.

Listing 1.20   hanoi.py

```python
from typing import TypeVar, Generic, List
T = TypeVar('T')


class Stack(Generic[T]):
    def __init__(self) -> None:
        self._container: List[T] = []

    def push(self, item: T) -> None:
        self._container.append(item)

    def pop(self) -> T:
        return self._container.pop()

    def __repr__(self) -> str:
        return repr(self._container)
```

NOTE This `Stack` class implements `__repr__()` so that we can easily explore the contents of a tower. `__repr__()` is what will be output when `print()` is applied to a `Stack`.

NOTE As was described in the introduction, this book utilizes type hints throughout. The import of `Generic` from the typing module enables `Stack` to be generic over a particular type in type hints. The arbitrary type `T` is defined in T = TypeVar('T'). T can be any type. When a type hint is later used for a Stack to solve the Hanoi problem, it is type-hinted as type Stack[int], which means T is filled in with type int. In other words, the stack is a stack of integers. If you are struggling with type hints, take a look at appendix C.

Stacks are perfect stand-ins for the towers in The Towers of Hanoi. When we want to put a disc onto a tower, we can just push it. When we want to move a disc from one tower to another, we can pop it from the first and push it onto the second.

Let's define our towers as Stacks and fill the first tower with discs.

Listing 1.21   hanoi.py continued

```
num_discs: int = 3
tower_a: Stack[int] = Stack()
tower_b: Stack[int] = Stack()
tower_c: Stack[int] = Stack()
for i in range(1, num_discs + 1):
    tower_a.push(i)
```

1.5.2   *Solving The Towers of Hanoi*

How can The Towers of Hanoi be solved? Imagine we were only trying to move 1 disc. We would know how to do that, right? In fact, moving one disc is our base case for a recursive solution to The Towers of Hanoi. The recursive case is moving more than one disc. Therefore, the key insight is that we essentially have two scenarios we need to codify: moving one disc (the base case) and moving more than one disc (the recursive case).

Let's look at a specific example to understand the recursive case. Say we have three discs (top, middle, and bottom) on tower A that we want to move to tower C. (It may help to sketch out the problem as you follow along.) We could first move the top disc to tower C. Then we could move the middle disc to tower B. Then we could move the top disc from tower C to tower B. Now we have the bottom disc still on tower A and the upper two discs on tower B. Essentially, we have now successfully moved two discs from one tower (A) to another tower (B). Moving the bottom disc from A to C is our base case (moving a single disc). Now we can move the two upper discs from B to C in the same procedure that we did from A to B. We move the top disc to A, the middle disc to C, and finally the top disc from A to C.

> **TIP** In a computer science classroom, it is not uncommon to see a little model of the towers built using dowels and plastic doughnuts. You can build your own model using three pencils and three pieces of paper. It may help you visualize the solution.

In our three-disc example, we had a simple base case of moving a single disc and a recursive case of moving all of the other discs (two in this case), using the third tower temporarily. We could break the recursive case into three steps:

1   Move the upper n-1 discs from tower A to B (the temporary tower), using C as the in-between.
2   Move the single lowest disc from A to C.
3   Move the n-1 discs from tower B to C, using A as the in-between.

The amazing thing is that this recursive algorithm works not only for three discs, but for any number of discs. We will codify it as a function called hanoi() that is responsible for moving discs from one tower to another, given a third temporary tower.

Listing 1.22   hanoi.py continued

```python
def hanoi(begin: Stack[int], end: Stack[int], temp: Stack[int], n: int) ->
    None:
    if n == 1:
        end.push(begin.pop())
    else:
        hanoi(begin, temp, end, n - 1)
        hanoi(begin, end, temp, 1)
        hanoi(temp, end, begin, n - 1)
```

After calling hanoi(), you should examine towers A, B, and C to verify that the discs were moved successfully.

Listing 1.23   hanoi.py continued

```python
if __name__ == "__main__":
    hanoi(tower_a, tower_c, tower_b, num_discs)
    print(tower_a)
    print(tower_b)
    print(tower_c)
```

You will find that they were. In codifying the solution to The Towers of Hanoi, we did not necessarily need to understand every step required to move multiple discs from tower A to tower C. But we came to understand the general recursive algorithm for moving any number of discs, and we codified it, letting the computer do the rest. This is the power of formulating recursive solutions to problems: we often can think of solutions in an abstract manner without the drudgery of negotiating every individual action in our minds.

Incidentally, the hanoi() function will execute an exponential number of times as a function of the number of discs, which makes solving the problem for even 64 discs untenable. You can try it with various other numbers of discs by changing the num_ discs variable. The exponentially increasing number of steps required as the number of discs increases is where the legend of The Towers of Hanoi comes from; you can read more about it in any number of sources. You may also be interested in reading more about the mathematics behind its recursive solution; see Carl Burch's explanation in "About the Towers of Hanoi," http://mng.bz/c1i2.

1.6   *Real-world applications*

The various techniques presented in this chapter (recursion, memoization, compression, and manipulation at the bit level) are so common in modern software development that it is impossible to imagine the world of computing without them. Although problems can be solved without them, it is often more logical or performant to solve problems with them.

Recursion, in particular, is at the heart of not just many algorithms, but even whole programming languages. In some functional programming languages, like Scheme and Haskell, recursion takes the place of the loops used in imperative languages. It is worth remembering, though, that anything accomplishable with a recursive technique is also accomplishable with an iterative technique.

Memoization has been applied successfully to speed up the work of parsers (programs that interpret languages). It is useful in all problems where the result of a recent calculation will likely be asked for again. Another application of memoization is in language runtimes. Some language runtimes (versions of Prolog, for instance) will store the results of function calls automatically (*auto-memoization*), so that the function need not execute the next time the same call is made. This is similar to how the `@lru_cache()` decorator in `fib6()` worked.

Compression has made an internet-connected world constrained by bandwidth more tolerable. The bit-string technique examined in section 1.2 is usable for real-world simple data types that have a limited number of possible values, for which even a byte is overkill. The majority of compression algorithms, however, operate by finding patterns or structures within a data set that allow for repeated information to be eliminated. They are significantly more complicated than what is covered in section 1.2.

One-time pads are not practical for general encryption. They require both the encrypter and the decrypter to have possession of one of the keys (the dummy data in our example) for the original data to be reconstructed, which is cumbersome and defeats the goal of most encryption schemes (keeping keys secret). But you may be interested to know that the name "one-time pad" comes from spies using real paper pads with dummy data on them to create encrypted communications during the Cold War.

These techniques are programmatic building blocks that other algorithms are built on top of. In future chapters you will see them applied liberally.

1.7   *Exercises*

1   Write yet another function that solves for element n of the Fibonacci sequence, using a technique of your own design. Write unit tests that evaluate its correctness and performance relative to the other versions in this chapter.

2   You saw how the simple `int` type in Python can be used to represent a bit string. Write an ergonomic wrapper around `int` that can be used generically as a sequence of bits (make it iterable and implement `__getitem__()`). Reimplement `CompressedGene`, using the wrapper.

3   Write a solver for The Towers of Hanoi that works for any number of towers.

4   Use a one-time pad to encrypt and decrypt images.

Search problems

"Search" is such a broad term that this entire book could be called *Classic Search Problems in Python*. This chapter is about core search algorithms that every programmer should know. It does not claim to be comprehensive, despite the declaratory title.

2.1 DNA search

Genes are commonly represented in computer software as a sequence of the characters *A*, *C*, *G*, and *T*. Each letter represents a *nucleotide*, and the combination of three nucleotides is called a *codon*. This is illustrated in figure 2.1. A codon codes for a specific amino acid that together with other amino acids can form a *protein*. A classic task in bioinformatics software is to find a particular codon within a gene.

2.1.1 Storing DNA

We can represent a nucleotide as a simple IntEnum with four cases.

Listing 2.1 dna_search.py

```
from enum import IntEnum
from typing import Tuple, List

Nucleotide: IntEnum = IntEnum('Nucleotide', ('A', 'C', 'G', 'T'))
```

Nucleotide is of type IntEnum instead of just Enum, because IntEnum gives us comparison operators (<, >=, and so on) "for free." Having these operators in a data type is required in order for the search algorithms we are going to implement to be able to operate on it. Tuple and List are imported from the typing package to assist with type hints.

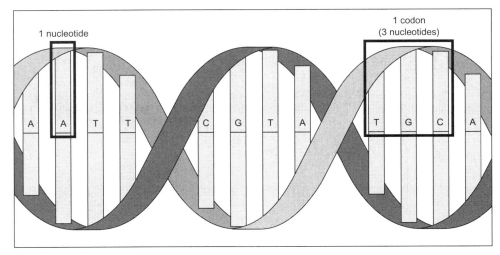

Part of a gene

Figure 2.1   **A nucleotide is represented by one of the letters *A*, *C*, *G*, and *T*. A codon is composed of three nucleotides, and a gene is composed of multiple codons.**

Codons can be defined as a tuple of three `Nucleotides`. A gene may be defined as a list of `Codons`.

Listing 2.2   dna_search.py continued

```
Codon = Tuple[Nucleotide, Nucleotide, Nucleotide]  # type alias for codons
Gene = List[Codon]  # type alias for genes
```

NOTE   Although we will later need to compare one `Codon` to another, we do not need to define a custom class with the < operator explicitly implemented for `Codon`. This is because Python has built-in support for comparisons between tuples that are composed of types that are also comparable.

Typically, genes on the internet will be in a file format that contains a giant string representing all of the nucleotides in the gene's sequence. We will define such a string for an imaginary gene and call it `gene_str`.

Listing 2.3   dna_search.py continued

```
gene_str: str = "ACGTGGCTCTCTAACGTACGTACGTACGGGGTTTATATATACCCTAGGACTCCCTTT"
```

We will also need a utility function to convert a `str` into a `Gene`.

Listing 2.4   dna_search.py continued

```
def string_to_gene(s: str) -> Gene:
    gene: Gene = []
    for i in range(0, len(s), 3):
        if (i + 2) >= len(s):  # don't run off end!
```

```
        return gene
    #  initialize codon out of three nucleotides
    codon: Codon = (Nucleotide[s[i]], Nucleotide[s[i + 1]],
Nucleotide[s[i + 2]])
    gene.append(codon)  # add codon to gene
return gene
```

`string_to_gene()` continually goes through the provided `str` and converts its next three characters into `Codons` that it adds to the end of a new `Gene`. If it finds that there is no `Nucleotide` two places into the future of the current place in `s` that it is examining (see the `if` statement within the loop), then it knows it has reached the end of an incomplete gene, and it skips over those last one or two nucleotides.

`string_to_gene()` can be used to convert the `str` `gene_str` into a `Gene`.

Listing 2.5 dna_search.py continued

```
my_gene: Gene = string_to_gene(gene_str)
```

2.1.2 Linear search

One basic operation we may want to perform on a gene is to search it for a particular codon. The goal is to simply find out whether the codon exists within the gene or not.

A linear search goes through every element in a search space, in the order of the original data structure, until what is sought is found or the end of the data structure is reached. In effect, a linear search is the most simple, natural, and obvious way to search for something. In the worst case, a linear search will require going through every element in a data structure, so it is of O(n) complexity, where n is the number of elements in the structure. This is illustrated in figure 2.2.

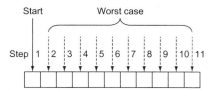

Figure 2.2 In the worst case of a linear search, you'll sequentially look through every element of the array.

It is trivial to define a function that performs a linear search. It simply must go through every element in a data structure and check for its equivalence to the item being sought. The following code defines such a function for a `Gene` and a `Codon` and then tries it out for `my_gene` and `Codons` called `acg` and `gat`.

Listing 2.6 dna_search.py continued

```
def linear_contains(gene: Gene, key_codon: Codon) -> bool:
    for codon in gene:
        if codon == key_codon:
            return True
    return False
```

```
acg: Codon = (Nucleotide.A, Nucleotide.C, Nucleotide.G)
gat: Codon = (Nucleotide.G, Nucleotide.A, Nucleotide.T)
print(linear_contains(my_gene, acg))  # True
print(linear_contains(my_gene, gat))  # False
```

> **NOTE** This function is for illustrative purposes only. The Python built-in sequence types (`list`, `tuple`, `range`) all implement the `__contains__()` method, which allows us to do a search for a specific item in them by simply using the `in` operator. In fact, the `in` operator can be used with any type that implements `__contains__()`. For instance, we could search `my_gene` for `acg` and print out the result by writing `print(acg in my_gene)`.

2.1.3 *Binary search*

There is a faster way to search than looking at every element, but it requires us to know something about the order of the data structure ahead of time. If we know that the structure is sorted, and we can instantly access any item within it by its index, we can perform a binary search. Based on this criteria, a sorted Python `list` is a perfect candidate for a binary search.

A binary search works by looking at the middle element in a sorted range of elements, comparing it to the element sought, reducing the range by half based on that comparison, and starting the process over again. Let's look at a concrete example.

Suppose we have a `list` of alphabetically sorted words like `["cat", "dog", "kangaroo", "llama", "rabbit", "rat", "zebra"]` and we are searching for the word "rat":

1 We could determine that the middle element in this seven-word list is "llama."

2 We could determine that "rat" comes after "llama" alphabetically, so it must be in the (approximately) half of the list that comes after "llama." (If we had found "rat" in this step, we could have returned its location; if we had found that our word came before the middle word we were checking, we could be assured that it was in the half of the list before "llama.")

3 We could rerun steps 1 and 2 for the half of the list that we know "rat" is still possibly in. In effect, this half becomes our new base list. These steps continually run until "rat" is found or the range we are looking in no longer contains any elements to search, meaning that "rat" does not exist within the word list.

Figure 2.3 illustrates a binary search. Notice that it does not involve searching every element, unlike a linear search.

A binary search continually reduces the search space by half, so it has a worst-case runtime of $O(\lg n)$. There is a sort-of catch, though. Unlike a linear search, a binary

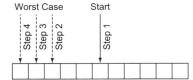

Figure 2.3   In the worst case of a binary search, you'll look through just lg(*n*) elements of the list.

search requires a sorted data structure to search through, and sorting takes time. In fact, sorting takes O(n lg n) time for the best sorting algorithms. If we are only going to run our search once, and our original data structure is unsorted, it probably makes sense to just do a linear search. But if the search is going to be performed many times, the time cost of doing the sort is worth it, to reap the benefit of the greatly reduced time cost of each individual search.

Writing a binary search function for a gene and a codon is not unlike writing one for any other type of data, because the Codon type can be compared to others of its type, and the Gene type is just a list.

Listing 2.7 dna_search.py continued

```
def binary_contains(gene: Gene, key_codon: Codon) -> bool:
    low: int = 0
    high: int = len(gene) - 1
    while low <= high:  # while there is still a search space
        mid: int = (low + high) // 2
        if gene[mid] < key_codon:
            low = mid + 1
        elif gene[mid] > key_codon:
            high = mid - 1
        else:
            return True
    return False
```

Let's walk through this function line by line.

```
low: int = 0
high: int = len(gene) - 1
```

We start by looking at a range that encompasses the entire list (gene).

```
while low <= high:
```

We keep searching as long as there is a still a range to search within. When `low` is greater than `high`, it means that there are no longer any slots to look at within the list.

```
mid: int = (low + high) // 2
```

We calculate the middle, `mid`, by using integer division and the simple mean formula you learned in grade school.

```
if gene[mid] < key_codon:
    low = mid + 1
```

If the element we are looking for is after the middle element of the range we are looking at, we modify the range that we will look at during the next iteration of the loop by moving `low` to be one past the current middle element. This is where we halve the range for the next iteration.

```
elif gene[mid] > key_codon:
    high = mid - 1
```

Similarly, we halve in the other direction when the element we are looking for is less than the middle element.

```
else:
    return True
```

If the element in question is not less than or greater than the middle element, that means we found it! And, of course, if the loop ran out of iterations, we return `False` (not reproduced here), indicating that it was never found.

We can try running our function with the same gene and codon, but we must remember to sort first.

> **Listing 2.8 dna_search.py continued**

```
my_sorted_gene: Gene = sorted(my_gene)
print(binary_contains(my_sorted_gene, acg))   # True
print(binary_contains(my_sorted_gene, gat))   # False
```

TIP You can build a performant binary search using the Python standard library's `bisect` module: https://docs.python.org/3/library/bisect.html.

2.1.4 *A generic example*

The functions `linear_contains()` and `binary_contains()` can be generalized to work with almost any Python sequence. The following generalized versions are nearly identical to the versions you saw before, with only some names and type hints changed.

NOTE There are many imported types in the following code listing. We will be reusing the file generic_search.py for many further generic search algorithms in this chapter, and this gets the imports out of the way.

NOTE Before proceeding with the book, you will need to install the `typing_extensions` module via either `pip install typing_extensions` or `pip3 install typing_extensions`, depending on how your Python interpreter is configured. You will need this module to access the `Protocol` type, which will be in the standard library in a future version of Python (as specified by PEP 544). Therefore, in a future version of Python, importing the `typing_extensions` module should be unnecessary, and you will be able to use `from typing import Protocol` instead of `from typing_extensions import Protocol`.

> **Listing 2.9 generic_search.py**

```
from __future__ import annotations
from typing import TypeVar, Iterable, Sequence, Generic, List, Callable, Set,
    Deque, Dict, Any, Optional
from typing_extensions import Protocol
from heapq import heappush, heappop

T = TypeVar('T')
```

```
def linear_contains(iterable: Iterable[T], key: T) -> bool:
    for item in iterable:
        if item == key:
            return True
    return False

C = TypeVar("C", bound="Comparable")

class Comparable(Protocol):
    def __eq__(self, other: Any) -> bool:
        ...

    def __lt__(self: C, other: C) -> bool:
        ...

    def __gt__(self: C, other: C) -> bool:
        return (not self < other) and self != other

    def __le__(self: C, other: C) -> bool:
        return self < other or self == other

    def __ge__(self: C, other: C) -> bool:
        return not self < other

def binary_contains(sequence: Sequence[C], key: C) -> bool:
    low: int = 0
    high: int = len(sequence) - 1
    while low <= high:  # while there is still a search space
        mid: int = (low + high) // 2
        if sequence[mid] < key:
            low = mid + 1
        elif sequence[mid] > key:
            high = mid - 1
        else:
            return True
    return False

if __name__ == "__main__":
    print(linear_contains([1, 5, 15, 15, 15, 15, 20], 5))  # True
    print(binary_contains(["a", "d", "e", "f", "z"], "f"))  # True
    print(binary_contains(["john", "mark", "ronald", "sarah"], "sheila"))  #
    False
```

Now you can try doing searches on other types of data. These functions can be reused for almost any Python collection. That is the power of writing code generically. The only unfortunate element of this example is the convoluted hoops that had to be jumped through for Python's type hints, in the form of the Comparable class. A Comparable type is a type that implements the comparison operators (<, >=, and so on). There should be a more succinct way in future versions of Python to create a type hint for types that implement these common operators.

2.2   *Maze solving*

Finding a path through a maze is analogous to many common search problems in computer science. Why not literally find a path through a maze, then, to illustrate the breadth-first search, depth-first search, and A* algorithms?

Our maze will be a two-dimensional grid of `Cell`s. A `Cell` is an enum with `str` values where `" "` will represent an empty space and `"X"` will represent a blocked space. There are also other cases for illustrative purposes when printing a maze.

Listing 2.10   maze.py

```
from enum import Enum
from typing import List, NamedTuple, Callable, Optional
import random
from math import sqrt
from generic_search import dfs, bfs, node_to_path, astar, Node


class Cell(str, Enum):
    EMPTY = " "
    BLOCKED = "X"
    START = "S"
    GOAL = "G"
    PATH = "*"
```

Once again, we are getting a large number of imports out of the way. Note that the last import (from `generic_search`) is of symbols we have not yet defined. It is included here for convenience, but you may want to comment it out until you need it.

We will need a way to refer to an individual location in the maze. This will simply be a `NamedTuple` with properties representing the row and column of the location in question.

Listing 2.11   maze.py continued

```
class MazeLocation(NamedTuple):
    row: int
    column: int
```

2.2.1   *Generating a random maze*

Our `Maze` class will internally keep track of a grid (a list of lists) representing its state. It will also have instance variables for the number of rows, number of columns, start location, and goal location. Its grid will be randomly filled with blocked cells.

The maze that is generated should be fairly sparse so that there is almost always a path from a given starting location to a given goal location. (This is for testing our algorithms, after all.) We'll let the caller of a new maze decide on the exact sparseness, but we will provide a default value of 20% blocked. When a random number beats the threshold of the `sparseness` parameter in question, we will simply replace an empty space with a wall. If we do this for every possible place in the maze, statistically, the sparseness of the maze as a whole will approximate the `sparseness` parameter supplied.

Listing 2.12   maze.py continued

```python
class Maze:
    def __init__(self, rows: int = 10, columns: int = 10, sparseness: float =
    0.2, start: MazeLocation = MazeLocation(0, 0), goal: MazeLocation =
    MazeLocation(9, 9)) -> None:
        # initialize basic instance variables
        self._rows: int = rows
        self._columns: int = columns
        self.start: MazeLocation = start
        self.goal: MazeLocation = goal
        # fill the grid with empty cells
        self._grid: List[List[Cell]] = [[Cell.EMPTY for c in range(columns)]
    for r in range(rows)]
        # populate the grid with blocked cells
        self._randomly_fill(rows, columns, sparseness)
        # fill the start and goal locations in
        self._grid[start.row][start.column] = Cell.START
        self._grid[goal.row][goal.column] = Cell.GOAL

    def _randomly_fill(self, rows: int, columns: int, sparseness: float):
        for row in range(rows):
            for column in range(columns):
                if random.uniform(0, 1.0) < sparseness:
                    self._grid[row][column] = Cell.BLOCKED
```

Now that we have a maze, we also want a way to print it succinctly to the console. We want its characters to be close together so it looks like a real maze.

Listing 2.13   maze.py continued

```python
# return a nicely formatted version of the maze for printing
def __str__(self) -> str:
    output: str = ""
    for row in self._grid:
        output += "".join([c.value for c in row]) + "\n"
    return output
```

Go ahead and test these maze functions.

```python
maze: Maze = Maze()
print(maze)
```

2.2.2   *Miscellaneous maze minutiae*

It will be handy later to have a function that checks whether we have reached our goal during the search. In other words, we want to check whether a particular Maze-Location that the search has reached is the goal. We can add a method to Maze.

Listing 2.14   maze.py continued

```python
def goal_test(self, ml: MazeLocation) -> bool:
    return ml == self.goal
```

How can we move within our mazes? Let's say that we can move horizontally and vertically one space at a time from a given space in the maze. Using these criteria, a `successors()` function can find the possible next locations from a given `MazeLocation`. However, the `successors()` function will differ for every `Maze` because every `Maze` has a different size and set of walls. Therefore, we will define it as a method on `Maze`.

Listing 2.15   maze.py continued

```python
def successors(self, ml: MazeLocation) -> List[MazeLocation]:
    locations: List[MazeLocation] = []
    if ml.row + 1 < self._rows and self._grid[ml.row + 1][ml.column] !=
    Cell.BLOCKED:
        locations.append(MazeLocation(ml.row + 1, ml.column))
    if ml.row - 1 >= 0 and self._grid[ml.row - 1][ml.column] != Cell.BLOCKED:
        locations.append(MazeLocation(ml.row - 1, ml.column))
    if ml.column + 1 < self._columns and self._grid[ml.row][ml.column + 1] !=
    Cell.BLOCKED:
        locations.append(MazeLocation(ml.row, ml.column + 1))
    if ml.column - 1 >= 0 and self._grid[ml.row][ml.column - 1] !=
    Cell.BLOCKED:
        locations.append(MazeLocation(ml.row, ml.column - 1))
    return locations
```

`successors()` simply checks above, below, to the right, and to the left of a `Maze-Location` in a `Maze` to see if it can find empty spaces that can be gone to from that location. It also avoids checking locations beyond the edges of the `Maze`. It puts every possible `MazeLocation` that it finds into a list that it ultimately returns to the caller.

2.2.3   *Depth-first search*

A *depth-first search* (DFS) is what its name suggests: a search that goes as deeply as it can before backtracking to its last decision point if it reaches a dead end. We'll implement a generic depth-first search that can solve our maze problem. It will also be reusable for other problems. Figure 2.4 illustrates an in-progress depth-first search of a maze.

STACKS

The depth-first search algorithm relies on a data structure known as a *stack*. (If you read about stacks in chapter 1, feel free to skip this section.) A stack is a data structure that operates under the Last-In-First-Out (LIFO) principle. Imagine a stack of papers. The last paper placed on top of the stack is the first paper pulled off the stack. It is common for a stack to be implemented on top of a more primitive data structure like a list. We will implement our stack on top of Python's `list` type.

Stacks generally have at least two operations:

- `push()`—Places an item on top of the stack
- `pop()`—Removes the item from the top of the stack and returns it

We will implement both of these, as well as an `empty` property to check if the stack has any more items in it. We will add the code for the stack to the generic_search.py file that we were working with earlier in the chapter. We already have completed all of the necessary imports.

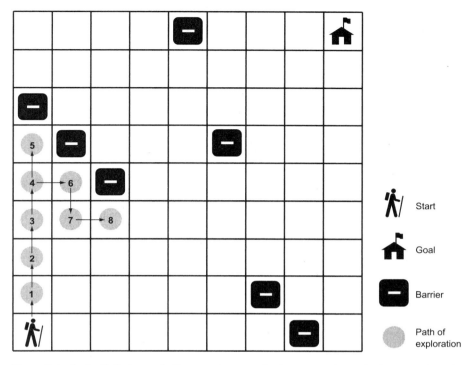

Figure 2.4 In depth-first search, the search proceeds along a continuously deeper path until it hits a barrier and must backtrack to the last decision point.

Listing 2.16 generic_search.py continued

```python
class Stack(Generic[T]):
    def __init__(self) -> None:
        self._container: List[T] = []

    @property
    def empty(self) -> bool:
        return not self._container  # not is true for empty container

    def push(self, item: T) -> None:
        self._container.append(item)

    def pop(self) -> T:
        return self._container.pop()  # LIFO

    def __repr__(self) -> str:
        return repr(self._container)
```

Note that implementing a stack using a Python `list` is as simple as always appending items onto its right end and always removing items from its extreme right end. The `pop()` method on `list` will fail if there are no longer any items in the list, so `pop()` will fail on a `Stack` if it is empty as well.

THE DFS ALGORITHM

We will need one more little tidbit before we can get to implementing DFS. We need a `Node` class that we will use to keep track of how we got from one state to another state (or from one place to another place) as we search. You can think of a `Node` as a wrapper around a state. In the case of our maze-solving problem, those states are of type `MazeLocation`. We'll call the `Node` that a state came from its `parent`. We will also define our `Node` class as having `cost` and `heuristic` properties and with `__lt__()` implemented, so we can reuse it later in the A* algorithm.

Listing 2.17   generic_search.py continued

```
class Node(Generic[T]):
    def __init__(self, state: T, parent: Optional[Node], cost: float = 0.0,
      heuristic: float = 0.0) -> None:
        self.state: T = state
        self.parent: Optional[Node] = parent
        self.cost: float = cost
        self.heuristic: float = heuristic

    def __lt__(self, other: Node) -> bool:
        return (self.cost + self.heuristic) < (other.cost + other.heuristic)
```

TIP The `Optional` type indicates that a value of a parameterized type may be referenced by the variable, or the variable may reference `None`.

TIP At the top of the file, the `from __future__ import annotations` allows `Node` to reference itself in the type hints of its methods. Without it, we would need to put the type hint in quotes as a string (for example, `'Node'`). In future versions of Python, importing `annotations` will be unnecessary. See PEP 563, "Postponed Evaluation of Annotations," for more information: http://mng.bz/pgzR.

An in-progress depth-first search needs to keep track of two data structures: the stack of states (or "places") that we are considering searching, which we will call the `frontier`; and the set of states that we have already searched, which we will call `explored`. As long as there are more states to visit in the frontier, DFS will keep checking whether they are the goal (if a state is the goal, DFS will stop and return it) and adding their successors to the frontier. It will also mark each state that has already been searched as explored, so that the search does not get caught in a circle, reaching states that have prior visited states as successors. If the frontier is empty, it means there is nowhere left to search.

Listing 2.18   generic_search.py continued

```python
def dfs(initial: T, goal_test: Callable[[T], bool], successors: Callable[[T],
    List[T]]) -> Optional[Node[T]]:
    # frontier is where we've yet to go
    frontier: Stack[Node[T]] = Stack()
    frontier.push(Node(initial, None))
    # explored is where we've been
    explored: Set[T] = {initial}

    # keep going while there is more to explore
    while not frontier.empty:
        current_node: Node[T] = frontier.pop()
        current_state: T = current_node.state
        # if we found the goal, we're done
        if goal_test(current_state):
            return current_node
        # check where we can go next and haven't explored
        for child in successors(current_state):
            if child in explored:  # skip children we already explored
                continue
            explored.add(child)
            frontier.push(Node(child, current_node))
    return None  # went through everything and never found goal
```

If dfs() is successful, it returns the Node encapsulating the goal state. The path from the start to the goal can be reconstructed by working backward from this Node and its priors using the parent property.

Listing 2.19   generic_search.py continued

```python
def node_to_path(node: Node[T]) -> List[T]:
    path: List[T] = [node.state]
    # work backwards from end to front
    while node.parent is not None:
        node = node.parent
        path.append(node.state)
    path.reverse()
    return path
```

For display purposes, it will be useful to mark up the maze with the successful path, the start state, and the goal state. It will also be useful to be able to remove a path so that we can try different search algorithms on the same maze. The following two methods should be added to the Maze class in maze.py.

Listing 2.20   maze.py continued

```python
def mark(self, path: List[MazeLocation]):
    for maze_location in path:
        self._grid[maze_location.row][maze_location.column] = Cell.PATH
    self._grid[self.start.row][self.start.column] = Cell.START
    self._grid[self.goal.row][self.goal.column] = Cell.GOAL

def clear(self, path: List[MazeLocation]):
```

```
for maze_location in path:
    self._grid[maze_location.row][maze_location.column] = Cell.EMPTY
self._grid[self.start.row][self.start.column] = Cell.START
self._grid[self.goal.row][self.goal.column] = Cell.GOAL
```

It has been a long journey, but we are finally ready to solve the maze.

Listing 2.21   maze.py continued

```
if __name__ == "__main__":
    # Test DFS
    m: Maze = Maze()
    print(m)
    solution1: Optional[Node[MazeLocation]] = dfs(m.start, m.goal_test,
     m.successors)
    if solution1 is None:
        print("No solution found using depth-first search!")
    else:
        path1: List[MazeLocation] = node_to_path(solution1)
        m.mark(path1)
        print(m)
        m.clear(path1)
```

A successful solution will look something like this:

```
S****X X
 X  *****
       X*
XX******X
 X*
 X**X
 X  *****
       *
    X  *X
       *G
```

The asterisks represent the path that our depth-first search function found from the start to the goal. Remember, because each maze is randomly generated, not every maze has a solution.

2.2.4 *Breadth-first search*

You may notice that the solution paths to the mazes found by depth-first traversal seem unnatural. They are usually not the shortest paths. Breadth-first search (BFS) always finds the shortest path by systematically looking one layer of nodes farther away from the start state in each iteration of the search. There are particular problems in which a depth-first search is likely to find a solution more quickly than a breadth-first search, and vice versa. Therefore, choosing between the two is sometimes a trade-off between the possibility of finding a solution quickly and the certainty of finding the shortest path to the goal (if one exists). Figure 2.5 illustrates an in-progress breadth-first search of a maze.

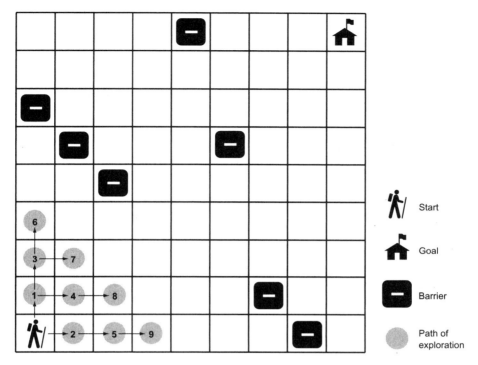

Figure 2.5 In a breadth-first search, the closest elements to the starting location are searched first.

To understand why a depth-first search sometimes returns a result faster than a breadth-first search, imagine looking for a marking on a particular layer of an onion. A searcher using a depth-first strategy may plunge a knife into the center of the onion and haphazardly examine the chunks cut out. If the marked layer happens to be near the chunk cut out, there is a chance that the searcher will find it more quickly than another searcher using a breadth-first strategy, who painstakingly peels the onion one layer at a time.

To get a better picture of why breadth-first search always finds the shortest solution path where one exists, consider trying to find the path with the fewest number of stops between Boston and New York by train. If you keep going in the same direction and backtracking when you hit a dead end (as in depth-first search), you may first find a route all the way to Seattle before it connects back to New York. However, in a breadth-first search, you will first check all of the stations one stop away from Boston. Then you will check all of the stations two stops away from Boston. Then you will check all of the stations three stops away from Boston. This will keep going until you find New York. Therefore, when you do find New York, you will know you have found the route with the fewest stops, because you already checked all of the stations that are fewer stops away from Boston, and none of them was New York.

QUEUES

To implement BFS, a data structure known as a *queue* is required. Whereas a stack is LIFO, a queue is FIFO (First-In-First-Out). A queue is like a line to use a restroom. The first person who got in line goes to the restroom first. At a minimum, a queue has the same push() and pop() methods as a stack. In fact, our implementation for Queue (backed by a Python deque) is almost identical to our implementation of Stack, with the only changes being the removal of elements from the left end of the _container instead of the right end and the switch from a list to a deque. (I use the word "left" here to mean the beginning of the backing store.) The elements on the left end are the oldest elements still in the deque (in terms of arrival time), so they are the first elements popped.

Listing 2.22 generic_search.py continued

```python
class Queue(Generic[T]):
    def __init__(self) -> None:
        self._container: Deque[T] = Deque()

    @property
    def empty(self) -> bool:
        return not self._container  # not is true for empty container

    def push(self, item: T) -> None:
        self._container.append(item)


    def pop(self) -> T:
        return self._container.popleft()  # FIFO


    def __repr__(self) -> str:
        return repr(self._container)
```

TIP   Why did the implementation of Queue use a deque as its backing store, whereas the implementation of Stack used a list as its backing store? It has to do with where we pop. In a stack, we push to the right and pop from the right. In a queue we push to the right as well, but we pop from the left. The Python list data structure has efficient pops from the right but not from the left. A deque can efficiently pop from either side. As a result, there is a built-in method on deque called popleft() but no equivalent method on list. You could certainly find other ways to use a list as the backing store for a queue, but they would be less efficient. Popping from the left on a deque is an O(1) operation, whereas it is an O(*n*) operation on a list. In the case of the list, after popping from the left, every subsequent element must be moved one to the left, making it inefficient.

THE BFS ALGORITHM

Amazingly, the algorithm for a breadth-first search is identical to the algorithm for a depth-first search, with the frontier changed from a stack to a queue. Changing the frontier from a stack to a queue changes the order in which states are searched and ensures that the states closest to the start state are searched first.

Listing 2.23   generic_search.py continued

```python
def bfs(initial: T, goal_test: Callable[[T], bool], successors: Callable[[T],
    List[T]]) -> Optional[Node[T]]:
    # frontier is where we've yet to go
    frontier: Queue[Node[T]] = Queue()
    frontier.push(Node(initial, None))
    # explored is where we've been
    explored: Set[T] = {initial}

    # keep going while there is more to explore
    while not frontier.empty:
        current_node: Node[T] = frontier.pop()
        current_state: T = current_node.state
        # if we found the goal, we're done
        if goal_test(current_state):
            return current_node
        # check where we can go next and haven't explored
        for child in successors(current_state):
            if child in explored:  # skip children we already explored
                continue
            explored.add(child)
            frontier.push(Node(child, current_node))
    return None  # went through everything and never found goal
```

If you try running `bfs()`, you will see that it always finds the shortest solution to the maze in question. The following trial is added just after the previous one in the `if __name__ == "__main__":` section of the file, so results can be compared on the same maze.

Listing 2.24   maze.py continued

```python
# Test BFS
solution2: Optional[Node[MazeLocation]] = bfs(m.start, m.goal_test,
    m.successors)
if solution2 is None:
    print("No solution found using breadth-first search!")
else:
    path2: List[MazeLocation] = node_to_path(solution2)
    m.mark(path2)
    print(m)
    m.clear(path2)
```

It is amazing that you can keep an algorithm the same and just change the data structure that it accesses and get radically different results. The following is the result of calling `bfs()` on the same maze that we earlier called `dfs()` on. Notice how the path marked by the asterisks is more direct from start to goal than in the prior example.

```
S    X X
*X
*       X
*XX     X
* X
* X  X
*X
*
*       X   X
********G
```

2.2.5   *A* search*

It can be very time-consuming to peel back an onion, layer-by-layer, as a breadth-first search does. Like a BFS, an A* search aims to find the shortest path from start state to goal state. Unlike the preceding BFS implementation, an A* search uses a combination of a cost function and a heuristic function to focus its search on pathways most likely to get to the goal quickly.

The cost function, $g(n)$, examines the cost to get to a particular state. In the case of our maze, this would be how many previous steps we had to go through to get to the state in question. The heuristic function, $h(n)$, gives an estimate of the cost to get from the state in question to the goal state. It can be proved that if $h(n)$ is an *admissible heuristic*, then the final path found will be optimal. An admissible heuristic is one that never overestimates the cost to reach the goal. On a two-dimensional plane, one example is a straight-line distance heuristic, because a straight line is always the shortest path.[1]

The total cost for any state being considered is $f(n)$, which is simply the combination of $g(n)$ and $h(n)$. In fact, $f(n) = g(n) + h(n)$. When choosing the next state to explore from the frontier, an A* search picks the one with the lowest $f(n)$. This is how it distinguishes itself from BFS and DFS.

PRIORITY QUEUES

To pick the state on the frontier with the lowest $f(n)$, an A* search uses a *priority queue* as the data structure for its frontier. A priority queue keeps its elements in an internal order, such that the first element popped out is always the highest-priority element. (In our case, the highest-priority item is the one with the lowest $f(n)$.) Usually this means the internal use of a binary heap, which results in $O(\lg n)$ pushes and $O(\lg n)$ pops.

Python's standard library contains `heappush()` and `heappop()` functions that will take a list and maintain it as a binary heap. We can implement a priority queue by building a thin wrapper around these standard library functions. Our `PriorityQueue` class will be similar to our `Stack` and `Queue` classes, with the `push()` and `pop()` methods modified to use `heappush()` and `heappop()`.

---

[1] For more information on heuristics, see Stuart Russell and Peter Norvig, *Artificial Intelligence: A Modern Approach*, 3rd edition (Pearson, 2010), page 94.

Listing 2.25 generic_search.py continued

```python
class PriorityQueue(Generic[T]):
    def __init__(self) -> None:
        self._container: List[T] = []

    @property
    def empty(self) -> bool:
        return not self._container  # not is true for empty container

    def push(self, item: T) -> None:
        heappush(self._container, item)  # in by priority

    def pop(self) -> T:
        return heappop(self._container)  # out by priority

    def __repr__(self) -> str:
        return repr(self._container)
```

To determine the priority of a particular element versus another of its kind, heappush() and heappop(), compare them by using the < operator. This is why we needed to implement __lt__() on Node earlier. One Node is compared to another by looking at its respective f(*n*), which is simply the sum of the properties cost and heuristic.

HEURISTICS

A *heuristic* is an intuition about the way to solve a problem.[2] In the case of maze solving, a heuristic aims to choose the best maze location to search next, in the quest to get to the goal. In other words, it is an educated guess about which nodes on the frontier are closest to the goal. As was mentioned previously, if a heuristic used with an A* search produces an accurate relative result and is admissible (never overestimates the distance), then A* will deliver the shortest path. Heuristics that calculate smaller values end up leading to a search through more states, whereas heuristics closer to the exact real distance (but not over it, which would make them inadmissible) lead to a search through fewer states. Therefore, ideal heuristics come as close to the real distance as possible without ever going over it.

EUCLIDEAN DISTANCE

As we learn in geometry, the shortest path between two points is a straight line. It makes sense, then, that a straight-line heuristic will always be admissible for the maze-solving problem. The Euclidean distance, derived from the Pythagorean theorem, states that distance = $\sqrt{((\text{difference in x})^2 + (\text{difference in y})^2)}$. For our mazes, the difference in *x* is equivalent to the difference in columns between two maze locations, and the difference in *y* is equivalent to the difference in rows. Note that we are implementing this back in maze.py.

---

[2] For more about heuristics for A* pathfinding, check out the "Heuristics" chapter in Amit Patel's *Amit's Thoughts on Pathfinding*, http://mng.bz/z7O4.

Listing 2.26   maze.py continued

```
def euclidean_distance(goal: MazeLocation) -> Callable[[MazeLocation],
        float]:
    def distance(ml: MazeLocation) -> float:
        xdist: int = ml.column - goal.column
        ydist: int = ml.row - goal.row
        return sqrt((xdist * xdist) + (ydist * ydist))
    return distance
```

euclidean_distance() is a function that returns another function. Languages like Python that support first-class functions enable this interesting pattern. distance() captures the goal MazeLocation that euclidean_distance() is passed. Capturing means that distance() can refer to this variable every time it's called (permanently). The function it returns makes use of goal to do its calculations. This pattern enables the creation of a function that requires fewer parameters. The returned distance() function takes just the start maze location as an argument and permanently "knows" the goal.

Figure 2.6 illustrates Euclidean distance within the context of a grid, like the streets of Manhattan.

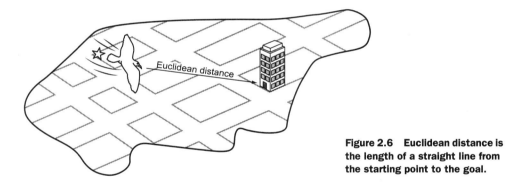

Figure 2.6   Euclidean distance is the length of a straight line from the starting point to the goal.

MANHATTAN DISTANCE

Euclidean distance is great, but for our particular problem (a maze in which you can move only in one of four directions) we can do even better. The Manhattan distance is derived from navigating the streets of Manhattan, the most famous of New York City's boroughs, which is laid out in a grid pattern. To get from anywhere to anywhere in Manhattan, one needs to walk a certain number of horizontal blocks and a certain number of vertical blocks. (There are almost no diagonal streets in Manhattan.) The Manhattan distance is derived by simply finding the difference in rows between two maze locations and summing it with the difference in columns. Figure 2.7 illustrates Manhattan distance.

Listing 2.27 maze.py continued

```python
def manhattan_distance(goal: MazeLocation) -> Callable[[MazeLocation],
    float]:
    def distance(ml: MazeLocation) -> float:
        xdist: int = abs(ml.column - goal.column)
        ydist: int = abs(ml.row - goal.row)
        return (xdist + ydist)
    return distance
```

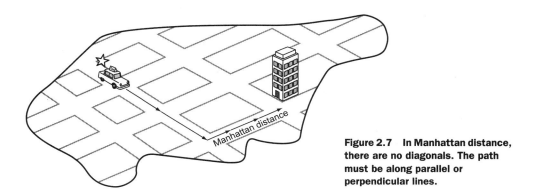

Figure 2.7 In Manhattan distance, there are no diagonals. The path must be along parallel or perpendicular lines.

Because this heuristic more accurately follows the actuality of navigating our mazes (moving vertically and horizontally instead of in diagonal straight lines), it comes closer to the actual distance between any maze location and the goal than Euclidean distance does. Therefore, when an A* search is coupled with Manhattan distance, it will result in searching through fewer states than when an A* search is coupled with Euclidean distance for our mazes. Solution paths will still be optimal, because Manhattan distance is admissible (never overestimates distance) for mazes in which only four directions of movement are allowed.

THE A* ALGORITHM

To go from BFS to A* search, we need to make several small modifications. The first is changing the frontier from a queue to a priority queue. This way, the frontier will pop nodes with the lowest f(n). The second is changing the explored set to a dictionary. A dictionary will allow us to keep track of the lowest cost (g(n)) of each node we may visit. With the heuristic function now at play, it is possible some nodes may be visited twice if the heuristic is inconsistent. If the node found through the new direction has a lower cost to get to than the prior time we visited it, we will prefer the new route.

For the sake of simplicity, the function `astar()` does not take a cost-calculation function as a parameter. Instead, we just consider every hop in our maze to be a cost of 1. Each new `Node` gets assigned a cost based on this simple formula, as well as a heuristic score using a new function passed as a parameter to the search function called `heuristic()`. Other than these changes, `astar()` is remarkably similar to `bfs()`. Examine them side by side for comparison.

Listing 2.28   generic_search.py

```
def astar(initial: T, goal_test: Callable[[T], bool], successors:
    Callable[[T], List[T]], heuristic: Callable[[T], float]) ->
    Optional[Node[T]]:
    # frontier is where we've yet to go
    frontier: PriorityQueue[Node[T]] = PriorityQueue()
    frontier.push(Node(initial, None, 0.0, heuristic(initial)))
    # explored is where we've been
    explored: Dict[T, float] = {initial: 0.0}

    # keep going while there is more to explore
    while not frontier.empty:
        current_node: Node[T] = frontier.pop()
        current_state: T = current_node.state
        # if we found the goal, we're done
        if goal_test(current_state):
            return current_node
        # check where we can go next and haven't explored
        for child in successors(current_state):
            new_cost: float = current_node.cost + 1  # 1 assumes a grid, need
    a cost function for more sophisticated apps

            if child not in explored or explored[child] > new_cost:
                explored[child] = new_cost
                frontier.push(Node(child, current_node, new_cost,
    heuristic(child)))
    return None  # went through everything and never found goal
```

Congratulations. If you have followed along this far, you have learned not only how to solve a maze, but also some generic search functions that you can use in many different search applications. DFS and BFS are suitable for many smaller data sets and state spaces where performance is not critical. In some situations, DFS will outperform BFS, but BFS has the advantage of always delivering an optimal path. Interestingly, BFS and DFS have identical implementations, only differentiated by the use of a queue instead of a stack for the frontier. The slightly more complicated A* search, coupled with a good, consistent, admissible heuristic, not only delivers optimal paths, but also far outperforms BFS. And because all three of these functions were implemented generically, using them on nearly any search space is just an `import generic_search` away.

Go ahead and try out `astar()` with the same maze in maze.py's testing section.

Listing 2.29   maze.py continued

```
# Test A*
distance: Callable[[MazeLocation], float] = manhattan_distance(m.goal)
solution3: Optional[Node[MazeLocation]] = astar(m.start, m.goal_test,
    m.successors, distance)
if solution3 is None:
    print("No solution found using A*!")
else:
    path3: List[MazeLocation] = node_to_path(solution3)
    m.mark(path3)
    print(m)
```

The output will interestingly be a little different from `bfs()`, even though both `bfs()` and `astar()` are finding optimal paths (equivalent in length). Due to its heuristic, `astar()` immediately drives through a diagonal toward the goal. It will ultimately search fewer states than `bfs()`, resulting in better performance. Add a state count to each if you want to prove this to yourself.

```
S**  X X
 X**
   *   X
 XX*     X
  X*
  X**X
 X  ****
        *
     X * X
       **G
```

2.3 Missionaries and cannibals

Three missionaries and three cannibals are on the west bank of a river. They have a canoe that can hold two people, and they all must cross to the east bank of the river. There may never be more cannibals than missionaries on either side of the river, or the cannibals will eat the missionaries. Further, the canoe must have at least one person on board to cross the river. What sequence of crossings will successfully take the entire party across the river? Figure 2.8 illustrates the problem.

2.3.1 Representing the problem

We will represent the problem by having a structure that keeps track of the west bank. How many missionaries and cannibals are on the west bank? Is the boat on the west bank? Once we have this knowledge, we can figure out what is on the east bank, because anything not on the west bank is on the east bank.

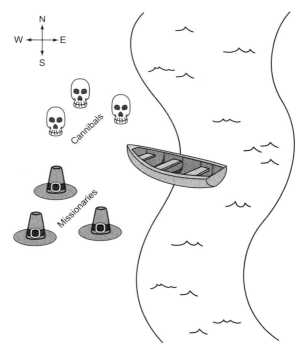

Figure 2.8 The missionaries and cannibals must use their single canoe to take everyone across the river from west to east. If the cannibals ever outnumber the missionaries, they will eat them.

First, we will create a little convenience variable for keeping track of the maximum number of missionaries or cannibals. Then we will define the main class.

```python
from __future__ import annotations
from typing import List, Optional
from generic_search import bfs, Node, node_to_path

MAX_NUM: int = 3


class MCState:
    def __init__(self, missionaries: int, cannibals: int, boat: bool) ->
    None:
        self.wm: int = missionaries # west bank missionaries
        self.wc: int = cannibals # west bank cannibals
        self.em: int = MAX_NUM - self.wm  # east bank missionaries
        self.ec: int = MAX_NUM - self.wc  # east bank cannibals
        self.boat: bool = boat


    def __str__(self) -> str:
        return ("On the west bank there are {} missionaries and {}
        cannibals.\n"
                "On the east bank there are {} missionaries and {}
        cannibals.\n"
                "The boat is on the {} bank.")\
            .format(self.wm, self.wc, self.em, self.ec, ("west" if self.boat
        else "east"))
```

The class MCState initializes itself based on the number of missionaries and cannibals on the west bank as well as the location of the boat. It also knows how to pretty-print itself, which will be valuable later when displaying the solution to the problem.

Working within the confines of our existing search functions means that we must define a function for testing whether a state is the goal state and a function for finding the successors from any state. The goal test function, as in the maze-solving problem, is quite simple. The goal is simply when we reach a legal state that has all of the missionaries and cannibals on the east bank. We add it as a method to MCState.

```python
def goal_test(self) -> bool:
    return self.is_legal and self.em == MAX_NUM and self.ec == MAX_NUM
```

To create a successors function, it is necessary to go through all of the possible moves that can be made from one bank to another and then check if each of those moves will result in a legal state. Recall that a legal state is one in which cannibals do not outnumber missionaries on either bank. To determine this, we can define a convenience property (as a method on MCState) that checks if a state is legal.

Listing 2.32   missionaries.py continued

```python
@property
def is_legal(self) -> bool:
    if self.wm < self.wc and self.wm > 0:
        return False
    if self.em < self.ec and self.em > 0:
        return False
    return True
```

The actual successors function is a bit verbose, for the sake of clarity. It tries adding every possible combination of one or two people moving across the river from the bank where the canoe currently resides. Once it has added all possible moves, it filters for the ones that are actually legal via a list comprehension. Once again, this is a method on `MCState`.

Listing 2.33   missionaries.py continued

```python
def successors(self) -> List[MCState]:
    sucs: List[MCState] = []
    if self.boat: # boat on west bank
        if self.wm > 1:
            sucs.append(MCState(self.wm - 2, self.wc, not self.boat))
        if self.wm > 0:
            sucs.append(MCState(self.wm - 1, self.wc, not self.boat))
        if self.wc > 1:
            sucs.append(MCState(self.wm, self.wc - 2, not self.boat))
        if self.wc > 0:
            sucs.append(MCState(self.wm, self.wc - 1, not self.boat))
        if (self.wc > 0) and (self.wm > 0):
            sucs.append(MCState(self.wm - 1, self.wc - 1, not self.boat))
    else: # boat on east bank
        if self.em > 1:
            sucs.append(MCState(self.wm + 2, self.wc, not self.boat))
        if self.em > 0:
            sucs.append(MCState(self.wm + 1, self.wc, not self.boat))
        if self.ec > 1:
            sucs.append(MCState(self.wm, self.wc + 2, not self.boat))
        if self.ec > 0:
            sucs.append(MCState(self.wm, self.wc + 1, not self.boat))
        if (self.ec > 0) and (self.em > 0):
            sucs.append(MCState(self.wm + 1, self.wc + 1, not self.boat))
    return [x for x in sucs if x.is_legal]
```

2.3.2   Solving

We now have all of the ingredients in place to solve the problem. Recall that when we solve a problem using the search functions `bfs()`, `dfs()`, and `astar()`, we get back a `Node` that ultimately we convert using `node_to_path()` into a list of states that leads to a solution. What we still need is a way to convert that list into a comprehensible printed sequence of steps to solve the missionaries and cannibals problem.

The function `display_solution()` converts a solution path into printed output—a human-readable solution to the problem. It works by iterating through all of the states in the solution path while keeping track of the last state as well. It looks at the difference between the last state and the state it is currently iterating on to find out how many missionaries and cannibals moved across the river and in which direction.

Listing 2.34 missionaries.py continued

```python
def display_solution(path: List[MCState]):
    if len(path) == 0:  # sanity check
        return
    old_state: MCState = path[0]
    print(old_state)
    for current_state in path[1:]:
        if current_state.boat:
            print("{} missionaries and {} cannibals moved from the east bank
    to the west bank.\n"
                    .format(old_state.em - current_state.em, old_state.ec -
    current_state.ec))
        else:
            print("{} missionaries and {} cannibals moved from the west bank
    to the east bank.\n"
                    .format(old_state.wm - current_state.wm, old_state.wc -
    current_state.wc))
        print(current_state)
        old_state = current_state
```

The `display_solution()` function takes advantage of the fact that `MCState` knows how to pretty-print a nice summary of itself via `__str__()`.

The last thing we need to do is actually solve the missionaries-and-cannibals problem. To do so we can conveniently reuse a search function that we have already implemented, because we implemented them generically. This solution uses `bfs()` (because using `dfs()` would require marking referentially different states with the same value as equal, and `astar()` would require a heuristic).

Listing 2.35 missionaries.py continued

```python
if __name__ == "__main__":
    start: MCState = MCState(MAX_NUM, MAX_NUM, True)
    solution: Optional[Node[MCState]] = bfs(start, MCState.goal_test,
     MCState.successors)
    if solution is None:
        print("No solution found!")
    else:
        path: List[MCState] = node_to_path(solution)
        display_solution(path)
```

It is great to see how flexible our generic search functions can be. They can easily be adapted for solving a diverse set of problems. You should see output something like the following (abridged):

```
On the west bank there are 3 missionaries and 3 cannibals.
On the east bank there are 0 missionaries and 0 cannibals.
```

```
The boast is on the west bank.
0 missionaries and 2 cannibals moved from the west bank to the east bank.

On the west bank there are 3 missionaries and 1 cannibals.
On the east bank there are 0 missionaries and 2 cannibals.
The boast is on the east bank.
0 missionaries and 1 cannibals moved from the east bank to the west bank.

…

On the west bank there are 0 missionaries and 0 cannibals.
On the east bank there are 3 missionaries and 3 cannibals.
The boast is on the east bank.
```

2.4   *Real-world applications*

Search plays some role in all useful software. In some cases, it is the central element (Google Search, Spotlight, Lucene); in others, it is the basis for using the structures that underlie data storage. Knowing the correct search algorithm to apply to a data structure is essential for performance. For example, it would be very costly to use linear search, instead of binary search, on a sorted data structure.

A* is one of the most widely deployed path-finding algorithms. It is only beaten by algorithms that do precalculation in the search space. For a blind search, A* is yet to be reliably beaten in all scenarios, and this has made it an essential component of everything from route planning to figuring out the shortest way to parse a programming language. Most directions-providing map software (think Google Maps) uses Dijkstra's algorithm (which A* is a variant of) to navigate. (There is more about Dijkstra's algorithm in chapter 4.) Whenever an AI character in a game is finding the shortest path from one end of the world to the other without human intervention, it is probably using A*.

Breadth-first search and depth-first search are often the basis for more complex search algorithms like uniform-cost search and backtracking search (which you will see in the next chapter). Breadth-first search is often a sufficient technique for finding the shortest path in a fairly small graph. But due to its similarity to A*, it is easy to swap out for A* if a good heuristic exists for a larger graph.

2.5   *Exercises*

1   Show the performance advantage of binary search over linear search by creating a list of one million numbers and timing how long it takes the `linear_contains()` and `binary_contains()` functions defined in this chapter to find various numbers in the list.

2   Add a counter to `dfs()`, `bfs()`, and `astar()` to see how many states each searches through for the same maze. Find the counts for 100 different mazes to get statistically significant results.

3   Find a solution to the missionaries-and-cannibals problem for a different number of starting missionaries and cannibals. Hint: you may need to add overrides of the `__eq__()` and `__hash__()` methods to `MCState`.

Constraint-satisfaction problems

A large number of problems that computational tools are used to solve can be broadly categorized as constraint-satisfaction problems (CSPs). CSPs are composed of *variables* with possible values that fall into ranges known as *domains*. *Constraints* between the variables must be satisfied in order for constraint-satisfaction problems to be solved. Those three core concepts—variables, domains, and constraints—are simple to understand, and their generality underlies the wide applicability of constraint-satisfaction problem solving.

Let's consider an example problem. Suppose you are trying to schedule a Friday meeting for Joe, Mary, and Sue. Sue has to be at the meeting with at least one other person. For this scheduling problem, the three people—Joe, Mary, and Sue—may be the variables. The domain for each variable may be their respective hours of availability. For instance, the variable Mary has the domain 2 p.m., 3 p.m., and 4 p.m. This problem also has two constraints. One is that Sue has to be at the meeting. The other is that at least two people must attend the meeting. A constraint-satisfaction problem solver will be provided with the three variables, three domains, and two constraints, and it will then solve the problem without having the user explain exactly *how*. Figure 3.1 illustrates this example.

Programming languages like Prolog and Picat have facilities for solving constraint-satisfaction problems built in. The usual technique in other languages is to build a framework that incorporates a backtracking search and several heuristics to improve the performance of that search. In this chapter we will first build a framework for CSPs that solves them using a simple recursive backtracking search. Then we will use the framework to solve several different example problems.

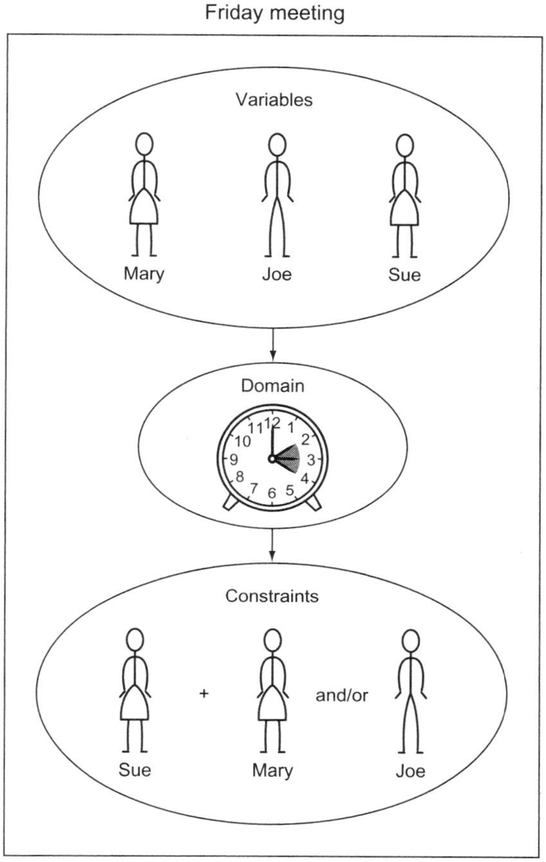

Friday meeting

Figure 3.1   Scheduling problems are a classic application of constraint-satisfaction frameworks.

3.1   *Building a constraint-satisfaction problem framework*

Constraints will be defined using a `Constraint` class. Each `Constraint` consists of the `variables` it constrains and a method that checks whether it is `satisfied()`. The determination of whether a constraint is satisfied is the main logic that goes into defining a specific constraint-satisfaction problem. The default implementation should be overridden. In fact, it must be, because we are defining our `Constraint` class as an abstract base class. Abstract base classes are not meant to be instantiated. Instead, only their subclasses that override and implement their `@abstractmethods` are for actual use.

Listing 3.1   csp.py

```python
from typing import Generic, TypeVar, Dict, List, Optional
from abc import ABC, abstractmethod

V = TypeVar('V') # variable type
```

```
D = TypeVar('D') # domain type

# Base class for all constraints
class Constraint(Generic[V, D], ABC):
    # The variables that the constraint is between
    def __init__(self, variables: List[V]) -> None:
        self.variables = variables


    # Must be overridden by subclasses
    @abstractmethod
    def satisfied(self, assignment: Dict[V, D]) -> bool:
        ...
```

TIP Abstract base classes serve as templates for a class hierarchy. They are more prevalent in other languages, like C++, as a user-facing feature than they are in Python. In fact, they were only introduced to Python about halfway through the language's lifetime. With that said, many of the collection classes in Python's standard library are implemented via abstract base classes. The general advice is not to use them in your own code unless you are sure that you are building a framework upon which others will build, and not just a class hierarchy for internal use. For more information, see chapter 11 of *Fluent Python* by Luciano Ramalho (O'Reilly, 2015).

The centerpiece of our constraint-satisfaction framework will be a class called CSP. CSP is the gathering point for variables, domains, and constraints. In terms of its type hints, it uses generics to make itself flexible enough to work with any kind of variables and domain values (V keys and D domain values). Within CSP, the variables, domains, and constraints collections are of types that you would expect. The variables collection is a list of variables, domains is a dict mapping variables to lists of possible values (the domains of those variables), and constraints is a dict that maps each variable to a list of the constraints imposed on it.

Listing 3.2   csp.py continued

```
# A constraint satisfaction problem consists of variables of type V
# that have ranges of values known as domains of type D and constraints
# that determine whether a particular variable's domain selection is valid
class CSP(Generic[V, D]):
    def __init__(self, variables: List[V], domains: Dict[V, List[D]]) ->
    None:
        self.variables: List[V] = variables # variables to be constrained
        self.domains: Dict[V, List[D]] = domains # domain of each variable
        self.constraints: Dict[V, List[Constraint[V, D]]] = {}
        for variable in self.variables:
            self.constraints[variable] = []
            if variable not in self.domains:
                raise LookupError("Every variable should have a domain
    assigned to it.")

    def add_constraint(self, constraint: Constraint[V, D]) -> None:
        for variable in constraint.variables:
```

```
        if variable not in self.variables:
            raise LookupError("Variable in constraint not in CSP")
        else:
            self.constraints[variable].append(constraint)
```

The __init__() initializer creates the constraints dict. The add_constraint() method goes through all of the variables touched by a given constraint and adds itself to the constraints mapping for each of them. Both methods have basic error-checking in place and will raise an exception when a variable is missing a domain or a constraint is on a nonexistent variable.

How do we know if a given configuration of variables and selected domain values satisfies the constraints? We will call such a given configuration an "assignment." We need a function that checks every constraint for a given variable against an assignment to see if the variable's value in the assignment works for the constraints. Here, we implement a consistent() function as a method on CSP.

Listing 3.3 csp.py continued

```
# Check if the value assignment is consistent by checking all constraints
# for the given variable against it
def consistent(self, variable: V, assignment: Dict[V, D]) -> bool:
    for constraint in self.constraints[variable]:
        if not constraint.satisfied(assignment):
            return False
    return True
```

consistent() goes through every constraint for a given variable (it will always be the variable that was just added to the assignment) and checks if the constraint is satisfied, given the new assignment. If the assignment satisfies every constraint, True is returned. If any constraint imposed on the variable is not satisfied, False is returned.

This constraint-satisfaction framework will use a simple backtracking search to find solutions to problems. *Backtracking* is the idea that once you hit a wall in your search, you go back to the last known point where you made a decision before the wall, and choose a different path. If you think that sounds like depth-first search from chapter 2, you are perceptive. The backtracking search implemented in the following backtracking_search() function is a kind of recursive depth-first search, combining ideas you saw in chapters 1 and 2. This function is added as a method to the CSP class.

Listing 3.4 csp.py continued

```
def backtracking_search(self, assignment: Dict[V, D] = {}) ->
        Optional[Dict[V, D]]:
    # assignment is complete if every variable is assigned (our base case)
    if len(assignment) == len(self.variables):
        return assignment

    # get all variables in the CSP but not in the assignment
    unassigned: List[V] = [v for v in self.variables if v not in assignment]

    # get the every possible domain value of the first unassigned variable
```

```
first: V = unassigned[0]
for value in self.domains[first]:
    local_assignment = assignment.copy()
    local_assignment[first] = value
    # if we're still consistent, we recurse (continue)
    if self.consistent(first, local_assignment):
        result: Optional[Dict[V, D]] = self.backtracking_search(local_
assignment)
        # if we didn't find the result, we will end up backtracking
        if result is not None:
            return result
return None
```

Let's walk through `backtracking_search()`, line by line.

```
if len(assignment) == len(self.variables):
    return assignment
```

The base case for the recursive search is having found a valid assignment for every variable. Once we have, we return the first instance of a solution that was valid. (We do not keep searching.)

```
unassigned: List[V] = [v for v in self.variables if v not in assignment]
first: V = unassigned[0]
```

To select a new variable whose domain we will explore, we simply go through all of the variables and find the first that does not have an assignment. To do this, we create a list of variables in `self.variables` but not in `assignment` through a list comprehension, and call it unassigned. Then we pull out the first value in unassigned.

```
for value in self.domains[first]:
    local_assignment = assignment.copy()
    local_assignment[first] = value
```

We try assigning all possible domain values for that variable, one at a time. The new assignment for each is stored in a local dictionary called local_assignment.

```
if self.consistent(first, local_assignment):
    result: Optional[Dict[V, D]] = self.backtracking_search(local_assignment)
    if result is not None:
        return result
```

If the new assignment in local_assignment is consistent with all of the constraints (that is what `consistent()` checks for), we continue recursively searching with the new assignment in place. If the new assignment turns out to be complete (the base case), we return the new assignment up the recursion chain.

```
return None  # no solution
```

Finally, if we have gone through every possible domain value for a particular variable, and there is no solution utilizing the existing set of assignments, we return None, indicating no solution. This will lead to backtracking up the recursion chain to the point where a different prior assignment could have been made.

3.2   *The Australian map-coloring problem*

Imagine you have a map of Australia that you want to color by state/territory (which we will collectively call "regions"). No two adjacent regions should share a color. Can you color the regions with just three different colors?

The answer is yes. Try it out on your own. (The easiest way is to print out a map of Australia with a white background.) As human beings, we can quickly figure out the solution by inspection and a little trial and error. It is a trivial problem, really, and a great first problem for our backtracking constraint-satisfaction solver. The problem is illustrated in figure 3.2.

Figure 3.2   In a solution to the Australian map-coloring problem, no two adjacent parts of Australia can be colored with the same color.

To model the problem as a CSP, we need to define the variables, domains, and constraints. The variables are the seven regions of Australia (at least the seven that we will restrict ourselves to): Western Australia, Northern Territory, South Australia, Queensland, New South Wales, Victoria, and Tasmania. In our CSP, they can be modeled with strings. The domain of each variable is the three different colors that can possibly be assigned. (We will use red, green, and blue.) The constraints are the tricky part. No two adjacent regions can be colored with the same color, so our constraints will be dependent on which regions border one another. We can use what are called binary constraints (constraints between two variables). Every two regions that share a border will also share a binary constraint indicating that they cannot be assigned the same color.

To implement these binary constraints in code, we need to subclass the `Constraint` class. The `MapColoringConstraint` subclass will take two variables in its constructor: the two regions that share a border. Its overridden `satisfied()` method will check first whether the two regions have domain values (colors) assigned to them; if either does not, the constraint is trivially satisfied until they do. (There cannot be a conflict when one does not yet have a color.) Then it will check whether the two regions are assigned the same color. Obviously, there is a conflict, meaning that the constraint is not satisfied, when they are the same.

The class is presented here in its entirety. `MapColoringConstraint` itself is not generic in terms of type hinting, but it subclasses a parameterized version of the generic class `Constraint` that indicates both variables and domains are of type `str`.

Listing 3.5   map_coloring.py

```python
from csp import Constraint, CSP
from typing import Dict, List, Optional

class MapColoringConstraint(Constraint[str, str]):
    def __init__(self, place1: str, place2: str) -> None:
        super().__init__([place1, place2])
        self.place1: str = place1
        self.place2: str = place2

    def satisfied(self, assignment: Dict[str, str]) -> bool:
        # If either place is not in the assignment, then it is not
        # yet possible for their colors to be conflicting
        if self.place1 not in assignment or self.place2 not in assignment:
            return True
        # check the color assigned to place1 is not the same as the
        # color assigned to place2
        return assignment[self.place1] != assignment[self.place2]
```

TIP super() is sometimes used to call a method on the superclass, but you can also use the name of the class itself, as in Constraint.__init__([place1, place2]). This is especially helpful when dealing with multiple inheritance, so that you know which superclass's method you are calling.

Now that we have a way of implementing the constraints between regions, fleshing out the Australian map-coloring problem with our CSP solver is simply a matter of filling in domains and variables, and then adding constraints.

Listing 3.6 map_coloring.py continued

```python
if __name__ == "__main__":
    variables: List[str] = ["Western Australia", "Northern Territory", "South
        Australia", "Queensland", "New South Wales", "Victoria", "Tasmania"]
    domains: Dict[str, List[str]] = {}
    for variable in variables:
        domains[variable] = ["red", "green", "blue"]
    csp: CSP[str, str] = CSP(variables, domains)
    csp.add_constraint(MapColoringConstraint("Western Australia", "Northern
        Territory"))
    csp.add_constraint(MapColoringConstraint("Western Australia", "South
        Australia"))
    csp.add_constraint(MapColoringConstraint("South Australia", "Northern
        Territory"))
    csp.add_constraint(MapColoringConstraint("Queensland", "Northern
        Territory"))
    csp.add_constraint(MapColoringConstraint("Queensland", "South
        Australia"))
    csp.add_constraint(MapColoringConstraint("Queensland", "New South
        Wales"))
    csp.add_constraint(MapColoringConstraint("New South Wales", "South
        Australia"))
    csp.add_constraint(MapColoringConstraint("Victoria", "South Australia"))
    csp.add_constraint(MapColoringConstraint("Victoria", "New South Wales"))
    csp.add_constraint(MapColoringConstraint("Victoria", "Tasmania"))
```

Finally, `backtracking_search()` is called to find a solution.

Listing 3.7 map_coloring.py continued

```python
solution: Optional[Dict[str, str]] = csp.backtracking_search()
if solution is None:
    print("No solution found!")
else:
    print(solution)
```

A correct solution will include an assigned color for every region.

```
{'Western Australia': 'red', 'Northern Territory': 'green', 'South
    Australia': 'blue', 'Queensland': 'red', 'New South Wales': 'green',
    'Victoria': 'red', 'Tasmania': 'green'}
```

3.3 The eight queens problem

A chessboard is an eight-by-eight grid of squares. A queen is a chess piece that can move on the chessboard any number of squares along any row, column, or diagonal. A queen is attacking another piece if in a single move, it can move to the square the piece is on without jumping over any other piece. (In other words, if the other piece is in the line of sight of the queen, then it is attacked by it.) The eight queens problem poses the question of how eight queens can be placed on a chessboard without any queen attacking another queen. The problem is illustrated in figure 3.3.

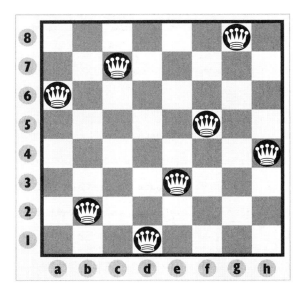

Figure 3.3   In a solution to the eight queens problem (there are many solutions), no two queens can be threatening each other.

To represent squares on the chessboard, we will assign each an integer row and an integer column. We can ensure each of the eight queens is not on the same column by simply assigning them sequentially the columns 1 through 8. The variables in our constraint-satisfaction problem can just be the column of the queen in question. The domains can be the possible rows (again, 1 through 8). The following code listing shows the end of our file, where we define these variables and domains.

Listing 3.8   queens.py

```
if __name__ == "__main__":
    columns: List[int] = [1, 2, 3, 4, 5, 6, 7, 8]
    rows: Dict[int, List[int]] = {}
    for column in columns:
        rows[column] = [1, 2, 3, 4, 5, 6, 7, 8]
    csp: CSP[int, int] = CSP(columns, rows)
```

To solve the problem, we will need a constraint that checks whether any two queens are on the same row or diagonal. (They were all assigned different sequential columns to begin with.) Checking for the same row is trivial, but checking for the same diagonal requires a little bit of math. If any two queens are on the same diagonal, the difference between their rows will be the same as the difference between their columns. Can you see where these checks take place in `QueensConstraint`? Note that the following code is at the top of our source file.

Listing 3.9   queens.py continued

```
from csp import Constraint, CSP
from typing import Dict, List, Optional
```

```
class QueensConstraint(Constraint[int, int]):
    def __init__(self, columns: List[int]) -> None:
        super().__init__(columns)
        self.columns: List[int] = columns

    def satisfied(self, assignment: Dict[int, int]) -> bool:
        # q1c = queen 1 column, q1r = queen 1 row
        for q1c, q1r in assignment.items():
            # q2c = queen 2 column
            for q2c in range(q1c + 1, len(self.columns) + 1):
                if q2c in assignment:
                    q2r: int = assignment[q2c] # q2r = queen 2 row
                    if q1r == q2r: # same row?
                        return False
                    if abs(q1r - q2r) == abs(q1c - q2c): # same diagonal?
                        return False
        return True # no conflict
```

All that is left is to add the constraint and run the search. We're now back at the bottom of the file.

Listing 3.10   queens.py continued

```
csp.add_constraint(QueensConstraint(columns))
solution: Optional[Dict[int, int]] = csp.backtracking_search()
if solution is None:
    print("No solution found!")
else:
    print(solution)
```

Notice that we were able to reuse the constraint-satisfaction problem-solving framework that we built for map coloring fairly easily for a completely different type of problem. This is the power of writing code generically! Algorithms should be implemented in as broadly applicable a manner as possible unless a performance optimization for a particular application requires specialization.

A correct solution will assign a column and row to every queen.

```
{1: 1, 2: 5, 3: 8, 4: 6, 5: 3, 6: 7, 7: 2, 8: 4}
```

3.4   Word search

A word search is a grid of letters with hidden words placed along rows, columns, and diagonals. A player of a word-search puzzle attempts to find the hidden words by carefully scanning through the grid. Finding places to put the words so that they all fit on the grid is a kind of constraint-satisfaction problem. The variables are the words, and the domains are the possible locations of those words. The problem is illustrated in figure 3.4.

For the purposes of expediency, our word search will not include words that overlap. You can improve it to allow for overlapping words as an exercise.

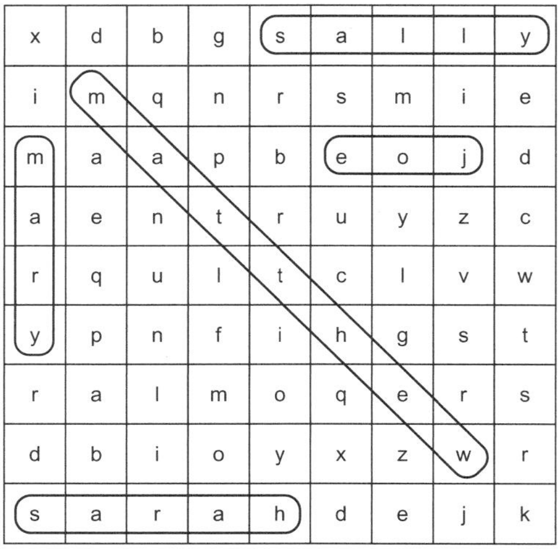

x	d	b	g	s	a	l	l	y
i	m	q	n	r	s	m	i	e
m	a	a	p	b	e	o	j	d
a	e	n	t	r	u	y	z	c
r	q	u	l	t	c	l	v	w
y	p	n	f	i	h	g	s	t
r	a	l	m	o	q	e	r	s
d	b	i	o	y	x	z	w	r
s	a	r	a	h	d	e	j	k

Figure 3.4 A classic word search, such as you might find in a children's puzzle book

The grid of this word-search problem is not entirely dissimilar from the mazes of chapter 2. Some of the following data types should look familiar.

Listing 3.11 word_search.py

```python
from typing import NamedTuple, List, Dict, Optional
from random import choice
from string import ascii_uppercase
from csp import CSP, Constraint

Grid = List[List[str]]  # type alias for grids


class GridLocation(NamedTuple):
    row: int
    column: int
```

Initially, we will fill the grid with the letters of the English alphabet (ascii_uppercase). We will also need a function for displaying the grid.

Listing 3.12 word_search.py continued

```python
def generate_grid(rows: int, columns: int) -> Grid:
    # initialize grid with random letters
    return [[choice(ascii_uppercase) for c in range(columns)] for r in
      range(rows)]


def display_grid(grid: Grid) -> None:
    for row in grid:
        print("".join(row))
```

To figure out where words can fit in the grid, we will generate their domains. The domain of a word is a list of lists of the possible locations of all of its letters (List[List[GridLocation]]). Words cannot just go anywhere, though. They must stay within a row, column, or diagonal that is within the bounds of the grid. In other words, they should not go off the end of the grid. The purpose of `generate_domain()` is to build these lists for every word.

Listing 3.13 word_search.py continued

```python
def generate_domain(word: str, grid: Grid) -> List[List[GridLocation]]:
    domain: List[List[GridLocation]] = []
    height: int = len(grid)
    width: int = len(grid[0])
    length: int = len(word)
    for row in range(height):
        for col in range(width):
            columns: range = range(col, col + length + 1)
            rows: range = range(row, row + length + 1)
            if col + length <= width:
                # left to right
                domain.append([GridLocation(row, c) for c in columns])
                # diagonal towards bottom right
                if row + length <= height:
                    domain.append([GridLocation(r, col + (r - row)) for r in
rows])
            if row + length <= height:
                # top to bottom
                domain.append([GridLocation(r, col) for r in rows])
                # diagonal towards bottom left
                if col - length >= 0:
                    domain.append([GridLocation(r, col - (r - row)) for r in
rows])
    return domain
```

For the range of potential locations of a word (along a row, column, or diagonal), list comprehensions translate the range into a list of `GridLocation` by using that class's constructor. Because `generate_domain()` loops through every grid location from the top left through to the bottom right for every word, it involves a lot of computation. Can you think of a way to do it more efficiently? What if we looked through all of the words of the same length at once, inside the loop?

To check if a potential solution is valid, we must implement a custom constraint for the word search. The `satisfied()` method of `WordSearchConstraint` simply checks whether any of the locations proposed for one word are the same as a location proposed for another word. It does this using a `set`. Converting a `list` into a `set` will remove all duplicates. If there are fewer items in a `set` converted from a `list` than there were in the original `list`, that means the original `list` contained some duplicates. To prepare the data for this check, we will use a somewhat complicated list comprehension to combine multiple sublists of locations for each word in the assignment into a single larger list of locations.

Listing 3.14 word_search.py continued

```python
class WordSearchConstraint(Constraint[str, List[GridLocation]]):
    def __init__(self, words: List[str]) -> None:
```

```
        super().__init__(words)
        self.words: List[str] = words

    def satisfied(self, assignment: Dict[str, List[GridLocation]]) -> bool:
        # if there are any duplicates grid locations, then there is an
    overlap
        all_locations = [locs for values in assignment.values() for locs in
    values]
        return len(set(all_locations)) == len(all_locations)
```

Finally, we are ready to run it. For this example, we have five words in a nine-by-nine grid. The solution we get back should contain mappings between each word and the locations where its letters can fit in the grid.

Listing 3.15   word_search.py continued

```
if __name__ == "__main__":
    grid: Grid = generate_grid(9, 9)
    words: List[str] = ["MATTHEW", "JOE", "MARY", "SARAH", "SALLY"]
    locations: Dict[str, List[List[GridLocation]]] = {}
    for word in words:
        locations[word] = generate_domain(word, grid)
    csp: CSP[str, List[GridLocation]] = CSP(words, locations)
    csp.add_constraint(WordSearchConstraint(words))
    solution: Optional[Dict[str, List[GridLocation]]] = csp.backtracking_
      search()
    if solution is None:
        print("No solution found!")
    else:
        for word, grid_locations in solution.items():
            # random reverse half the time
            if choice([True, False]):
                grid_locations.reverse()
            for index, letter in enumerate(word):
                (row, col) = (grid_locations[index].row, grid_
    locations[index].column)
                grid[row][col] = letter
        display_grid(grid)
```

There is a finishing touch in the code that fills the grid with words. Some words are randomly chosen to be reversed. This is valid, because this example does not allow overlapping words. Your ultimate output should look something like the following. Can you find Matthew, Joe, Mary, Sarah, and Sally?

```
LWEHTTAMJ
MARYLISGO
DKOJYHAYE
IAJYHALAG
GYZJWRLGM
LLOTCAYIX
PEUTUSLKO
AJZYGIKDU
HSLZOFNNR
```

3.5 *SEND+MORE=MONEY*

SEND+MORE=MONEY is a cryptarithmetic puzzle, meaning that it is about finding digits that replace letters to make a mathematical statement true. Each letter in the problem represents one digit (0–9). No two letters can represent the same digit. When a letter repeats, it means a digit repeats in the solution.

To solve this puzzle by hand, it helps to line up the words.

```
  SEND
 +MORE
=MONEY
```

It is absolutely solvable by hand, with a bit of algebra and intuition. But a fairly simple computer program can solve it faster by brute-forcing many possible solutions. Let's represent SEND+MORE=MONEY as a constraint-satisfaction problem.

Listing 3.16 send_more_money.py

```python
from csp import Constraint, CSP
from typing import Dict, List, Optional


class SendMoreMoneyConstraint(Constraint[str, int]):
    def __init__(self, letters: List[str]) -> None:
        super().__init__(letters)
        self.letters: List[str] = letters

    def satisfied(self, assignment: Dict[str, int]) -> bool:
        # if there are duplicate values, then it's not a solution
        if len(set(assignment.values())) < len(assignment):
            return False

        # if all variables have been assigned, check if it adds correctly
        if len(assignment) == len(self.letters):
            s: int = assignment["S"]
            e: int = assignment["E"]
            n: int = assignment["N"]
            d: int = assignment["D"]
            m: int = assignment["M"]
            o: int = assignment["O"]
            r: int = assignment["R"]
            y: int = assignment["Y"]
            send: int = s * 1000 + e * 100 + n * 10 + d
            more: int = m * 1000 + o * 100 + r * 10 + e
            money: int = m * 10000 + o * 1000 + n * 100 + e * 10 + y
            return send + more == money
        return True # no conflict
```

SendMoreMoneyConstraint's satisfied() method does a few things. First, it checks if multiple letters represent the same digits. If they do, that's an invalid solution, and it returns False. Next, it checks if all letters have been assigned. If they have, it checks to see if the formula (SEND+MORE=MONEY) is correct with the given assignment. If it is, a solution has been found, and it returns True. Otherwise, it returns False. Finally, if all letters have not yet been assigned, it returns True. This is to ensure that a partial solution continues to be worked on.

Let's try running it.

Listing 3.17   send_more_money.py continued

```python
if __name__ == "__main__":
    letters: List[str] = ["S", "E", "N", "D", "M", "O", "R", "Y"]
    possible_digits: Dict[str, List[int]] = {}
    for letter in letters:
        possible_digits[letter] = [0, 1, 2, 3, 4, 5, 6, 7, 8, 9]
    possible_digits["M"] = [1]  # so we don't get answers starting with a 0
    csp: CSP[str, int] = CSP(letters, possible_digits)
    csp.add_constraint(SendMoreMoneyConstraint(letters))
    solution: Optional[Dict[str, int]] = csp.backtracking_search()
    if solution is None:
        print("No solution found!")
    else:
        print(solution)
```

You will notice that we preassigned the answer for the letter M. This was to ensure that the answer doesn't include a 0 for M, because if you think about it, our constraint has no notion of the concept that a number can't start with zero. Feel free to try it out without that preassigned answer.

The solution should look something like this:

```
{'S': 9, 'E': 5, 'N': 6, 'D': 7, 'M': 1, 'O': 0, 'R': 8, 'Y': 2}
```

3.6   *Circuit board layout*

A manufacturer needs to fit certain rectangular chips onto a rectangular circuit board. Essentially, this problem asks, "How can several different-sized rectangles all fit snugly inside of another rectangle?" A constraint-satisfaction problem solver can find the solution. The problem is illustrated in figure 3.5.

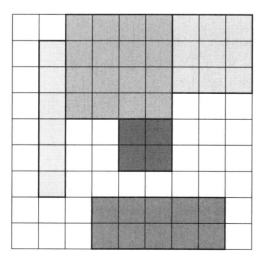

Figure 3.5   The circuit board layout problem is very similar to the word-search problem, but the rectangles are of variable width.

The circuit board layout problem is similar to the word-search problem. Instead of 1×*N* rectangles (words), the problem presents *M*×*N* rectangles. Like in the word-search problem, the rectangles cannot overlap. The rectangles cannot be put on diagonals, so in that sense the problem is actually simpler than the word search.

On your own, try rewriting the word-search solution to accommodate circuit board layout. You can reuse much of the code, including the code for the grid.

3.7   *Real-world applications*

As was mentioned in the introduction to this chapter, constraint-satisfaction problem solvers are commonly used in scheduling. Several people need to be at a meeting, and they are the variables. The domains consist of the open times on their calendars. The constraints may involve what combinations of people are required at the meeting.

Constraint-satisfaction problem solvers are also used in motion planning. Imagine a robot arm that needs to fit inside of a tube. It has constraints (the walls of the tube), variables (the joints), and domains (possible movements of the joints).

There are also applications in computational biology. You can imagine constraints between molecules required for a chemical reaction. And, of course, as is common with AI, there are applications in games. Writing a Sudoku solver is one of the following exercises, but many logic puzzles can be solved using constraint-satisfaction problem solving.

In this chapter, we built a simple backtracking, depth-first search, problem-solving framework. But it can be greatly improved by adding heuristics (remember A*?)—intuitions that can aid the search process. A newer technique than backtracking, known as *constraint propagation*, is also an efficient avenue for real-world applications. For more information, check out chapter 6 of Stuart Russell and Peter Norvig's *Artificial Intelligence: A Modern Approach*, third edition (Pearson, 2010).

3.8   *Exercises*

1 Revise `WordSearchConstraint` so that overlapping letters are allowed.
2 Build the circuit board layout problem solver described in section 3.6, if you have not already.
3 Build a program that can solve Sudoku problems using this chapter's constraint-satisfaction problem-solving framework.

Graph problems

A *graph* is an abstract mathematical construct that is used for modeling a real-world problem by dividing the problem into a set of connected nodes. We call each of the nodes a *vertex* and each of the connections an *edge*. For instance, a subway map can be thought of as a graph representing a transportation network. Each of the dots represents a station, and each of the lines represents a route between two stations. In graph terminology, we would call the stations "vertices" and the routes "edges."

Why is this useful? Not only do graphs help us abstractly think about a problem, but they also let us apply several well-understood and performant search and optimization techniques. For instance, in the subway example, suppose we want to know the shortest route from one station to another. Or suppose we want to know the minimum amount of track needed to connect all of the stations. Graph algorithms that you will learn in this chapter can solve both of those problems. Further, graph algorithms can be applied to any kind of network problem—not just transportation networks. Think of computer networks, distribution networks, and utility networks. Search and optimization problems across all of these spaces can be solved using graph algorithms.

4.1 A map as a graph

In this chapter, we won't work with a graph of subway stations, but instead cities of the United States and potential routes between them. Figure 4.1 is a map of the continental United States and the 15 largest metropolitan statistical areas (MSAs) in the country, as estimated by the U.S. Census Bureau.[1]

---

[1] Data is from the United States Census Bureau's American Fact Finder, https://factfinder.census.gov/.

Figure 4.1   A map of the 15 largest MSAs in the United States

Famous entrepreneur Elon Musk has suggested building a new high-speed transportation network composed of capsules traveling in pressurized tubes. According to Musk, the capsules would travel at 700 miles per hour and be suitable for cost-effective transportation between cities less than 900 miles apart.[2] He calls this new transportation system the "Hyperloop." In this chapter we will explore classic graph problems in the context of building out this transportation network.

Musk initially proposed the Hyperloop idea for connecting Los Angeles and San Francisco. If one were to build a national Hyperloop network, it would make sense to do so between America's largest metropolitan areas. In figure 4.2, the state outlines from figure 4.1 are removed. In addition, each of the MSAs is connected with some of its neighbors. To make the graph a little more interesting, those neighbors are not always the MSA's closest neighbors.

Figure 4.2 is a graph with vertices representing the 15 largest MSAs in the United States and edges representing potential Hyperloop routes between cities. The routes were chosen for illustrative purposes. Certainly, other potential routes could be part of a new Hyperloop network.

This abstract representation of a real-world problem highlights the power of graphs. With this abstraction, we can ignore the geography of the United States and concentrate on thinking about the potential Hyperloop network simply in the context of connecting cities. In fact, as long as we keep the edges the same, we can think about the problem with a different-looking graph. In figure 4.3, for example, the location of

---

[2]   Elon Musk, "Hyperloop Alpha," http://mng.bz/chmu.

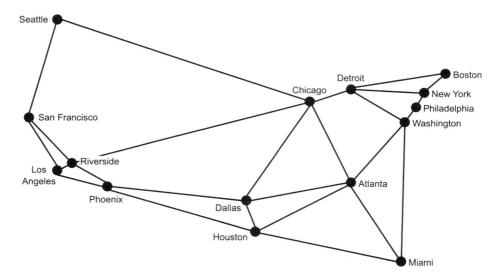

Figure 4.2   A graph with vertices representing the 15 largest MSAs in the United States and edges representing potential Hyperloop routes between them

Miami has moved. The graph in figure 4.3, being an abstract representation, can address the same fundamental computational problems as the graph in figure 4.2, even if Miami is not where we would expect it. But for our sanity, we will stick with the representation in figure 4.2.

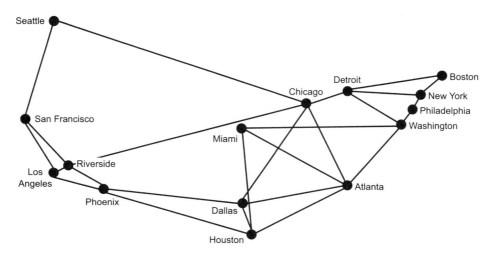

Figure 4.3   An equivalent graph to that in figure 4.2, with the location of Miami moved

4.2 Building a graph framework

Python can be programmed in many different styles. But at its heart, Python is an object-oriented programming language. In this section we will define two different types of graphs: unweighted and weighted. Weighted graphs, which we will discuss later in the chapter, associate a weight (read number, such as a length in the case of our example) with each edge.

We will make use of the inheritance model, fundamental to Python's object-oriented class hierarchies, so we do not duplicate our effort. The weighted classes in our data model will be subclasses of their unweighted counterparts. This will allow them to inherit much of their functionality, with small tweaks for what makes a weighted graph distinct from an unweighted graph.

We want this graph framework to be as flexible as possible so that it can represent as many different problems as possible. To achieve this goal, we will use generics to abstract away the type of the vertices. Every vertex will ultimately be assigned an integer index, but it will be stored as the user-defined generic type.

Let's start work on the framework by defining the `Edge` class, which is the simplest machinery in our graph framework.

Listing 4.1 edge.py

```python
from __future__ import annotations
from dataclasses import dataclass


@dataclass
class Edge:
    u: int # the "from" vertex
    v: int # the "to" vertex

    def reversed(self) -> Edge:
        return Edge(self.v, self.u)

    def __str__(self) -> str:
        return f"{self.u} -> {self.v}"
```

An `Edge` is defined as a connection between two vertices, each of which is represented by an integer index. By convention, u is used to refer to the first vertex, and v is used to represent the second vertex. You can also think of u as "from" and v as "to." In this chapter, we are only working with undirected graphs (graphs with edges that allow travel in both directions), but in *directed graphs*, also known as *digraphs*, edges can also be one-way. The `reversed()` method is meant to return an `Edge` that travels in the opposite direction of the edge it is applied to.

NOTE The `Edge` class uses a new feature in Python 3.7: dataclasses. A class marked with the `@dataclass` decorator saves some tedium by automatically creating an `__init__()` method that instantiates instance variables for any variables declared with type annotations in the class's body. Dataclasses can also automatically create other special methods for a class. Which special methods are automatically created is configurable via the decorator. See the Python documentation on dataclasses for details (https://docs.python.org/3/library/dataclasses.html). In short, a dataclass is a way of saving ourselves some typing.

The `Graph` class focuses on the essential role of a graph: associating vertices with edges. Again, we want to let the actual types of the vertices be whatever the user of the framework desires. This lets the framework be used for a wide range of problems without needing to make intermediate data structures that glue everything together. For example, in a graph like the one for Hyperloop routes, we might define the type of the vertices to be `str`, because we would use strings like "New York" and "Los Angeles" as the vertices. Let's begin the `Graph` class.

Listing 4.2   graph.py

```python
from typing import TypeVar, Generic, List, Optional
from edge import Edge


V = TypeVar('V') # type of the vertices in the graph


class Graph(Generic[V]):
    def __init__(self, vertices: List[V] = []) -> None:
        self._vertices: List[V] = vertices
        self._edges: List[List[Edge]] = [[] for _ in vertices]
```

The `_vertices` list is the heart of a `Graph`. Each vertex will be stored in the list, but we will later refer to them by their integer index in the list. The vertex itself may be a complex data type, but its index will always be an `int`, which is easy to work with. On another level, by putting this index between graph algorithms and the `_vertices` array, it allows us to have two vertices that are equal in the same graph. (Imagine a graph with a country's cities as vertices, where the country has more than one city named "Springfield.") Even though they are the same, they will have different integer indexes.

There are many ways to implement a graph data structure, but the two most common are to use a *vertex matrix* or *adjacency lists*. In a vertex matrix, each cell of the matrix represents the intersection of two vertices in the graph, and the value of that cell indicates the connection (or lack thereof) between them. Our graph data structure uses adjacency lists. In this graph representation, every vertex has a list of vertices that it is connected to. Our specific representation uses a list of lists of edges, so for every vertex there is a list of edges via which the vertex is connected to other vertices. `_edges` is this list of lists.

The rest of the `Graph` class is now presented in its entirety. You will notice the use of short, mostly one-line methods, with verbose and clear method names. This should make the rest of the class largely self-explanatory, but short comments are included so that there is no room for misinterpretation.

Listing 4.3 graph.py continued

```python
@property
def vertex_count(self) -> int:
    return len(self._vertices) # Number of vertices

@property
def edge_count(self) -> int:
    return sum(map(len, self._edges)) # Number of edges

# Add a vertex to the graph and return its index
def add_vertex(self, vertex: V) -> int:
    self._vertices.append(vertex)
    self._edges.append([]) # Add empty list for containing edges
    return self.vertex_count - 1 # Return index of added vertex

# This is an undirected graph,
# so we always add edges in both directions
def add_edge(self, edge: Edge) -> None:
    self._edges[edge.u].append(edge)
    self._edges[edge.v].append(edge.reversed())

# Add an edge using vertex indices (convenience method)
def add_edge_by_indices(self, u: int, v: int) -> None:
    edge: Edge = Edge(u, v)
    self.add_edge(edge)

# Add an edge by looking up vertex indices (convenience method)
def add_edge_by_vertices(self, first: V, second: V) -> None:
    u: int = self._vertices.index(first)
    v: int = self._vertices.index(second)
    self.add_edge_by_indices(u, v)

# Find the vertex at a specific index
def vertex_at(self, index: int) -> V:
    return self._vertices[index]

# Find the index of a vertex in the graph
def index_of(self, vertex: V) -> int:
    return self._vertices.index(vertex)

# Find the vertices that a vertex at some index is connected to
def neighbors_for_index(self, index: int) -> List[V]:
    return list(map(self.vertex_at, [e.v for e in self._edges[index]]))

# Look up a vertice's index and find its neighbors (convenience method)
def neighbors_for_vertex(self, vertex: V) -> List[V]:
    return self.neighbors_for_index(self.index_of(vertex))

# Return all of the edges associated with a vertex at some index
def edges_for_index(self, index: int) -> List[Edge]:
    return self._edges[index]

# Look up the index of a vertex and return its edges (convenience method)
def edges_for_vertex(self, vertex: V) -> List[Edge]:
    return self.edges_for_index(self.index_of(vertex))

# Make it easy to pretty-print a Graph
def __str__(self) -> str:
```

```
    desc: str = ""
    for i in range(self.vertex_count):
        desc += f"{self.vertex_at(i)} -> {self.neighbors_for_index(i)}\n"
    return desc
```

Let's step back for a moment and consider why this class has two versions of most of its methods. We know from the class definition that the list _vertices is a list of elements of type V, which can be any Python class. So we have vertices of type V that are stored in the _vertices list. But if we want to retrieve or manipulate them later, we need to know where they are stored in that list. Hence, every vertex has an index in the array (an integer) associated with it. If we don't know a vertex's index, we need to look it up by searching through _vertices. That is why there are two versions of every method. One operates on int indices, and one operates on V itself. The methods that operate on V look up the relevant indices and call the index-based function. Therefore, they can be considered convenience methods.

Most of the functions are fairly self-explanatory, but neighbors_for_index() deserves a little unpacking. It returns the *neighbors* of a vertex. A vertex's neighbors are all of the other vertices that are directly connected to it by an edge. For example, in figure 4.2, New York and Washington are the only neighbors of Philadelphia. We find the neighbors for a vertex by looking at the ends (the vs) of all of the edges going out from it.

```
def neighbors_for_index(self, index: int) -> List[V]:
    return list(map(self.vertex_at, [e.v for e in self._edges[index]]))
```

_edges[index] is the adjacency list, the list of edges through which the vertex in question is connected to other vertices. In the list comprehension passed to the map() call, e represents one particular edge, and e.v represents the index of the neighbor that the edge is connected to. map() will return all of the vertices (as opposed to just their indices), because map() applies the vertex_at() method on every e.v.

Another important thing to note is the way add_edge() works. add_edge() first adds an edge to the adjacency list of the "from" vertex (u) and then adds a reversed version of the edge to the adjacency list of the "to" vertex (v). The second step is necessary because this graph is undirected. We want every edge to be added in both directions; that means that u will be a neighbor of v in the same way that v is a neighbor of u. You can think of an undirected graph as being "bidirectional" if it helps you remember that it means any edge can be traversed in either direction.

```
def add_edge(self, edge: Edge) -> None:
    self._edges[edge.u].append(edge)
    self._edges[edge.v].append(edge.reversed())
```

As was mentioned earlier, we are only dealing with undirected graphs in this chapter. Beyond being undirected or directed, graphs can also be *unweighted* or *weighted*. A weighted graph is one that has some comparable value, usually numeric, associated with each of its edges. We could think of the weights in our potential Hyperloop network as being the distances between the stations. For now, though, we will deal with an unweighted version of the graph. An unweighted edge is simply a connection between two vertices; hence, the Edge class is unweighted, and the Graph class is unweighted. Another way of putting it is that in an unweighted graph we know which vertices are connected, whereas in a weighted graph we know which vertices are connected and also know something about those connections.

4.2.1 *Working with Edge and Graph*

Now that we have concrete implementations of Edge and Graph, we can create a representation of the potential Hyperloop network. The vertices and edges in city_graph correspond to the vertices and edges represented in figure 4.2. Using generics, we can specify that vertices will be of type str (Graph[str]). In other words, the str type fills in for the type variable V.

Listing 4.4 graph.py continued

```python
if __name__ == "__main__":
    # test basic Graph construction
    city_graph: Graph[str] = Graph(["Seattle", "San Francisco", "Los
      Angeles", "Riverside", "Phoenix", "Chicago", "Boston", "New York",
      "Atlanta", "Miami", "Dallas", "Houston", "Detroit", "Philadelphia",
      "Washington"])
    city_graph.add_edge_by_vertices("Seattle", "Chicago")
    city_graph.add_edge_by_vertices("Seattle", "San Francisco")
    city_graph.add_edge_by_vertices("San Francisco", "Riverside")
    city_graph.add_edge_by_vertices("San Francisco", "Los Angeles")
    city_graph.add_edge_by_vertices("Los Angeles", "Riverside")
    city_graph.add_edge_by_vertices("Los Angeles", "Phoenix")
    city_graph.add_edge_by_vertices("Riverside", "Phoenix")
    city_graph.add_edge_by_vertices("Riverside", "Chicago")
    city_graph.add_edge_by_vertices("Phoenix", "Dallas")
    city_graph.add_edge_by_vertices("Phoenix", "Houston")
    city_graph.add_edge_by_vertices("Dallas", "Chicago")
    city_graph.add_edge_by_vertices("Dallas", "Atlanta")
    city_graph.add_edge_by_vertices("Dallas", "Houston")
    city_graph.add_edge_by_vertices("Houston", "Atlanta")
    city_graph.add_edge_by_vertices("Houston", "Miami")
    city_graph.add_edge_by_vertices("Atlanta", "Chicago")
    city_graph.add_edge_by_vertices("Atlanta", "Washington")
    city_graph.add_edge_by_vertices("Atlanta", "Miami")
    city_graph.add_edge_by_vertices("Miami", "Washington")
    city_graph.add_edge_by_vertices("Chicago", "Detroit")
    city_graph.add_edge_by_vertices("Detroit", "Boston")
    city_graph.add_edge_by_vertices("Detroit", "Washington")
    city_graph.add_edge_by_vertices("Detroit", "New York")
    city_graph.add_edge_by_vertices("Boston", "New York")
    city_graph.add_edge_by_vertices("New York", "Philadelphia")
    city_graph.add_edge_by_vertices("Philadelphia", "Washington")
    print(city_graph)
```

city_graph has vertices of type str, and we indicate each vertex with the name of the MSA that it represents. It is irrelevant in what order we add the edges to city_graph.

Because we implemented __str__() with a nicely printed description of the graph, we can now pretty-print (that's a real term!) the graph. You should get output similar to the following:

```
Seattle -> ['Chicago', 'San Francisco']
San Francisco -> ['Seattle', 'Riverside', 'Los Angeles']
Los Angeles -> ['San Francisco', 'Riverside', 'Phoenix']
Riverside -> ['San Francisco', 'Los Angeles', 'Phoenix', 'Chicago']
Phoenix -> ['Los Angeles', 'Riverside', 'Dallas', 'Houston']
Chicago -> ['Seattle', 'Riverside', 'Dallas', 'Atlanta', 'Detroit']
Boston -> ['Detroit', 'New York']
New York -> ['Detroit', 'Boston', 'Philadelphia']
Atlanta -> ['Dallas', 'Houston', 'Chicago', 'Washington', 'Miami']
Miami -> ['Houston', 'Atlanta', 'Washington']
Dallas -> ['Phoenix', 'Chicago', 'Atlanta', 'Houston']
Houston -> ['Phoenix', 'Dallas', 'Atlanta', 'Miami']
Detroit -> ['Chicago', 'Boston', 'Washington', 'New York']
Philadelphia -> ['New York', 'Washington']
Washington -> ['Atlanta', 'Miami', 'Detroit', 'Philadelphia']
```

4.3   *Finding the shortest path*

The Hyperloop is so fast that for optimizing travel time from one station to another, it probably matters less how long the distances are between the stations and more how many hops it takes (how many stations need to be visited) to get from one station to another. Each station may involve a layover, so just like with flights, the fewer stops the better.

In graph theory, a set of edges that connects two vertices is known as a *path*. In other words, a path is a way of getting from one vertex to another vertex. In the context of the Hyperloop network, a set of tubes (edges) represents the path from one city (vertex) to another (vertex). Finding optimal paths between vertices is one of the most common problems that graphs are used for.

Informally, we can also think of a list of vertices sequentially connected to one another by edges as a path. This description is really just another side of the same coin. It is like taking a list of edges, figuring out which vertices they connect, keeping that list of vertices, and throwing away the edges. In this brief example, we will find such a list of vertices that connects two cities on our Hyperloop.

4.3.1   *Revisiting breadth-first search (BFS)*

In an unweighted graph, finding the shortest path means finding the path that has the fewest edges between the starting vertex and the destination vertex. To build out the Hyperloop network, it might make sense to first connect the furthest cities on the highly populated seaboards. That raises the question "What is the shortest path between Boston and Miami?"

> **TIP** This section assumes that you have read chapter 2. Before continuing, ensure that you are comfortable with the material on breadth-first search in chapter 2.

Luckily, we already have an algorithm for finding shortest paths, and we can reuse it to answer this question. Breadth-first search, introduced in chapter 2, is just as viable for graphs as it is for mazes. In fact, the mazes we worked with in chapter 2 really are graphs. The vertices are the locations in the maze, and the edges are the moves that can be made from one location to another. In an unweighted graph, a breadth-first search will find the shortest path between any two vertices.

We can reuse the breadth-first search implementation from chapter 2 and use it to work with `Graph`. In fact, we can reuse it completely unchanged. This is the power of writing code generically!

Recall that `bfs()` in chapter 2 requires three parameters: an initial state, a `Callable` (read function-like object) for testing for a goal, and a `Callable` that finds the successor states for a given state. The initial state will be the vertex represented by the string "Boston." The goal test will be a lambda that checks if a vertex is equivalent to "Miami." Finally, successor vertices can be generated by the `Graph` method `neighbors_for_vertex()`.

With this plan in mind, we can add code to the end of the main section of graph.py to find the shortest route between Boston and Miami on `city_graph`.

> **NOTE** In listing 4.5, bfs, Node, and node_to_path are imported from the generic_search module in the Chapter2 package. To do this, the parent directory of graph.py is added to Python's search path (`'..'`). This works because the code structure for the book's repository has each chapter in its own directory, so our directory structure includes roughly Book->Chapter2->generic_search.py and Book->Chapter4->graph.py. If your directory structure is significantly different, you will need to find a way to add generic_search.py to your path and possibly change the import statement. In a worst-case scenario, you can just copy generic_search.py to the same directory that contains graph.py and change the import statement to from generic_search import bfs, Node, node_to_path.

Listing 4.5   graph.py continued

```python
# Reuse BFS from chapter 2 on city_graph
import sys
sys.path.insert(0, '..') # so we can access the Chapter2 package in the
    parent directory
from Chapter2.generic_search import bfs, Node, node_to_path

bfs_result: Optional[Node[V]] = bfs("Boston", lambda x: x == "Miami", city_
    graph.neighbors_for_vertex)
if bfs_result is None:
    print("No solution found using breadth-first search!")
else:
    path: List[V] = node_to_path(bfs_result)
    print("Path from Boston to Miami:")
    print(path)
```

The output should look something like this:

```
Path from Boston to Miami:
['Boston', 'Detroit', 'Washington', 'Miami']
```

Boston to Detroit to Washington to Miami, composed of three edges, is the shortest route between Boston and Miami in terms of the number of edges. Figure 4.4 highlights this route.

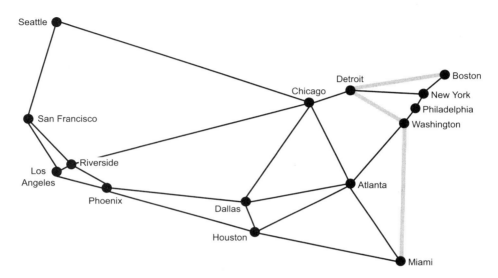

Figure 4.4   The shortest route between Boston and Miami, in terms of the number of edges, is highlighted.

4.4   *Minimizing the cost of building the network*

Imagine that we want to connect all 15 of the largest MSAs to the Hyperloop network. Our goal is to minimize the cost of rolling out the network, so that means using a minimum amount of track. Then the question is "How can we connect all of the MSAs using the minimum amount of track?"

4.4.1   *Workings with weights*

To understand the amount of track that a particular edge may require, we need to know the distance that the edge represents. This is an opportunity to re-introduce the concept of weights. In the Hyperloop network, the weight of an edge is the distance between the two MSAs that it connects. Figure 4.5 is the same as figure 4.2 except that it has a weight added to each edge, representing the distance in miles between the two vertices that the edge connects.

To handle weights, we will need a subclass of `Edge` (`WeightedEdge`) and a subclass of `Graph` (`WeightedGraph`). Every `WeightedEdge` will have a `float` associated with it,

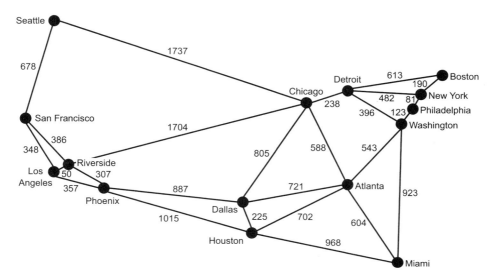

Figure 4.5 **A weighted graph of the 15 largest MSAs in the United States, where each of the weights represents the distance between two MSAs in miles**

representing its weight. Jarník's algorithm, which we will cover shortly, requires the ability to compare one edge with another to determine the edge with the lowest weight. This is easy to do with numeric weights.

Listing 4.6   weighted_edge.py

```
from __future__ import annotations
from dataclasses import dataclass
from edge import Edge


@dataclass
class WeightedEdge(Edge):
    weight: float

    def reversed(self) -> WeightedEdge:
        return WeightedEdge(self.v, self.u, self.weight)

    # so that we can order edges by weight to find the minimum weight edge
    def __lt__(self, other: WeightedEdge) -> bool:
        return self.weight < other.weight

    def __str__(self) -> str:
        return f"{self.u} {self.weight}> {self.v}"
```

The implementation of `WeightedEdge` is not immensely different from that of `Edge`. It only differs in the addition of a `weight` property and the implementation of the < operator via `__lt__()`, so that two `WeightedEdges` are comparable. The < operator is only interested in looking at weights (as opposed to including the inherited properties u and v), because Jarník's algorithm is interested in finding the smallest edge by weight.

A `WeightedGraph` inherits much of its functionality from `Graph`. Other than that, it has init methods; it has convenience methods for adding `WeightedEdges`; and it implements its own version of `__str__()`. There is also a new method, `neighbors_for_index_with_weights()`, that returns not only each neighbor, but also the weight of the edge that got to it. This method is useful for the new version of `__str__()`.

Listing 4.7 weighted_graph.py

```python
from typing import TypeVar, Generic, List, Tuple
from graph import Graph
from weighted_edge import WeightedEdge

V = TypeVar('V') # type of the vertices in the graph


class WeightedGraph(Generic[V], Graph[V]):
    def __init__(self, vertices: List[V] = []) -> None:
        self._vertices: List[V] = vertices
        self._edges: List[List[WeightedEdge]] = [[] for _ in vertices]

    def add_edge_by_indices(self, u: int, v: int, weight: float) -> None:
        edge: WeightedEdge = WeightedEdge(u, v, weight)
        self.add_edge(edge) # call superclass version

    def add_edge_by_vertices(self, first: V, second: V, weight: float) ->
     None:
        u: int = self._vertices.index(first)
        v: int = self._vertices.index(second)
        self.add_edge_by_indices(u, v, weight)

    def neighbors_for_index_with_weights(self, index: int) -> List[Tuple[V,
     float]]:
        distance_tuples: List[Tuple[V, float]] = []
        for edge in self.edges_for_index(index):
            distance_tuples.append((self.vertex_at(edge.v), edge.weight))
        return distance_tuples

    def __str__(self) -> str:
        desc: str = ""
        for i in range(self.vertex_count):
            desc += f"{self.vertex_at(i)} -> {self.neighbors_for_index_with_
     weights(i)}\n"
        return desc
```

It is now possible to actually define a weighted graph. The weighted graph we will work with is a representation of figure 4.5 called `city_graph2`.

Listing 4.8 weighted_graph.py continued

```python
if __name__ == "__main__":
    city_graph2: WeightedGraph[str] = WeightedGraph(["Seattle", "San
     Francisco", "Los Angeles", "Riverside", "Phoenix", "Chicago", "Boston",
     "New York", "Atlanta", "Miami", "Dallas", "Houston", "Detroit",
     "Philadelphia", "Washington"])
```

```
city_graph2.add_edge_by_vertices("Seattle", "Chicago", 1737)
city_graph2.add_edge_by_vertices("Seattle", "San Francisco", 678)
city_graph2.add_edge_by_vertices("San Francisco", "Riverside", 386)
city_graph2.add_edge_by_vertices("San Francisco", "Los Angeles", 348)
city_graph2.add_edge_by_vertices("Los Angeles", "Riverside", 50)
city_graph2.add_edge_by_vertices("Los Angeles", "Phoenix", 357)
city_graph2.add_edge_by_vertices("Riverside", "Phoenix", 307)
city_graph2.add_edge_by_vertices("Riverside", "Chicago", 1704)
city_graph2.add_edge_by_vertices("Phoenix", "Dallas", 887)
city_graph2.add_edge_by_vertices("Phoenix", "Houston", 1015)
city_graph2.add_edge_by_vertices("Dallas", "Chicago", 805)
city_graph2.add_edge_by_vertices("Dallas", "Atlanta", 721)
city_graph2.add_edge_by_vertices("Dallas", "Houston", 225)
city_graph2.add_edge_by_vertices("Houston", "Atlanta", 702)
city_graph2.add_edge_by_vertices("Houston", "Miami", 968)
city_graph2.add_edge_by_vertices("Atlanta", "Chicago", 588)
city_graph2.add_edge_by_vertices("Atlanta", "Washington", 543)
city_graph2.add_edge_by_vertices("Atlanta", "Miami", 604)
city_graph2.add_edge_by_vertices("Miami", "Washington", 923)
city_graph2.add_edge_by_vertices("Chicago", "Detroit", 238)
city_graph2.add_edge_by_vertices("Detroit", "Boston", 613)
city_graph2.add_edge_by_vertices("Detroit", "Washington", 396)
city_graph2.add_edge_by_vertices("Detroit", "New York", 482)
city_graph2.add_edge_by_vertices("Boston", "New York", 190)
city_graph2.add_edge_by_vertices("New York", "Philadelphia", 81)
city_graph2.add_edge_by_vertices("Philadelphia", "Washington", 123)

print(city_graph2)
```

Because `WeightedGraph` implements `__str__()`, we can pretty-print `city_graph2`. In the output, you will see both the vertices that each vertex is connected to and the weights of those connections.

```
Seattle -> [('Chicago', 1737), ('San Francisco', 678)]
San Francisco -> [('Seattle', 678), ('Riverside', 386), ('Los Angeles', 348)]
Los Angeles -> [('San Francisco', 348), ('Riverside', 50), ('Phoenix', 357)]
Riverside -> [('San Francisco', 386), ('Los Angeles', 50), ('Phoenix', 307),
    ('Chicago', 1704)]
Phoenix -> [('Los Angeles', 357), ('Riverside', 307), ('Dallas', 887),
    ('Houston', 1015)]
Chicago -> [('Seattle', 1737), ('Riverside', 1704), ('Dallas', 805),
    ('Atlanta', 588), ('Detroit', 238)]
Boston -> [('Detroit', 613), ('New York', 190)]
New York -> [('Detroit', 482), ('Boston', 190), ('Philadelphia', 81)]
Atlanta -> [('Dallas', 721), ('Houston', 702), ('Chicago', 588),
    ('Washington', 543), ('Miami', 604)]
Miami -> [('Houston', 968), ('Atlanta', 604), ('Washington', 923)]
Dallas -> [('Phoenix', 887), ('Chicago', 805), ('Atlanta', 721), ('Houston',
    225)]
Houston -> [('Phoenix', 1015), ('Dallas', 225), ('Atlanta', 702), ('Miami',
    968)]
Detroit -> [('Chicago', 238), ('Boston', 613), ('Washington', 396), ('New
    York', 482)]
Philadelphia -> [('New York', 81), ('Washington', 123)]
Washington -> [('Atlanta', 543), ('Miami', 923), ('Detroit', 396),
    ('Philadelphia', 123)]
```

4.4.2 *Finding the minimum spanning tree*

A *tree* is a special kind of graph that has one, and only one, path between any two vertices. This implies that there are no *cycles* in a tree (which is sometimes called *acyclic*). A cycle can be thought of as a loop: if it is possible to traverse a graph from a starting vertex, never repeat any edges, and get back to the same starting vertex, then it has a cycle. Any graph that is not a tree can become a tree by pruning edges. Figure 4.6 illustrates pruning an edge to turn a graph into a tree.

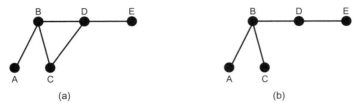

(a)   (b)

Figure 4.6   In the left graph, a cycle exists between vertices B, C, and D, so it is not a tree. In the right graph, the edge connecting C and D has been pruned, so the graph is a tree.

A *connected* graph is a graph that has some way of getting from any vertex to any other vertex. (All of the graphs we are looking at in this chapter are connected.) A *spanning tree* is a tree that connects every vertex in a graph. A *minimum spanning tree* is a tree that connects every vertex in a weighted graph with the minimum total weight (compared to other spanning trees). For every weighted graph, it is possible to efficiently find its minimum spanning tree.

Whew—that was a lot of terminology! The point is that finding a minimum spanning tree is the same as finding a way to connect every vertex in a weighted graph with the minimum weight. This is an important and practical problem for anyone designing a network (transportation network, computer network, and so on): how can every node in the network be connected for the minimum cost? That cost may be in terms of wire, track, road, or anything else. For instance, for a telephone network, another way of posing the problem is "What is the minimum length of cable one needs to connect every phone?"

REVISITING PRIORITY QUEUES

Priority queues were covered in chapter 2. We will need a priority queue for Jarník's algorithm. You can import the `PriorityQueue` class from chapter 2's package (see the note immediately previous to listing 4.5 for details), or you can copy the class into a new file to go with this chapter's package. For completeness, we will recreate `PriorityQueue` from chapter 2 here, with specific `import` statements that assume that it will be put in its own stand-alone file.

Listing 4.9   priority_queue.py

```python
from typing import TypeVar, Generic, List
from heapq import heappush, heappop


T = TypeVar('T')


class PriorityQueue(Generic[T]):
    def __init__(self) -> None:
        self._container: List[T] = []

    @property
    def empty(self) -> bool:
        return not self._container  # not is true for empty container

    def push(self, item: T) -> None:
        heappush(self._container, item)  # in by priority

    def pop(self) -> T:
        return heappop(self._container)  # out by priority

    def __repr__(self) -> str:
        return repr(self._container)
```

CALCULATING THE TOTAL WEIGHT OF A WEIGHTED PATH

Before we develop a method for finding a minimum spanning tree, we will develop a function we can use to test the total weight of a solution. The solution to the minimum spanning tree problem will consist of a list of weighted edges that compose the tree. First, we will define a `WeightedPath` as a list of `WeightedEdge`. Then we will define a `total_weight()` function that takes a list of `WeightedPath` and finds the total weight that results from adding all of its edges' weights together.

Listing 4.10   mst.py

```python
from typing import TypeVar, List, Optional
from weighted_graph import WeightedGraph
from weighted_edge import WeightedEdge
from priority_queue import PriorityQueue

V = TypeVar('V') # type of the vertices in the graph
WeightedPath = List[WeightedEdge] # type alias for paths


def total_weight(wp: WeightedPath) -> float:
    return sum([e.weight for e in wp])
```

JARNÍK'S ALGORITHM

Jarník's algorithm for finding a minimum spanning tree works by dividing a graph into two parts: the vertices in the still-being-assembled minimum spanning tree and the vertices not yet in the minimum spanning tree. It takes the following steps:

1 Pick an arbitrary vertex to include in the minimum spanning tree.
2 Find the lowest-weight edge connecting the minimum spanning tree to the vertices not yet in the minimum spanning tree.

3 Add the vertex at the end of that minimum edge to the minimum spanning tree.

4 Repeat steps 2 and 3 until every vertex in the graph is in the minimum spanning tree.

NOTE Jarník's algorithm is commonly referred to as Prim's algorithm. Two Czech mathematicians, Otakar Borůvka and Vojtěch Jarník, interested in minimizing the cost of laying electric lines in the late 1920s, came up with algorithms to solve the problem of finding a minimum spanning tree. Their algorithms were "rediscovered" decades later by others.[3]

To run Jarník's algorithm efficiently, a priority queue is used. Every time a new vertex is added to the minimum spanning tree, all of its outgoing edges that link to vertices outside the tree are added to the priority queue. The lowest-weight edge is always popped off the priority queue, and the algorithm keeps executing until the priority queue is empty. This ensures that the lowest-weight edges are always added to the tree first. Edges that connect to vertices already in the tree are ignored when they are popped.

The following code for `mst()` is the full implementation of Jarník's algorithm,[4] along with a utility function for printing a `WeightedPath`.

WARNING Jarník's algorithm will not necessarily work correctly in a graph with directed edges. It also will not work in a graph that is not connected.

Listing 4.11   mst.py continued

```python
def mst(wg: WeightedGraph[V], start: int = 0) -> Optional[WeightedPath]:
    if start > (wg.vertex_count - 1) or start < 0:
        return None
    result: WeightedPath = [] # holds the final MST
    pq: PriorityQueue[WeightedEdge] = PriorityQueue()
    visited: [bool] = [False] * wg.vertex_count # where we've been

    def visit(index: int):
        visited[index] = True # mark as visited
        for edge in wg.edges_for_index(index):
            # add all edges coming from here to pq
            if not visited[edge.v]:
                pq.push(edge)

    visit(start) # the first vertex is where everything begins

    while not pq.empty: # keep going while there are edges to process
        edge = pq.pop()
        if visited[edge.v]:
            continue # don't ever revisit
```

---

[3] Helena Durnová, "Otakar Borůvka (1899-1995) and the Minimum Spanning Tree" (Institute of Mathematics of the Czech Academy of Sciences, 2006), http://mng.bz/O2vj.

[4] Inspired by a solution by Robert Sedgewick and Kevin Wayne, *Algorithms*, 4th Edition (Addison-Wesley Professional, 2011), p. 619.

```
        # this is the current smallest, so add it to solution
        result.append(edge)
        visit(edge.v) # visit where this connects

    return result


def print_weighted_path(wg: WeightedGraph, wp: WeightedPath) -> None:
    for edge in wp:
        print(f"{wg.vertex_at(edge.u)} {edge.weight}> {wg.vertex_
         at(edge.v)}")
    print(f"Total Weight: {total_weight(wp)}")
```

Let's walk through mst(), line by line.

```
def mst(wg: WeightedGraph[V], start: int = 0) -> Optional[WeightedPath]:
    if start > (wg.vertex_count - 1) or start < 0:
        return None
```

The algorithm returns an optional WeightedPath representing the minimum spanning tree. It does not matter where the algorithm starts (assuming the graph is connected and undirected), so the default is set to vertex index 0. If it so happens that the start is invalid, mst() returns None.

```
result: WeightedPath = [] # holds the final MST
pq: PriorityQueue[WeightedEdge] = PriorityQueue()
visited: [bool] = [False] * wg.vertex_count # where we've been
```

result will ultimately hold the weighted path containing the minimum spanning tree. This is where we will add WeightedEdges, as the lowest-weight edge is popped off and takes us to a new part of the graph. Jarník's algorithm is considered a *greedy algorithm* because it always selects the lowest-weight edge. pq is where newly discovered edges are stored and the next-lowest-weight edge is popped. visited keeps track of vertex indices that we have already been to. This could also have been accomplished with a Set, similar to explored in bfs().

```
def visit(index: int):
    visited[index] = True # mark as visited
    for edge in wg.edges_for_index(index):
        # add all edges coming from here
        if not visited[edge.v]:
            pq.push(edge)
```

visit() is an inner convenience function that marks a vertex as visited and adds all of its edges that connect to vertices not yet visited to pq. Note how easy the adjacency-list model makes finding edges belonging to a particular vertex.

```
visit(start) # the first vertex is where everything begins
```

It does not matter which vertex is visited first unless the graph is not connected. If the graph is not connected, but is instead made up of disconnected *components*, mst() will return a tree that spans the particular component that the starting vertex belongs to.

```
while not pq.empty: # keep going while there are edges to process
    edge = pq.pop()
```

```
    if visited[edge.v]:
        continue # don't ever revisit
    # this is the current smallest, so add it
    result.append(edge)
    visit(edge.v) # visit where this connects
return result
```

While there are still edges on the priority queue, we pop them off and check if they lead to vertices not yet in the tree. Because the priority queue is ascending, it pops the lowest-weight edges first. This ensures that the result is indeed of minimum total weight. Any edge popped that does not lead to an unexplored vertex is ignored. Otherwise, because the edge is the lowest seen so far, it is added to the result set, and the new vertex it leads to is explored. When there are no edges left to explore, the result is returned.

Let's finally return to the problem of connecting all 15 of the largest MSAs in the United States by Hyperloop, using a minimum amount of track. The route that accomplishes this is simply the minimum spanning tree of city_graph2. Let's try running mst() on city_graph2.

Listing 4.12 mst.py continued

```
if __name__ == "__main__":
    city_graph2: WeightedGraph[str] = WeightedGraph(["Seattle", "San
      Francisco", "Los Angeles", "Riverside", "Phoenix", "Chicago", "Boston",
      "New York", "Atlanta", "Miami", "Dallas", "Houston", "Detroit",
      "Philadelphia", "Washington"])

    city_graph2.add_edge_by_vertices("Seattle", "Chicago", 1737)
    city_graph2.add_edge_by_vertices("Seattle", "San Francisco", 678)
    city_graph2.add_edge_by_vertices("San Francisco", "Riverside", 386)
    city_graph2.add_edge_by_vertices("San Francisco", "Los Angeles", 348)
    city_graph2.add_edge_by_vertices("Los Angeles", "Riverside", 50)
    city_graph2.add_edge_by_vertices("Los Angeles", "Phoenix", 357)
    city_graph2.add_edge_by_vertices("Riverside", "Phoenix", 307)
    city_graph2.add_edge_by_vertices("Riverside", "Chicago", 1704)
    city_graph2.add_edge_by_vertices("Phoenix", "Dallas", 887)
    city_graph2.add_edge_by_vertices("Phoenix", "Houston", 1015)
    city_graph2.add_edge_by_vertices("Dallas", "Chicago", 805)
    city_graph2.add_edge_by_vertices("Dallas", "Atlanta", 721)
    city_graph2.add_edge_by_vertices("Dallas", "Houston", 225)
    city_graph2.add_edge_by_vertices("Houston", "Atlanta", 702)
    city_graph2.add_edge_by_vertices("Houston", "Miami", 968)
    city_graph2.add_edge_by_vertices("Atlanta", "Chicago", 588)
    city_graph2.add_edge_by_vertices("Atlanta", "Washington", 543)
    city_graph2.add_edge_by_vertices("Atlanta", "Miami", 604)
    city_graph2.add_edge_by_vertices("Miami", "Washington", 923)
    city_graph2.add_edge_by_vertices("Chicago", "Detroit", 238)
    city_graph2.add_edge_by_vertices("Detroit", "Boston", 613)
    city_graph2.add_edge_by_vertices("Detroit", "Washington", 396)
    city_graph2.add_edge_by_vertices("Detroit", "New York", 482)
    city_graph2.add_edge_by_vertices("Boston", "New York", 190)
    city_graph2.add_edge_by_vertices("New York", "Philadelphia", 81)
```

```
city_graph2.add_edge_by_vertices("Philadelphia", "Washington", 123)

result: Optional[WeightedPath] = mst(city_graph2)
if result is None:
    print("No solution found!")
else:
    print_weighted_path(city_graph2, result)
```

Thanks to the pretty-printing `printWeightedPath()` method, the minimum spanning tree is easy to read.

```
Seattle 678> San Francisco
San Francisco 348> Los Angeles
Los Angeles 50> Riverside
Riverside 307> Phoenix
Phoenix 887> Dallas
Dallas 225> Houston
Houston 702> Atlanta
Atlanta 543> Washington
Washington 123> Philadelphia
Philadelphia 81> New York
New York 190> Boston
Washington 396> Detroit
Detroit 238> Chicago
Atlanta 604> Miami
Total Weight: 5372
```

In other words, this is the cumulatively shortest collection of edges that connects all of the MSAs in the weighted graph. The minimum length of track needed to connect all of them is 5,372 miles. Figure 4.7 illustrates the minimum spanning tree.

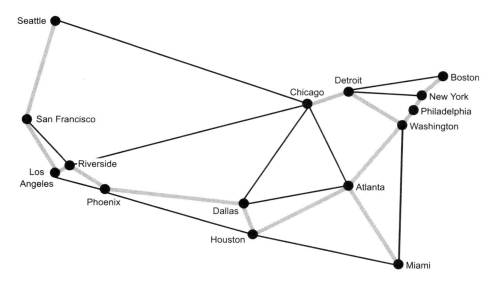

Figure 4.7   The highlighted edges represent a minimum spanning tree that connects all 15 MSAs.

4.5   *Finding shortest paths in a weighted graph*

As the Hyperloop network gets built, it is unlikely the builders will have the ambition to connect the whole country at once. Instead, it is likely the builders will want to minimize the cost to lay track between key cities. The cost to extend the network to particular cities will obviously depend on where the builders start.

Finding the cost to any city from some starting city is a version of the "single-source shortest path" problem. That problem asks, "What is the shortest path (in terms of total edge weight) from some vertex to every other vertex in a weighted graph?"

4.5.1   *Dijkstra's algorithm*

Dijkstra's algorithm solves the single-source shortest path problem. It is provided a starting vertex, and it returns the lowest-weight path to any other vertex on a weighted graph. It also returns the minimum total weight to every other vertex from the starting vertex. Dijkstra's algorithm starts at the single-source vertex and then continually explores the closest vertices to the starting vertex. For this reason, like Jarník's algorithm, Dijkstra's algorithm is greedy. When Dijkstra's algorithm encounters a new vertex, it keeps track of how far it is from the starting vertex and updates this value if it ever finds a shorter path. It also keeps track of which edge got it to each vertex, like a breadth-first search.

Here are all of the algorithm's steps:

1. Add the starting vertex to a priority queue.
2. Pop the closest vertex from the priority queue (at the beginning, this is just the starting vertex); we'll call it the current vertex.
3. Look at all of the neighbors connected to the current vertex. If they have not previously been recorded, or if the edge offers a new shortest path to them, then for each of them record its distance from the start, record the edge that produced this distance, and add the new vertex to the priority queue.
4. Repeat steps 2 and 3 until the priority queue is empty.
5. Return the shortest distance to every vertex from the starting vertex and the path to get to each of them.

The code for Dijkstra's algorithm includes `DijkstraNode`, a simple data structure for keeping track of costs associated with each vertex explored so far and for comparing them. This is similar to the `Node` class in chapter 2. It also includes utility functions for converting the returned array of distances to something easier to use for looking up by vertex and for calculating a shortest path to a particular destination vertex from the path dictionary returned by `dijkstra()`.

Without further ado, here is the code for Dijkstra's algorithm. We will go over it line by line after.

Listing 4.13   dijkstra.py

```python
from __future__ import annotations
from typing import TypeVar, List, Optional, Tuple, Dict
from dataclasses import dataclass
from mst import WeightedPath, print_weighted_path
from weighted_graph import WeightedGraph
from weighted_edge import WeightedEdge
from priority_queue import PriorityQueue

V = TypeVar('V') # type of the vertices in the graph


@dataclass
class DijkstraNode:
    vertex: int
    distance: float

    def __lt__(self, other: DijkstraNode) -> bool:
        return self.distance < other.distance

    def __eq__(self, other: DijkstraNode) -> bool:
        return self.distance == other.distance


def dijkstra(wg: WeightedGraph[V], root: V) -> Tuple[List[Optional[float]],
    Dict[int, WeightedEdge]]:
    first: int = wg.index_of(root) # find starting index
    # distances are unknown at first
    distances: List[Optional[float]] = [None] * wg.vertex_count
    distances[first] = 0 # the root is 0 away from the root
    path_dict: Dict[int, WeightedEdge] = {} # how we got to each vertex
    pq: PriorityQueue[DijkstraNode] = PriorityQueue()
    pq.push(DijkstraNode(first, 0))

    while not pq.empty:
        u: int = pq.pop().vertex # explore the next closest vertex
        dist_u: float = distances[u] # should already have seen it
        # look at every edge/vertex from the vertex in question
        for we in wg.edges_for_index(u):
            # the old distance to this vertex
            dist_v: float = distances[we.v]
            # no old distance or found shorter path
            if dist_v is None or dist_v > we.weight + dist_u:
                # update distance to this vertex
                distances[we.v] = we.weight + dist_u
                # update the edge on the shortest path to this vertex
                path_dict[we.v] = we
                # explore it soon
                pq.push(DijkstraNode(we.v, we.weight + dist_u))

    return distances, path_dict


# Helper function to get easier access to dijkstra results
def distance_array_to_vertex_dict(wg: WeightedGraph[V], distances:
    List[Optional[float]]) -> Dict[V, Optional[float]]:
    distance_dict: Dict[V, Optional[float]] = {}
    for i in range(len(distances)):
```

```
        distance_dict[wg.vertex_at(i)] = distances[i]
    return distance_dict

# Takes a dictionary of edges to reach each node and returns a list of
# edges that goes from `start` to `end`
def path_dict_to_path(start: int, end: int, path_dict: Dict[int,
    WeightedEdge]) -> WeightedPath:
    if len(path_dict) == 0:
        return []
    edge_path: WeightedPath = []
    e: WeightedEdge = path_dict[end]
    edge_path.append(e)
    while e.u != start:
        e = path_dict[e.u]
        edge_path.append(e)
    return list(reversed(edge_path))
```

The first few lines of dijkstra() use data structures you have become familiar with, except for distances, which is a placeholder for the distances to every vertex in the graph from the root. Initially all of these distances are None, because we do not yet know how far each of them is; that is what we are using Dijkstra's algorithm to figure out!

```
def dijkstra(wg: WeightedGraph[V], root: V) -> Tuple[List[Optional[float]],
    Dict[int, WeightedEdge]]:
    first: int = wg.index_of(root) # find starting index
    # distances are unknown at first
    distances: List[Optional[float]] = [None] * wg.vertex_count
    distances[first] = 0 # the root is 0 away from the root
    path_dict: Dict[int, WeightedEdge] = {} # how we got to each vertex
    pq: PriorityQueue[DijkstraNode] = PriorityQueue()
    pq.push(DijkstraNode(first, 0))
```

The first node pushed onto the priority queue contains the root vertex.

```
while not pq.empty:
    u: int = pq.pop().vertex # explore the next closest vertex
    dist_u: float = distances[u] # should already have seen it
```

We keep running Dijkstra's algorithm until the priority queue is empty. u is the current vertex we are searching from, and dist_u is the stored distance for getting to u along known routes. Every vertex explored at this stage has already been found, so it must have a known distance.

```
# look at every edge/vertex from here
for we in wg.edges_for_index(u):
    # the old distance to this
    dist_v: float = distances[we.v]
```

Next, every edge connected to u is explored. dist_v is the distance to any known vertex attached by an edge from u.

```
# no old distance or found shorter path
if dist_v is None or dist_v > we.weight + dist_u:
```

```
# update distance to this vertex
distances[we.v] = we.weight + dist_u
# update the edge on the shortest path
path_dict[we.v] = we
# explore it soon
pq.push(DijkstraNode(we.v, we.weight + dist_u))
```

If we have found a vertex that has not yet been explored (dist_v is None), or we have found a new, shorter path to it, we record that new shortest distance to v and the edge that got us there. Finally, we push any vertices that have new paths to them to the priority queue.

```
return distances, path_dict
```

dijkstra() returns both the distances to every vertex in the weighted graph from the root vertex, and the path_dict that can unlock the shortest paths to them.

It is safe to run Dijkstra's algorithm now. We will start by finding the distance from Los Angeles to every other MSA in the graph. Then we will find the shortest path between Los Angeles and Boston. Finally, we will use print_weighted_path() to pretty-print the result.

Listing 4.14   dijkstra.py continued

```python
if __name__ == "__main__":
    city_graph2: WeightedGraph[str] = WeightedGraph(["Seattle", "San
        Francisco", "Los Angeles", "Riverside", "Phoenix", "Chicago", "Boston",
        "New York", "Atlanta", "Miami", "Dallas", "Houston", "Detroit",
        "Philadelphia", "Washington"])

    city_graph2.add_edge_by_vertices("Seattle", "Chicago", 1737)
    city_graph2.add_edge_by_vertices("Seattle", "San Francisco", 678)
    city_graph2.add_edge_by_vertices("San Francisco", "Riverside", 386)
    city_graph2.add_edge_by_vertices("San Francisco", "Los Angeles", 348)
    city_graph2.add_edge_by_vertices("Los Angeles", "Riverside", 50)
    city_graph2.add_edge_by_vertices("Los Angeles", "Phoenix", 357)
    city_graph2.add_edge_by_vertices("Riverside", "Phoenix", 307)
    city_graph2.add_edge_by_vertices("Riverside", "Chicago", 1704)
    city_graph2.add_edge_by_vertices("Phoenix", "Dallas", 887)
    city_graph2.add_edge_by_vertices("Phoenix", "Houston", 1015)
    city_graph2.add_edge_by_vertices("Dallas", "Chicago", 805)
    city_graph2.add_edge_by_vertices("Dallas", "Atlanta", 721)
    city_graph2.add_edge_by_vertices("Dallas", "Houston", 225)
    city_graph2.add_edge_by_vertices("Houston", "Atlanta", 702)
    city_graph2.add_edge_by_vertices("Houston", "Miami", 968)
    city_graph2.add_edge_by_vertices("Atlanta", "Chicago", 588)
    city_graph2.add_edge_by_vertices("Atlanta", "Washington", 543)
    city_graph2.add_edge_by_vertices("Atlanta", "Miami", 604)
    city_graph2.add_edge_by_vertices("Miami", "Washington", 923)
    city_graph2.add_edge_by_vertices("Chicago", "Detroit", 238)
    city_graph2.add_edge_by_vertices("Detroit", "Boston", 613)
    city_graph2.add_edge_by_vertices("Detroit", "Washington", 396)
    city_graph2.add_edge_by_vertices("Detroit", "New York", 482)
    city_graph2.add_edge_by_vertices("Boston", "New York", 190)
    city_graph2.add_edge_by_vertices("New York", "Philadelphia", 81)
```

```
city_graph2.add_edge_by_vertices("Philadelphia", "Washington", 123)

distances, path_dict = dijkstra(city_graph2, "Los Angeles")
name_distance: Dict[str, Optional[int]] = distance_array_to_vertex_
 dict(city_graph2, distances)
print("Distances from Los Angeles:")
for key, value in name_distance.items():
    print(f"{key} : {value}")
print("") # blank line

print("Shortest path from Los Angeles to Boston:")
path: WeightedPath = path_dict_to_path(city_graph2.index_of("Los
 Angeles"), city_graph2.index_of("Boston"), path_dict)
print_weighted_path(city_graph2, path)
```

Your output should look something like this:

```
Distances from Los Angeles:
Seattle : 1026
San Francisco : 348
Los Angeles : 0
Riverside : 50
Phoenix : 357
Chicago : 1754
Boston : 2605
New York : 2474
Atlanta : 1965
Miami : 2340
Dallas : 1244
Houston : 1372
Detroit : 1992
Philadelphia : 2511
Washington : 2388

Shortest path from Los Angeles to Boston:
Los Angeles 50> Riverside
Riverside 1704> Chicago
Chicago 238> Detroit
Detroit 613> Boston
Total Weight: 2605
```

You may have noticed that Dijkstra's algorithm has some resemblance to Jarník's algorithm. They are both greedy, and it is possible to implement them using quite similar code if one is sufficiently motivated. Another algorithm that Dijkstra's algorithm resembles is A* from chapter 2. A* can be thought of as a modification of Dijkstra's algorithm. Add a heuristic and restrict Dijkstra's algorithm to finding a single destination, and the two algorithms are the same.

NOTE Dijkstra's algorithm is designed for graphs with positive weights. Graphs with negatively weighted edges can pose a challenge for Dijkstra's algorithm and will require modification or an alternative algorithm.

4.6   *Real-world applications*

A huge amount of our world can be represented using graphs. You have seen in this chapter how effective they are for working with transportation networks, but many other kinds of networks have the same essential optimization problems: telephone networks, computer networks, utility networks (electricity, plumbing, and so on). As a result, graph algorithms are essential for efficiency in the telecommunications, shipping, transportation, and utility industries.

Retailers must handle complex distribution problems. Stores and warehouses can be thought of as vertices and the distances between them as edges. The algorithms are the same. The internet itself is a giant graph, with each connected device a vertex and each wired or wireless connection being an edge. Whether a business is saving fuel or wire, minimum spanning tree and shortest path problem-solving are useful for more than just games. Some of the world's most famous brands became successful by optimizing graph problems: think of Walmart building out an efficient distribution network, Google indexing the web (a giant graph), and FedEx finding the right set of hubs to connect the world's addresses.

Some obvious applications of graph algorithms are social networks and map applications. In a social network, people are vertices, and connections (friendships on Facebook, for instance) are edges. In fact, one of Facebook's most prominent developer tools is known as the Graph API (https://developers.facebook.com/docs/graph-api). In map applications like Apple Maps and Google Maps, graph algorithms are used to provide directions and calculate trip times.

Several popular video games also make explicit use of graph algorithms. Mini-Metro and Ticket to Ride are two examples of games that closely mimic the problems solved in this chapter.

4.7   *Exercises*

1. Add support to the graph framework for removing edges and vertices.
2. Add support to the graph framework for directed graphs (digraphs).
3. Use this chapter's graph framework to prove or disprove the classic Bridges of Königsberg problem, as described on Wikipedia: https://en.wikipedia.org/wiki/Seven_Bridges_of_Königsberg.

Genetic algorithms 5

Genetic algorithms are not used for everyday programmatic problems. They are called upon when traditional algorithmic approaches are insufficient for arriving at a solution to a problem in a reasonable amount of time. In other words, genetic algorithms are usually reserved for complex problems without easy solutions. If you need a sense of what some of these complex problems might be, feel free to read ahead in section 5.7 before proceeding. One interesting example, though, is protein-ligand docking and drug design. Computational biologists need to design molecules that will bind to receptors to deliver drugs. There may be no obvious algorithm for designing a particular molecule, but as you will see, sometimes genetic algorithms can provide an answer without much direction beyond a definition of the goal of a problem.

5.1 Biological background

In biology, the theory of evolution is an explanation of how genetic mutation, coupled with the constraints of an environment, leads to changes in organisms over time (including speciation—the creation of new species). The mechanism by which the well-adapted organisms succeed and the less well-adapted organisms fail is known as *natural selection*. Each generation of a species will include individuals with different (and sometimes new) traits that come about through genetic mutation. All individuals compete for limited resources to survive, and because there are more individuals than there are resources, some individuals must die.

An individual with a mutation that makes it better adapted for survival in its environment will have a higher probability of living and reproducing. Over time, the better-adapted individuals in an environment will have more children and

94

through inheritance will pass on their mutations to those children. Therefore, a mutation that benefits survival is likely to eventually proliferate amongst a population.

For example, if bacteria are being killed by a specific antibiotic, and one individual bacterium in the population has a mutation in a gene that makes it more resistant to the antibiotic, it is more likely to survive and reproduce. If the antibiotic is continually applied over time, the children who have inherited the gene for antibiotic resistance will also be more likely to reproduce and have children of their own. Eventually the whole population may gain the mutation, as continued assault by the antibiotic kills off the individuals without the mutation. The antibiotic does not cause the mutation to develop, but it does lead to the proliferation of individuals with the mutation.

Natural selection has been applied in spheres beyond biology. Social Darwinism is natural selection applied to the sphere of social theory. In computer science, genetic algorithms are a simulation of natural selection to solve computational challenges.

A genetic algorithm includes a *population* (group) of individuals known as *chromosomes*. The chromosomes, each composed of *genes* that specify their traits, are competing to solve some problem. How well a chromosome solves a problem is defined by a *fitness function*.

The genetic algorithm goes through *generations*. In each generation, the chromosomes that are more fit are more likely to be *selected* to reproduce. There is also a probability in each generation that two chromosomes will have their genes merged. This is known as *crossover*. And finally, there is the important possibility in each generation that a gene in a chromosome may *mutate* (randomly change).

After the fitness function of some individual in the population crosses some specified threshold, or the algorithm runs through some specified maximum number of generations, the best individual (the one that scored highest in the fitness function) is returned.

Genetic algorithms are not a good solution for all problems. They depend on three partially or fully *stochastic* (randomly determined) operations: selection, crossover, and mutation. Therefore, they may not find an optimal solution in a reasonable amount of time. For most problems, more deterministic algorithms exist with better guarantees. But there are problems for which no fast deterministic algorithm exists. In these cases, genetic algorithms are a good choice.

5.2 *A generic genetic algorithm*

Genetic algorithms are often highly specialized and tuned for a particular application. In this chapter, we will define a generic genetic algorithm that can be used with multiple problems while not being particularly well tuned for any of them. It will include some configurable options, but the goal is to show the algorithm's fundamentals instead of its tunability.

We will start by defining an interface for the individuals that the generic algorithm can operate on. The abstract class `Chromosome` defines four essential features. A chromosome must be able to do the following:

- Determine its own fitness
- Create an instance with randomly selected genes (for use in filling the first generation)
- Implement crossover (combine itself with another of the same type to create children)—in other words, mix itself with another chromosome
- Mutate—make a small, fairly random change in itself

Here is the code for Chromosome, codifying these four needs.

Listing 5.1   chromosome.py

```python
from __future__ import annotations
from typing import TypeVar, Tuple, Type
from abc import ABC, abstractmethod

T = TypeVar('T', bound='Chromosome') # for returning self


# Base class for all chromosomes; all methods must be overridden
class Chromosome(ABC):
    @abstractmethod
    def fitness(self) -> float:
        ...

    @classmethod
    @abstractmethod
    def random_instance(cls: Type[T]) -> T:
        ...

    @abstractmethod
    def crossover(self: T, other: T) -> Tuple[T, T]:
        ...

    @abstractmethod
    def mutate(self) -> None:
        ...
```

TIP You'll notice in its constructor that the TypeVar T is bound to Chromosome. This means that anything that fills in a variable that is of type T must be an instance of a Chromosome or a subclass of Chromosome.

We will implement the algorithm itself (the code that will manipulate chromosomes) as a generic class that is open to subclassing for future specialized applications. Before we do so, though, let's revisit the description of a genetic algorithm from the beginning of the chapter and clearly define the steps that a genetic algorithm takes:

1 Create an initial population of random chromosomes for the first generation of the algorithm.
2 Measure the fitness of each chromosome in this generation of the population. If any exceeds the threshold, return it, and the algorithm ends.
3 Select some individuals to reproduce, with a higher probability of selecting those with the highest fitness.

4 Crossover (combine), with some probability, some of the selected chromosomes to create children that represent the population of the next generation.

5 Mutate, usually with a low probability, some of those chromosomes. The population of the new generation is now complete, and it replaces the population of the last generation.

6 Return to step 2 unless the maximum number of generations has been reached. If that is the case, return the best chromosome found so far.

This general outline of a genetic algorithm (illustrated in figure 5.1) is missing a lot of important details. How many chromosomes should be in the population? What is the threshold that stops the algorithm? How should the chromosomes be selected for reproduction? How should they be combined (crossover) and at what probability? At what probability should mutations occur? How many generations should be run?

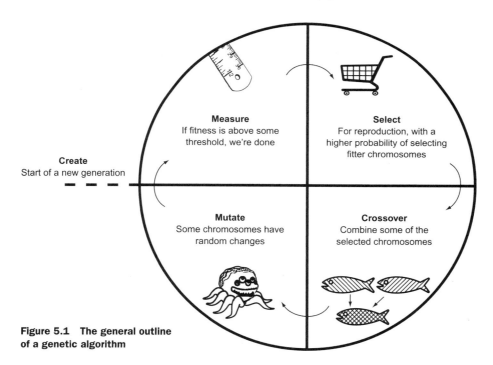

Figure 5.1 The general outline of a genetic algorithm

All of these points will be configurable in our `GeneticAlgorithm` class. We will define it piece by piece so we can talk about each piece separately.

Listing 5.2 genetic_algorithm.py

```python
from __future__ import annotations
from typing import TypeVar, Generic, List, Tuple, Callable
from enum import Enum
from random import choices, random
```

```
from heapq import nlargest
from statistics import mean
from chromosome import Chromosome

C = TypeVar('C', bound=Chromosome) # type of the chromosomes

class GeneticAlgorithm(Generic[C]):
    SelectionType = Enum("SelectionType", "ROULETTE TOURNAMENT")
```

GeneticAlgorithm takes a generic type that conforms to Chromosome, and its name is C. The enum SelectionType is an internal type used for specifying the selection method used by the algorithm. The two most common genetic algorithm selection methods are known as *roulette-wheel selection* (sometimes called *fitness proportionate selection*) and *tournament selection*. The former gives every chromosome a chance of being picked, proportionate to its fitness. In tournament selection, a certain number of random chromosomes are challenged against one another, and the one with the best fitness is selected.

Listing 5.3   genetic_algorithm.py continued

```
def __init__(self, initial_population: List[C], threshold: float, max_
        generations: int = 100, mutation_chance: float = 0.01, crossover_chance:
        float = 0.7, selection_type: SelectionType = SelectionType.TOURNAMENT) -
        > None:
    self._population: List[C] = initial_population
    self._threshold: float = threshold
    self._max_generations: int = max_generations
    self._mutation_chance: float = mutation_chance
    self._crossover_chance: float = crossover_chance
    self._selection_type: GeneticAlgorithm.SelectionType = selection_type
    self._fitness_key: Callable = type(self._population[0]).fitness
```

The preceding are all properties of the genetic algorithm that will be configured at the time of creation, through __init__(). initial_population is the chromosomes in the first generation of the algorithm. threshold is the fitness level that indicates that a solution has been found for the problem that the genetic algorithm is trying to solve. max_generations is the maximum number of generations to run. If we have run that many generations and no solution with a fitness level beyond threshold has been found, the best solution that has been found will be returned. mutation_chance is the probability of each chromosome in each generation mutating. crossover_chance is the probability that two parents selected to reproduce have children that are a mixture of their genes; otherwise, the children are just duplicates of the parents. Finally, selection_type is the type of selection method to use, as delineated by the enum SelectionType.

The preceding init method takes a long list of parameters, most of which have default values. They set up instance versions of the configurable properties we just discussed. In our examples, _population is initialized with a random set of chromosomes using the Chromosome class's random_instance() class method. In other words, the first generation of chromosomes is just composed of random individuals. This is a point of potential optimization for a more sophisticated genetic algorithm. Instead of starting with purely random individuals, the first generation could contain individuals that are closer to the solution, through some knowledge of the problem. This is referred to as *seeding*.

_fitness_key is a reference to the method we will be using throughout Genetic-Algorithm for calculating the fitness of a chromosome. Recall that this class needs to work with any subclass of Chromosome. Therefore, _fitness_key will differ by subclass. To get to it, we use type() to refer to the specific subclass of Chromosome that we are finding the fitness of.

Now we will examine the two selection methods that our class supports.

Listing 5.4 genetic_algorithm.py continued

```
# Use the probability distribution wheel to pick 2 parents
# Note: will not work with negative fitness results
def _pick_roulette(self, wheel: List[float]) -> Tuple[C, C]:
    return tuple(choices(self._population, weights=wheel, k=2))
```

Roulette-wheel selection is based on each chromosome's proportion of fitness to the sum of all fitnesses in a generation. The chromosomes with the highest fitness have a better chance of being picked. The values that represent each chromosome's fitness are provided in the parameter wheel. The actual picking is conveniently done by the choices() function from the Python standard library's random module. This function takes a list of things we want to pick from, an equal-length list containing weights for each item in the first list, and how many items we want to pick.

If we were to implement this ourselves, we could calculate percentages of total fitness for each item (proportional fitnesses) that are represented by floating-point values between 0 and 1. A random number (pick) between 0 and 1 could be used to figure out which chromosome to select. The algorithm would work by decreasing pick by each chromosome's proportional fitness value sequentially. When pick crosses 0, that's the chromosome to select.

Does it make sense to you why this process results in each chromosome's being pickable by its proportion? If not, think about it with pencil and paper. Consider drawing a proportional roulette wheel, as in figure 5.2.

The most basic form of tournament selection is simpler than roulette-wheel selection. Instead of figuring out proportions, we simply pick k chromosomes from the whole population at random. The two chromosomes with the best fitness out of the randomly selected bunch win.

Listing 5.5 genetic_algorithm.py continued

```
# Choose num_participants at random and take the best 2
def _pick_tournament(self, num_participants: int) -> Tuple[C, C]:
    participants: List[C] = choices(self._population, k=num_participants)
    return tuple(nlargest(2, participants, key=self._fitness_key))
```

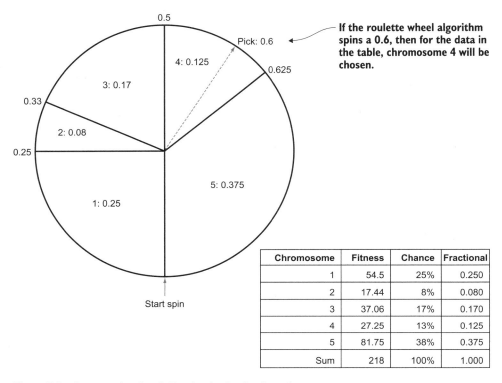

Figure 5.2   An example of roulette-wheel selection in action

The code for _pick_tournament() first uses choices() to randomly pick num_participants from _population. Then it uses the nlargest() function from the heapq module to find the two largest individuals by _fitness_key. What is the right number for num_participants? As with many parameters in a genetic algorithm, trial and error may be the best way to determine it. One thing to keep in mind is that a higher number of participants in the tournament leads to less diversity in the population, because chromosomes with poor fitness are more likely to be eliminated in matchups.[1] More sophisticated forms of tournament selection may pick individuals that are not the best, but second- or third-best, based on some kind of decreasing probability model.

These two methods, _pick_roulette() and _pick_tournament(), are used for selection, which occurs during reproduction. Reproduction is implemented in _reproduce_and_replace(), and it also takes care of ensuring that a new population of an equal number of chromosomes replaces the chromosomes in the last generation.

---

[1] Artem Sokolov and Darrell Whitley, "Unbiased Tournament Selection," GECCO'05 (June 25–29, 2005, Washington, D.C., U.S.A.), http://mng.bz/S7l6.

Listing 5.6   genetic_algorithm.py continued

```python
# Replace the population with a new generation of individuals
def _reproduce_and_replace(self) -> None:
    new_population: List[C] = []
    # keep going until we've filled the new generation
    while len(new_population) < len(self._population):
        # pick the 2 parents
        if self._selection_type == GeneticAlgorithm.SelectionType.ROULETTE:
            parents: Tuple[C, C] = self._pick_roulette([x.fitness() for x in
    self._population])
        else:
            parents = self._pick_tournament(len(self._population) // 2)
        # potentially crossover the 2 parents
        if random() < self._crossover_chance:
            new_population.extend(parents[0].crossover(parents[1]))
        else:
            new_population.extend(parents)
    # if we had an odd number, we'll have 1 extra, so we remove it
    if len(new_population) > len(self._population):
        new_population.pop()
    self._population = new_population # replace reference
```

In _reproduce_and_replace(), the following steps occur in broad strokes:

1 Two chromosomes, called parents, are selected for reproduction using one of the two selection methods. For tournament selection, we always run the tournament amongst half of the total population, but this too could be a configuration option.

2 There is _crossover_chance that the two parents will be combined to produce two new chromosomes, in which case they are added to new_population. If there are no children, the two parents are just added to new_population.

3 If new_population has as many chromosomes as _population, it replaces it. Otherwise, we return to step 1.

The method that implements mutation, _mutate(), is very simple, with the details of how to perform a mutation being left to individual chromosomes.

Listing 5.7   genetic_algorithm.py continued

```python
# With _mutation_chance probability mutate each individual
def _mutate(self) -> None:
    for individual in self._population:
        if random() < self._mutation_chance:
            individual.mutate()
```

We now have all of the building blocks needed to run the genetic algorithm. run() coordinates the measurement, reproduction (which includes selection), and mutation steps that bring the population from one generation to another. It also keeps track of the best (fittest) chromosome found at any point in the search.

Listing 5.8   genetic_algorithm.py continued

```python
# Run the genetic algorithm for max_generations iterations
# and return the best individual found
def run(self) -> C:
    best: C = max(self._population, key=self._fitness_key)
    for generation in range(self._max_generations):
        # early exit if we beat threshold
        if best.fitness() >= self._threshold:
            return best
        print(f"Generation {generation} Best {best.fitness()} Avg
    {mean(map(self._fitness_key, self._population))}")
        self._reproduce_and_replace()
        self._mutate()
        highest: C = max(self._population, key=self._fitness_key)
        if highest.fitness() > best.fitness():
            best = highest # found a new best
    return best # best we found in _max_generations
```

best keeps track of the best chromosome found so far. The main loop executes _max_
generations times. If any chromosome exceeds threshold in fitness, it is returned, and
the method ends. Otherwise, it calls _reproduce_and_replace() as well as _mutate() to
create the next generation and run the loop again. If _max_generations is reached, the
best chromosome found so far is returned.

5.3   *A naive test*

The generic genetic algorithm, GeneticAlgorithm, will work with any type that implements Chromosome. As a test, we will start by implementing a simple problem that can
be easily solved using traditional methods. We will try to maximize the equation $6x - x^2$
$+ 4y - y^2$. In other words, what values for x and y in that equation will yield the largest
number?

The maximizing values can be found, using calculus, by taking partial derivatives
and setting each equal to zero. The result is $x = 3$ and $y = 2$. Can our genetic algorithm
reach the same result without using calculus? Let's dig in.

Listing 5.9   simple_equation.py

```python
from __future__ import annotations
from typing import Tuple, List
from chromosome import Chromosome
from genetic_algorithm import GeneticAlgorithm
from random import randrange, random
from copy import deepcopy


class SimpleEquation(Chromosome):
    def __init__(self, x: int, y: int) -> None:
        self.x: int = x
        self.y: int = y

    def fitness(self) -> float: # 6x - x^2 + 4y - y^2
        return 6 * self.x - self.x * self.x + 4 * self.y - self.y * self.y
```

```
    @classmethod
    def random_instance(cls) -> SimpleEquation:
        return SimpleEquation(randrange(100), randrange(100))

    def crossover(self, other: SimpleEquation) -> Tuple[SimpleEquation,
      SimpleEquation]:
        child1: SimpleEquation = deepcopy(self)
        child2: SimpleEquation = deepcopy(other)
        child1.y = other.y
        child2.y = self.y
        return child1, child2

    def mutate(self) -> None:
        if random() > 0.5: # mutate x
            if random() > 0.5:
                self.x += 1
            else:
                self.x -= 1
        else: # otherwise mutate y
            if random() > 0.5:
                self.y += 1
            else:
                self.y -= 1

    def __str__(self) -> str:
        return f"X: {self.x} Y: {self.y} Fitness: {self.fitness()}"
```

SimpleEquation conforms to Chromosome, and true to its name, it does so as simply as possible. The genes of a SimpleEquation chromosome can be thought of as x and y. The method fitness() evaluates x and y using the equation $6x - x^2 + 4y - y^2$. The higher the value, the more fit the individual chromosome is, according to Genetic-Algorithm. In the case of a random instance, x and y are initially set to be random integers between 0 and 100, so random_instance() does not need to do anything other than instantiate a new SimpleEquation with these values. To combine one SimpleEquation with another in crossover(), the y values of the two instances are simply swapped to create the two children. mutate() randomly increments or decrements x or y. And that is pretty much it.

Because SimpleEquation conforms to Chromosome, we can already plug it into GeneticAlgorithm.

Listing 5.10 simple_equation.py continued

```
if __name__ == "__main__":
    initial_population: List[SimpleEquation] = [SimpleEquation.random_
      instance() for _ in range(20)]
    ga: GeneticAlgorithm[SimpleEquation] = GeneticAlgorithm(initial_
      population=initial_population, threshold=13.0, max_generations = 100,
      mutation_chance = 0.1, crossover_chance = 0.7)
    result: SimpleEquation = ga.run()
    print(result)
```

The parameters used here were derived through guess-and-check. You can try others. threshold is set to 13.0 because we already know the correct answer. When $x = 3$ and $y = 2$, the equation evaluates to 13.

If you did not previously know the answer, you might want to see the best result that could be found in a certain number of generations. In that case, you would set threshold to some arbitrarily large number. Remember, because genetic algorithms are stochastic, every run will be different.

Here is some sample output from a run in which the genetic algorithm solved the equation in nine generations:

```
Generation 0 Best -349 Avg -6112.3
Generation 1 Best 4 Avg -1306.7
Generation 2 Best 9 Avg -288.25
Generation 3 Best 9 Avg -7.35
Generation 4 Best 12 Avg 7.25
Generation 5 Best 12 Avg 8.5
Generation 6 Best 12 Avg 9.65
Generation 7 Best 12 Avg 11.7
Generation 8 Best 12 Avg 11.6
X: 3 Y: 2 Fitness: 13
```

As you can see, it came to the proper solution derived earlier with calculus, $x = 3$ and $y = 2$. You may also note that almost every generation, it got closer to the right answer.

Take into consideration that the genetic algorithm took more computational power than other methods would have to find the solution. In the real world, such a simple maximization problem would not be a good use of a genetic algorithm. But its simple implementation at least suffices to prove that our genetic algorithm works.

5.4   *SEND+MORE=MONEY revisited*

In chapter 3, we solved the classic cryptarithmetic problem SEND+MORE=MONEY using a constraint-satisfaction framework. (For a refresher on what the problem is all about, look back to the description in chapter 3.) The problem can also be solved in a reasonable amount of time using a genetic algorithm.

One of the largest difficulties in formulating a problem for a genetic algorithm solution is determining how to represent it. A convenient representation for cryptarithmetic problems is to use list indices as digits.[2] Hence, to represent the 10 possible digits (0, 1, 2, 3, 4, 5, 6, 7, 8, 9), a 10-element list is required. The characters to be searched within the problem can then be shifted around from place to place. For example, if it is suspected that the solution to a problem includes the character "E" representing the digit 4, then list[4] = "E". SEND+MORE=MONEY has eight distinct letters (S, E, N, D, M, O, R, Y), leaving two slots in the array empty. They can be filled with spaces indicating no letter.

---

[2]   Reza Abbasian and Masoud Mazloom, "Solving Cryptarithmetic Problems Using Parallel Genetic Algorithm," 2009 Second International Conference on Computer and Electrical Engineering, http://mng.bz/RQ7V.

A chromosome that represents the SEND+MORE=MONEY problem is represented in `SendMoreMoney2`. Note how the `fitness()` method is strikingly similar to `satisfied()` from `SendMoreMoneyConstraint` in chapter 3.

Listing 5.11   send_more_money2.py

```python
from __future__ import annotations
from typing import Tuple, List
from chromosome import Chromosome
from genetic_algorithm import GeneticAlgorithm
from random import shuffle, sample
from copy import deepcopy


class SendMoreMoney2(Chromosome):
    def __init__(self, letters: List[str]) -> None:
        self.letters: List[str] = letters

    def fitness(self) -> float:
        s: int = self.letters.index("S")
        e: int = self.letters.index("E")
        n: int = self.letters.index("N")
        d: int = self.letters.index("D")
        m: int = self.letters.index("M")
        o: int = self.letters.index("O")
        r: int = self.letters.index("R")
        y: int = self.letters.index("Y")
        send: int = s * 1000 + e * 100 + n * 10 + d
        more: int = m * 1000 + o * 100 + r * 10 + e
        money: int = m * 10000 + o * 1000 + n * 100 + e * 10 + y
        difference: int = abs(money - (send + more))
        return 1 / (difference + 1)

    @classmethod
    def random_instance(cls) -> SendMoreMoney2:
        letters = ["S", "E", "N", "D", "M", "O", "R", "Y", " ", " "]
        shuffle(letters)
        return SendMoreMoney2(letters)

    def crossover(self, other: SendMoreMoney2) -> Tuple[SendMoreMoney2,
    SendMoreMoney2]:
        child1: SendMoreMoney2 = deepcopy(self)
        child2: SendMoreMoney2 = deepcopy(other)
        idx1, idx2 = sample(range(len(self.letters)), k=2)
        l1, l2 = child1.letters[idx1], child2.letters[idx2]
        child1.letters[child1.letters.index(l2)], child1.letters[idx2] = 
    child1.letters[idx2], l2
        child2.letters[child2.letters.index(l1)], child2.letters[idx1] = 
    child2.letters[idx1], l1
        return child1, child2

    def mutate(self) -> None: # swap two letters' locations
        idx1, idx2 = sample(range(len(self.letters)), k=2)
        self.letters[idx1], self.letters[idx2] = self.letters[idx2], 
    self.letters[idx1]

    def __str__(self) -> str:
```

```
s: int = self.letters.index("S")
e: int = self.letters.index("E")
n: int = self.letters.index("N")
d: int = self.letters.index("D")
m: int = self.letters.index("M")
o: int = self.letters.index("O")
r: int = self.letters.index("R")
y: int = self.letters.index("Y")
send: int = s * 1000 + e * 100 + n * 10 + d
more: int = m * 1000 + o * 100 + r * 10 + e
money: int = m * 10000 + o * 1000 + n * 100 + e * 10 + y
difference: int = abs(money - (send + more))
return f"{send} + {more} = {money} Difference: {difference}"
```

There is, however, a major difference between `satisfied()` in chapter 3 and `fitness()` here. Here, we return `1 / (difference + 1)`. `difference` is the absolute value of the difference between MONEY and SEND+MORE. This represents how far off the chromosome is from solving the problem. If we were trying to minimize the `fitness()`, returning `difference` on its own would be fine. But because `Genetic-Algorithm` tries to maximize the value of `fitness()`, it needs to be flipped (so smaller values look like larger values), and that is why 1 is divided by `difference`. 1 is added to `difference` first, so that a `difference` of 0 does not yield a `fitness()` of 0 but instead of 1. Table 5.1 illustrates how this works.

Table 5.1   How the equation 1 / (difference + 1) yields fitnesses for maximization

difference	difference + 1	fitness (1/(difference + 1))
0	1	1
1	2	0.5
2	3	0.25
3	4	0.125

Remember, lower differences are better, and higher fitnesses are better. Because this formula causes those two facts to line up, it works well. Dividing 1 by a fitness value is a simple way to convert a minimization problem into a maximization problem. It does introduce some biases, though, so it is not foolproof.[3]

random_instance() makes use of the `shuffle()` function in the `random` module. `crossover()` selects two random indices in the `letters` lists of both chromosomes and swaps letters so that we end up with one letter from the first chromosome in the same place in the second chromosome, and vice versa. It performs these swaps in

---

[3] For example, we might end up with more numbers closer to 0 than we will closer to 1 if we were to simply divide 1 by a uniform distribution of integers, which—with the subtleties of how typical microprocessors interpret floating-point numbers—could lead to some unexpected results. An alternative way to convert a minimization problem into a maximization problem is to simply flip the sign (make it negative instead of positive). However, this will only work if the values are all positive to begin with.

children so that the placement of letters in the two children ends up being a combination of the parents. `mutate()` swaps two random locations in the `letters` list.

We can plug `SendMoreMoney2` into `GeneticAlgorithm` just as easily as we plugged in `SimpleEquation`. But be forewarned: This is a fairly tough problem, and it will take a long time to execute if the parameters are not well tweaked. And there's still some randomness even if one gets them right! The problem may be solved in a few seconds or a few minutes. Unfortunately, that is the nature of genetic algorithms.

Listing 5.12   send_more_money2.py continued

```
if __name__ == "__main__":
    initial_population: List[SendMoreMoney2] = [SendMoreMoney2.random_
        instance() for _ in range(1000)]
    ga: GeneticAlgorithm[SendMoreMoney2] = GeneticAlgorithm(initial_
        population=initial_population, threshold=1.0, max_generations = 1000,
        mutation_chance = 0.2, crossover_chance = 0.7, selection_
        type=GeneticAlgorithm.SelectionType.ROULETTE)
    result: SendMoreMoney2 = ga.run()
    print(result)
```

The following output is from a run that solved the problem in 3 generations using 1,000 individuals in each generation (as created above). See if you can mess around with the configurable parameters of `GeneticAlgorithm` and get a similar result with fewer individuals. Does it seem to work better with roulette selection than it does with tournament selection?

```
Generation 0 Best 0.0040650406504065045 Avg 8.854014252391551e-05
Generation 1 Best 0.16666666666666666 Avg 0.001277329479413134
Generation 2 Best 0.5 Avg 0.014920889170684687
8324 + 913 = 9237 Difference: 0
```

This solution indicates that SEND = 8324, MORE = 913, and MONEY = 9237. How is that possible? It looks like letters are missing from the solution. In fact, if M = 0, there are several solutions to the problem not possible in the version from chapter 3. MORE is actually 0913 here, and MONEY is 09237. The 0 is just ignored.

5.5   *Optimizing list compression*

Suppose that we have some information we want to compress. Suppose that it is a list of items, and we do not care about the order of the items, as long as all of them are intact. What order of the items will maximize the compression ratio? Did you even know that the order of the items will affect the compression ratio for most compression algorithms?

The answer will depend on the compression algorithm used. For this example, we will use the `compress()` function from the `zlib` module with its standard settings. The solution is shown here in its entirety for a list of 12 first names. If we do not run the genetic algorithm and we just run `compress()` on the 12 names in the order they were originally presented, the resulting compressed data will be 165 bytes.

Listing 5.13   list_compression.py

```python
from __future__ import annotations
from typing import Tuple, List, Any
from chromosome import Chromosome
from genetic_algorithm import GeneticAlgorithm
from random import shuffle, sample
from copy import deepcopy
from zlib import compress
from sys import getsizeof
from pickle import dumps

# 165 bytes compressed
PEOPLE: List[str] = ["Michael", "Sarah", "Joshua", "Narine", "David",
    "Sajid", "Melanie", "Daniel", "Wei", "Dean", "Brian", "Murat", "Lisa"]


class ListCompression(Chromosome):
    def __init__(self, lst: List[Any]) -> None:
        self.lst: List[Any] = lst

    @property
    def bytes_compressed(self) -> int:
        return getsizeof(compress(dumps(self.lst)))

    def fitness(self) -> float:
        return 1 / self.bytes_compressed

    @classmethod
    def random_instance(cls) -> ListCompression:
        mylst: List[str] = deepcopy(PEOPLE)
        shuffle(mylst)
        return ListCompression(mylst)

    def crossover(self, other: ListCompression) -> Tuple[ListCompression,
    ListCompression]:
        child1: ListCompression = deepcopy(self)
        child2: ListCompression = deepcopy(other)
        idx1, idx2 = sample(range(len(self.lst)), k=2)
        l1, l2 = child1.lst[idx1], child2.lst[idx2]
        child1.lst[child1.lst.index(l2)], child1.lst[idx2] = \
    child1.lst[idx2], l2
        child2.lst[child2.lst.index(l1)], child2.lst[idx1] = \
    child2.lst[idx1], l1
        return child1, child2

    def mutate(self) -> None: # swap two locations
        idx1, idx2 = sample(range(len(self.lst)), k=2)
        self.lst[idx1], self.lst[idx2] = self.lst[idx2], self.lst[idx1]

    def __str__(self) -> str:
        return f"Order: {self.lst} Bytes: {self.bytes_compressed}"

if __name__ == "__main__":
    initial_population: List[ListCompression] = [ListCompression.random_
        instance() for _ in range(1000)]
    ga: GeneticAlgorithm[ListCompression] = GeneticAlgorithm(initial_
        population=initial_population, threshold=1.0, max_generations = 1000,
```

```
    mutation_chance = 0.2, crossover_chance = 0.7, selection_
    type=GeneticAlgorithm.SelectionType.TOURNAMENT)
    result: ListCompression = ga.run()
    print(result)
```

Note how similar this implementation is to the implementation from SEND+
MORE=MONEY in section 5.4. The crossover() and mutate() functions are essentially the same. In both problems' solutions, we are taking a list of items and continually rearranging them and testing those rearrangements. One could write a generic
superclass for both problems' solutions that would work with a wide variety of problems. Any problem that can be represented as a list of items that needs to find its optimal order could be solved the same way. The only real point of customization for the
subclasses would be their respective fitness functions.

   If we run list_compression.py, it may take a very long time to complete. This is
because we don't know what constitutes the "right" answer ahead of time, unlike the
prior two problems, so we have no real threshold that we are working toward. Instead,
we set the number of generations and the number of individuals in each generation
to an arbitrarily high number and hope for the best. What is the minimum number of
bytes that rearranging the 12 names will yield in compression? Frankly, we don't know
the answer to that. In my best run, using the configuration in the preceding solution,
after 546 generations, the genetic algorithm found an order of the 12 names that
yielded 159 bytes compressed.

   That's only a savings of 6 bytes over the original order—a ~4% savings. One might
say that 4% is irrelevant, but if this were a far larger list that would be transferred
many times over the network, that could add up. Imagine if this were a 1 MB list that
would eventually be transferred across the internet 10,000,000 times. If the genetic
algorithm could optimize the order of the list for compression to save 4%, it would
save ~40 kilobytes per transfer and ultimately 400 GB in bandwidth across all transfers.
That's not a huge amount, but perhaps it could be significant enough that it's worth
running the algorithm once to find a near optimal order for compression.

   Consider this, though—we don't really know if we found the optimal order for the
12 names, let alone for the hypothetical 1 MB list. How would we know if we did?
Unless we have a deep understanding of the compression algorithm, we would have to
try compressing every possible order of the list. Just for a list of 12 items, that's a fairly
unfeasible 479,001,600 possible orders (12!, where ! means factorial). Using a genetic
algorithm that attempts to find optimality is perhaps more feasible, even if we don't
know whether its ultimate solution is truly optimal.

5.6   *Challenges for genetic algorithms*

Genetic algorithms are not a panacea. In fact, they are not suitable for most problems.
For any problem in which a fast deterministic algorithm exists, a genetic algorithm
approach does not make sense. Their inherently stochastic nature makes their runtimes unpredictable. To solve this problem, they can be cut off after a certain number
of generations. But then it is not clear if a truly optimal solution has been found.

Steven Skiena, author of one of the most popular texts on algorithms, even went so far as to write this:

> *I have never encountered any problem where genetic algorithms seemed to me the right way to attack it. Further, I have never seen any computational results reported using genetic algorithms that have favorably impressed me.*[4]

Skiena's view is a little extreme, but it is indicative of the fact that genetic algorithms should only be chosen when you are reasonably confident that a better solution does not exist. Another issue with genetic algorithms is determining how to represent a potential solution to a problem as a chromosome. The traditional practice is to represent most problems as binary strings (sequences of 1s and 0s, raw bits). This is often optimal in terms of space usage, and it lends itself to easy crossover functions. But most complex problems are not easily represented as divisible bit strings.

Another, more specific issue worth mentioning is challenges related to the roulette-wheel selection method described in this chapter. Roulette-wheel selection, sometimes referred to as fitness proportional selection, can lead to a lack of diversity in a population due to the dominance of relatively fit individuals each time selection is run. On the other hand, if fitness values are close together, roulette-wheel selection can lead to a lack of selection pressure.[5] Further, roulette-wheel selection, as constructed in this chapter, does not work for problems in which fitness can be measured with negative values, as in our simple equation example in section 5.3.

In short, for most problems large enough to warrant using them, genetic algorithms cannot guarantee the discovery of an optimal solution in a predictable amount of time. For this reason, they are best utilized in situations that do not call for an optimal solution, but instead for a "good enough" solution. They are fairly easy to implement, but tweaking their configurable parameters can take a lot of trial and error.

5.7   *Real-world applications*

Despite what Skiena wrote, genetic algorithms are frequently and effectively applied in a myriad of problem spaces. They are often used on hard problems that do not require perfectly optimal solutions, such as constraint-satisfaction problems too large to be solved using traditional methods. One example is complex scheduling problems.

Genetic algorithms have found many applications in computational biology. They have been used successfully for protein-ligand docking, which is a search for the configuration of a small molecule when it is bound to a receptor. This is used in pharmaceutical research and to better understand mechanisms in nature.

The Traveling Salesman Problem, which we will revisit in chapter 9, is one of the most famous problems in computer science. A traveling salesman wants to find the shortest route on a map that visits every city exactly once and brings him back to his starting location. It may sound like minimum spanning trees in chapter 4, but it is

---

[4] Steven Skiena, *The Algorithm Design Manual*, 2nd edition (Springer, 2009), p. 267.

[5] A.E. Eiben and J.E. Smith, *Introduction to Evolutionary Computation*, 2nd edition (Springer, 2015), p. 80.

different. In the Traveling Salesman, the solution is a giant cycle that minimizes the cost to traverse it, whereas a minimum spanning tree minimizes the cost to connect every city. A person traveling a minimum spanning tree of cities may have to visit the same city twice to reach every city. Even though they sound similar, there is no reasonably timed algorithm for finding a solution to the Traveling Salesman problem for an arbitrary number of cities. Genetic algorithms have been shown to find suboptimal, but pretty good, solutions in short periods of time. The problem is widely applicable to the efficient distribution of goods. For example, dispatchers of FedEx and UPS trucks use software to sólve the Traveling Salesman problem every day. Algorithms that help solve the problem can cut costs in a large variety of industries.

In computer-generated art, genetic algorithms are sometimes used to mimic photographs using stochastic methods. Imagine 50 polygons placed randomly on a screen and gradually twisted, turned, moved, resized, and changed in color until they match a photograph as closely as possible. The result looks like the work of an abstract artist or, if more angular shapes are used, a stained-glass window.

Genetic algorithms are part of a larger field called evolutionary computation. One area of evolutionary computation closely related to genetic algorithms is *genetic programming*, in which programs use the selection, crossover, and mutation operations to modify themselves to find nonobvious solutions to programming problems. Genetic programming is not a widely used technique, but imagine a future where programs write themselves.

A benefit of genetic algorithms is that they lend themselves to easy parallelization. In the most obvious form, each population can be simulated on a separate processor. In the most granular form, each individual can be mutated and crossed, and have its fitness calculated in a separate thread. There are also many possibilities in between.

5.8 Exercises

1 Add support to `GeneticAlgorithm` for an advanced form of tournament selection that may sometimes choose the second- or third-best chromosome, based on a diminishing probability.

2 Add a new function to the constraint-satisfaction framework from chapter 3 that solves any arbitrary CSP using a genetic algorithm. A possible measure of fitness is the number of constraints that are resolved by a chromosome.

3 Create a class, `BitString`, that implements `Chromosome`. Recall what a bit string is from chapter 1. Then use your new class to solve the simple equation problem from section 5.3. How can the problem be encoded as a bit string?

K-means clustering

6

Humanity has never had more data about more facets of society than it does today. Computers are great for storing data sets, but those data sets have little value to society until they are analyzed by human beings. Computational techniques can guide humans on the road to deriving meaning from a data set.

Clustering is a computational technique that divides the points in a data set into groups. A successful clustering results in groups that contain points that are related to one another. Whether those relationships are meaningful generally requires human verification.

In clustering, the group (a.k.a. *cluster*) that a data point belongs to is not predetermined, but instead is decided during the run of the clustering algorithm. In fact, the algorithm is not guided to place any particular data point in any particular cluster by presupposed information. For this reason, clustering is considered an *unsupervised* method within the realm of machine learning. You can think of *unsupervised* as meaning *not guided by foreknowledge.*

Clustering is a useful technique when you want to learn about the structure of a data set but you do not know ahead of time its constituent parts. For example, imagine you own a grocery store, and you collect data about customers and their transactions. You want to run mobile advertisements of specials at relevant times of the week to bring customers into your store. You could try clustering your data by day of the week and demographic information. Perhaps you will find a cluster that indicates younger shoppers prefer to shop on Tuesdays, and you could use that information to run an ad specifically targeting them on that day.

6.1 Preliminaries

Our clustering algorithm will require some statistical primitives (mean, standard deviation, and so on). Since Python version 3.4, the Python standard library provides several useful statistical primitives in the statistics module. It should be noted that while we keep to the standard library in this book, there are more performant third-party libraries for numerical manipulation, like NumPy, that should be utilized in performance-critical applications—notably, those dealing with big data.

For simplicity's sake, the data sets we will work with in this chapter are all expressible with the float type, so there will be many operations on lists and tuples of floats. The statistical primitives sum(), mean(), and pstdev() are defined in the standard library. Their definitions follow directly from the formulas you would find in a statistics textbook. In addition, we will need a function for calculating z-scores.

Listing 6.1 kmeans.py

```python
from __future__ import annotations
from typing import TypeVar, Generic, List, Sequence
from copy import deepcopy
from functools import partial
from random import uniform
from statistics import mean, pstdev
from dataclasses import dataclass
from data_point import DataPoint


def zscores(original: Sequence[float]) -> List[float]:
    avg: float = mean(original)
    std: float = pstdev(original)
    if std == 0: # return all zeros if there is no variation
        return [0] * len(original)
    return [(x - avg) / std for x in original]
```

TIP pstdev() finds the standard deviation of a population, and stdev(), which we are not using, finds the standard deviation of a sample.

zscores() converts a sequence of floats into a list of floats with the original numbers' respective z-scores relative to all of the numbers in the original sequence. There will be more about z-scores later in the chapter.

NOTE It is beyond the purview of this book to teach elementary statistics, but you do not need more than a rudimentary understanding of mean and standard deviation to follow the rest of the chapter. If it has been a while and you need a refresher, or you never previously learned these terms, it may be worthwhile to quickly peruse a statistics resource that explains these two fundamental concepts.

All clustering algorithms work with points of data, and our implementation of k-means will be no exception. We will define a common interface called DataPoint. For cleanliness, we will define it in its own file.

Listing 6.2   data_point.py

```python
from __future__ import annotations
from typing import Iterator, Tuple, List, Iterable
from math import sqrt


class DataPoint:
    def __init__(self, initial: Iterable[float]) -> None:
        self._originals: Tuple[float, ...] = tuple(initial)
        self.dimensions: Tuple[float, ...] = tuple(initial)

    @property
    def num_dimensions(self) -> int:
        return len(self.dimensions)

    def distance(self, other: DataPoint) -> float:
        combined: Iterator[Tuple[float, float]] = zip(self.dimensions,
    other.dimensions)
        differences: List[float] = [(x - y) ** 2 for x, y in combined]
        return sqrt(sum(differences))

    def __eq__(self, other: object) -> bool:
        if not isinstance(other, DataPoint):
            return NotImplemented
        return self.dimensions == other.dimensions

    def __repr__(self) -> str:
        return self._originals.__repr__()
```

Every data point must be comparable to other data points of the same type for equality (__eq__()) and must be human-readable for debug printing (__repr__()). Every data point type has a certain number of dimensions (num_dimensions). The tuple dimensions stores the actual values for each of those dimensions as floats. The __init__() method takes an iterable of values for the dimensions that are required. These dimensions may later be replaced with z-scores by k-means, so we also keep a copy of the initial data in _originals for later printing.

One final preliminary we need before we can dig into k-means is a way of calculating the distance between any two data points of the same type. There are many ways to calculate distance, but the form most commonly used with k-means is Euclidean distance. This is the distance formula familiar to most from a grade-school course in geometry, derivable from the Pythagorean theorem. In fact, we already discussed the formula and derived a version of it for two-dimensional spaces in chapter 2, where we used it to find the distance between any two locations within a maze. Our version for DataPoint needs to be more sophisticated, because a DataPoint can involve any number of dimensions.

This version of distance() is especially compact and will work with DataPoint types with any number of dimensions. The zip() call creates tuples filled with pairs of each dimension of the two points, combined into a sequence. The list comprehension finds the difference between each point at each dimension and squares that value. sum() adds all of these values together, and the final value returned by distance() is the square root of this sum.

6.2 *The k-means clustering algorithm*

K-means is a clustering algorithm that attempts to group data points into a certain predefined number of clusters, based on each point's relative distance to the center of the cluster. In every round of k-means, the distance between every data point and every center of a cluster (a point known as a *centroid*) is calculated. Points are assigned to the cluster whose centroid they are closest to. Then the algorithm recalculates all of the centroids, finding the mean of each cluster's assigned points and replacing the old centroid with the new mean. The process of assigning points and recalculating centroids continues until the centroids stop moving or a certain number of iterations occurs.

Each dimension of the initial points provided to k-means needs to be comparable in magnitude. If not, k-means will skew toward clustering based on dimensions with the largest differences. The process of making different types of data (in our case, different dimensions) comparable is known as *normalization*. One common way of normalizing data is to evaluate each value based on its *z-score* (also known as *standard score*) relative to the other values of the same type. A z-score is calculated by taking a value, subtracting the mean of all of the values from it, and dividing that result by the standard deviation of all of the values. The `zscores()` function devised near the beginning of the previous section does exactly this for every value in an iterable of `floats`.

The main difficulty with k-means is choosing how to assign the initial centroids. In the most basic form of the algorithm, which is what we will be implementing, the initial centroids are placed randomly within the range of the data. Another difficulty is deciding how many clusters to divide the data into (the "k" in k-means). In the classical algorithm, that number is determined by the user, but the user may not know the right number, and this will require some experimentation. We will let the user define "k."

Putting all of these steps and considerations together, here is our k-means clustering algorithm:

1. Initialize all of the data points and "k" empty clusters.
2. Normalize all of the data points.
3. Create random centroids associated with each cluster.
4. Assign each data point to the cluster of the centroid it is closest to.
5. Recalculate each centroid so it is the center (mean) of the cluster it is associated with.
6. Repeat steps 4 and 5 until a maximum number of iterations is reached or the centroids stop moving (convergence).

Conceptually, k-means is actually quite simple: In each iteration, every data point is associated with the cluster that it is closest to in terms of the cluster's center. That center moves as new points are associated with the cluster. This is illustrated in figure 6.1.

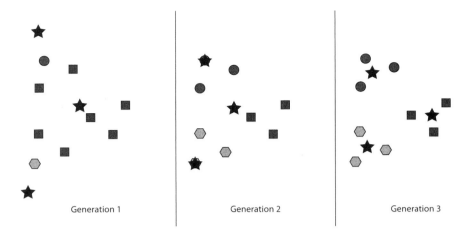

Figure 6.1   An example of k-means running through three generations on an arbitrary data set. Stars indicate centroids. Colors and shapes represent current cluster membership (which changes).

We will implement a class for maintaining state and running the algorithm, similar to `GeneticAlgorithm` in chapter 5. We now return to the kmeans.py file.

Listing 6.3   kmeans.py continued

```
Point = TypeVar('Point', bound=DataPoint)


class KMeans(Generic[Point]):
    @dataclass
    class Cluster:
        points: List[Point]
        centroid: DataPoint
```

KMeans is a generic class. It works with `DataPoint` or any subclass of `DataPoint`, as defined by the `Point` type's bound. It has an internal class, `Cluster`, that keeps track of the individual clusters in the operation. Each `Cluster` has data points and a centroid associated with it.

Now we will continue with the outer class's __init__() method.

Listing 6.4   kmeans.py continued

```
def __init__(self, k: int, points: List[Point]) -> None:
    if k < 1: # k-means can't do negative or zero clusters
        raise ValueError("k must be >= 1")
    self._points: List[Point] = points
    self._zscore_normalize()
    # initialize empty clusters with random centroids
    self._clusters: List[KMeans.Cluster] = []
    for _ in range(k):
        rand_point: DataPoint = self._random_point()
```

```
        cluster: KMeans.Cluster = KMeans.Cluster([], rand_point)
        self._clusters.append(cluster)

@property
def _centroids(self) -> List[DataPoint]:
    return [x.centroid for x in self._clusters]
```

KMeans has an array, _points, associated with it. This is all of the points in the data set. The points are further divided between the clusters, which are stored in the appropriately titled _clusters variable. When KMeans is instantiated, it needs to know how many clusters to create (k). Every cluster initially has a random centroid. All of the data points that will be used in the algorithm are normalized by z-score. The computed _centroids property returns all of the centroids associated with the clusters that are associated with the algorithm.

Listing 6.5   kmeans.py continued

```
def _dimension_slice(self, dimension: int) -> List[float]:
    return [x.dimensions[dimension] for x in self._points]
```

_dimension_slice() is a convenience method that can be thought of as returning a column of data. It will return a list composed of every value at a particular index in every data point. For instance, if the data points were of type DataPoint, then _dimension_slice(0) would return a list of the value of the first dimension of every data point. This is helpful in the following normalization method.

Listing 6.6   kmeans.py continued

```
def _zscore_normalize(self) -> None:
    zscored: List[List[float]] = [[] for _ in range(len(self._points))]
    for dimension in range(self._points[0].num_dimensions):
        dimension_slice: List[float] = self._dimension_slice(dimension)
        for index, zscore in enumerate(zscores(dimension_slice)):
            zscored[index].append(zscore)
    for i in range(len(self._points)):
        self._points[i].dimensions = tuple(zscored[i])
```

_zscore_normalize() replaces the values in the dimensions tuple of every data point with its z-scored equivalent. This uses the zscores() function that we defined for sequences of float earlier. Although the values in the dimensions tuple are replaced, the _originals tuple in the DataPoint are not. This is useful; the user of the algorithm can still retrieve the original values of the dimensions before normalization after the algorithm runs if they are stored in both places.

Listing 6.7   kmeans.py continued

```
def _random_point(self) -> DataPoint:
    rand_dimensions: List[float] = []
    for dimension in range(self._points[0].num_dimensions):
        values: List[float] = self._dimension_slice(dimension)
        rand_value: float = uniform(min(values), max(values))
```

```
        rand_dimensions.append(rand_value)
    return DataPoint(rand_dimensions)
```

The preceding _random_point() method is used in the __init__() method to create
the initial random centroids for each cluster. It constrains the random values of each
point to be within the range of the existing data points' values. It uses the constructor
we specified earlier on DataPoint to create a new point from an iterable of values.

Now we will look to our method for finding the appropriate cluster for a data point
to belong to.

Listing 6.8   kmeans.py continued

```
# Find the closest cluster centroid to each point and assign the point to
    that cluster
def _assign_clusters(self) -> None:
    for point in self._points:
        closest: DataPoint = min(self._centroids,
    key=partial(DataPoint.distance, point))
        idx: int = self._centroids.index(closest)
        cluster: KMeans.Cluster = self._clusters[idx]
        cluster.points.append(point)
```

Throughout the book, we have created several functions that find the minimum or
find the maximum in a list. This one is not dissimilar. In this case we are looking for
the cluster centroid that has the minimum distance to each individual point. The
point is then assigned to that cluster. The only tricky bit is the use of a function medi-
ated by partial() as a key for min(). partial() takes a function and provides it with
some of its parameters before the function is applied. In this case, we supply the
DataPoint.distance() method with the point we are calculating from as its other
parameter. This will result in each centroid's distance to the point being computed
and the lowest-distance centroid's being returned by min().

Listing 6.9   kmeans.py continued

```
# Find the center of each cluster and move the centroid to there
def _generate_centroids(self) -> None:
    for cluster in self._clusters:
        if len(cluster.points) == 0: # keep the same centroid if no points
            continue
        means: List[float] = []
        for dimension in range(cluster.points[0].num_dimensions):
            dimension_slice: List[float] = [p.dimensions[dimension] for p in
    cluster.points]
            means.append(mean(dimension_slice))
        cluster.centroid = DataPoint(means)
```

After every point is assigned to a cluster, the new centroids are calculated. This
involves calculating the mean of each dimension of every point in the cluster. The
means of each dimension are then combined to find the "mean point" in the cluster,
which becomes the new centroid. Note that we cannot use _dimension_slice() here,

because the points in question are a subset of all of the points (just those belonging to a particular cluster). How could _dimension_slice() be rewritten to be more generic?

Now let's look at the method that will actually execute the algorithm.

Listing 6.10   kmeans.py continued

```
def run(self, max_iterations: int = 100) -> List[KMeans.Cluster]:
    for iteration in range(max_iterations):
        for cluster in self._clusters: # clear all clusters
            cluster.points.clear()
        self._assign_clusters() # find cluster each point is closest to
        old_centroids: List[DataPoint] = deepcopy(self._centroids) # record
        self._generate_centroids() # find new centroids
        if old_centroids == self._centroids: # have centroids moved?
            print(f"Converged after {iteration} iterations")
            return self._clusters
    return self._clusters
```

run() is the purest expression of the original algorithm. The only change to the algorithm you may find unexpected is the removal of all points at the beginning of each iteration. If this were not to occur, the _assign_clusters() method, as written, would end up putting duplicate points in each cluster.

You can perform a quick test using test DataPoints and k set to 2.

Listing 6.11   kmeans.py continued

```
if __name__ == "__main__":
    point1: DataPoint = DataPoint([2.0, 1.0, 1.0])
    point2: DataPoint = DataPoint([2.0, 2.0, 5.0])
    point3: DataPoint = DataPoint([3.0, 1.5, 2.5])
    kmeans_test: KMeans[DataPoint] = KMeans(2, [point1, point2, point3])
    test_clusters: List[KMeans.Cluster] = kmeans_test.run()
    for index, cluster in enumerate(test_clusters):
        print(f"Cluster {index}: {cluster.points}")
```

Because there is randomness involved, your results may vary. The expected result is something along these lines:

```
Converged after 1 iterations
Cluster 0: [(2.0, 1.0, 1.0), (3.0, 1.5, 2.5)]
Cluster 1: [(2.0, 2.0, 5.0)]
```

6.3   *Clustering governors by age and longitude*

Every American state has a governor. In June 2017, those governors ranged in age from 42 to 79. If we take the United States from east to west, looking at each state by its longitude, perhaps we can find clusters of states with similar longitudes and similar-age governors. Figure 6.2 is a scatter plot of all 50 governors. The *x*-axis is state longitude, and the *y*-axis is governor age.

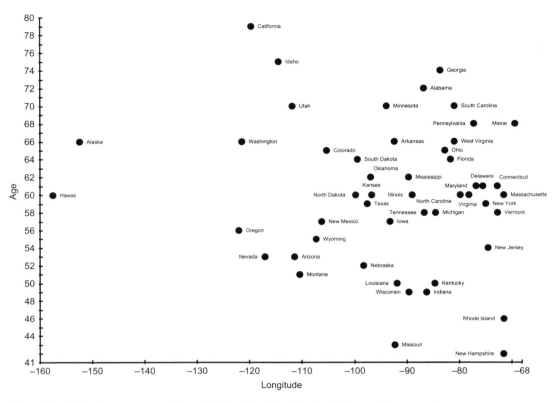

Figure 6.2   State governors, as of June 2017, plotted by state longitude and governor age

Are there any obvious clusters in figure 6.2? In this figure, the axes are not normalized. Instead, we are looking at raw data. If clusters were always obvious, there would be no need for clustering algorithms.

Let's try running this data set through k-means. First, we will need a way of representing an individual data point.

Listing 6.12   governors.py

```python
from __future__ import annotations
from typing import List
from data_point import DataPoint
from kmeans import KMeans


class Governor(DataPoint):
    def __init__(self, longitude: float, age: float, state: str) -> None:
        super().__init__([longitude, age])
        self.longitude = longitude
        self.age = age
        self.state = state
```

```
def __repr__(self) -> str:
    return f"{self.state}: (longitude: {self.longitude}, age:
{self.age})"
```

A `Governor` has two named and stored dimensions: `longitude` and `age`. Other than that, `Governor` makes no modifications to the machinery of its superclass, `DataPoint`, other than an overridden `__repr__()` for pretty printing. It would be pretty unreasonable to enter the following data manually, so check out the source code repository that accompanies this book.

Listing 6.13 governors.py continued

```
if __name__ == "__main__":
    governors: List[Governor] = [Governor(-86.79113, 72, "Alabama"),
    Governor(-152.404419, 66, "Alaska"),
            Governor(-111.431221, 53, "Arizona"), Governor(-92.373123,
    66, "Arkansas"),
            Governor(-119.681564, 79, "California"), Governor(-
    105.311104, 65, "Colorado"),
            Governor(-72.755371, 61, "Connecticut"), Governor(-
    75.507141, 61, "Delaware"),
            Governor(-81.686783, 64, "Florida"), Governor(-83.643074,
    74, "Georgia"),
            Governor(-157.498337, 60, "Hawaii"), Governor(-114.478828,
    75, "Idaho"),
            Governor(-88.986137, 60, "Illinois"), Governor(-86.258278,
    49, "Indiana"),
            Governor(-93.210526, 57, "Iowa"), Governor(-96.726486, 60,
    "Kansas"),
            Governor(-84.670067, 50, "Kentucky"), Governor(-91.867805,
    50, "Louisiana"),
            Governor(-69.381927, 68, "Maine"), Governor(-76.802101, 61,
    "Maryland"),
            Governor(-71.530106, 60, "Massachusetts"), Governor(-
    84.536095, 58, "Michigan"),
            Governor(-93.900192, 70, "Minnesota"), Governor(-89.678696,
    62, "Mississippi"),
            Governor(-92.288368, 43, "Missouri"), Governor(-110.454353,
    51, "Montana"),
            Governor(-98.268082, 52, "Nebraska"), Governor(-117.055374,
    53, "Nevada"),
            Governor(-71.563896, 42, "New Hampshire"), Governor(-
    74.521011, 54, "New Jersey"),
            Governor(-106.248482, 57, "New Mexico"), Governor(-
    74.948051, 59, "New York"),
            Governor(-79.806419, 60, "North Carolina"), Governor(-
    99.784012, 60, "North Dakota"),
            Governor(-82.764915, 65, "Ohio"), Governor(-96.928917, 62,
    "Oklahoma"),
            Governor(-122.070938, 56, "Oregon"), Governor(-77.209755,
    68, "Pennsylvania"),
            Governor(-71.51178, 46, "Rhode Island"), Governor(-
    80.945007, 70, "South Carolina"),
```

```
            Governor(-99.438828, 64, "South Dakota"), Governor(-
86.692345, 58, "Tennessee"),
            Governor(-97.563461, 59, "Texas"), Governor(-111.862434, 70,
"Utah"),
            Governor(-72.710686, 58, "Vermont"), Governor(-78.169968,
60, "Virginia"),
            Governor(-121.490494, 66, "Washington"), Governor(-
80.954453, 66, "West Virginia"),
            Governor(-89.616508, 49, "Wisconsin"), Governor(-107.30249,
55, "Wyoming")]
```

We will run k-means with k set to 2.

Listing 6.14   governors.py continued

```
kmeans: KMeans[Governor] = KMeans(2, governors)
gov_clusters: List[KMeans.Cluster] = kmeans.run()
for index, cluster in enumerate(gov_clusters):
    print(f"Cluster {index}: {cluster.points}\n")
```

Because it starts with randomized centroids, every run of KMeans may potentially return different clusters. It takes some human analysis to see if the clusters are actually relevant. The following result is from a run that did have an interesting cluster:

```
Converged after 5 iterations
Cluster 0: [Alabama: (longitude: -86.79113, age: 72), Arizona: (longitude: -
    111.431221, age: 53), Arkansas: (longitude: -92.373123, age: 66),
    Colorado: (longitude: -105.311104, age: 65), Connecticut: (longitude: -
    72.755371, age: 61), Delaware: (longitude: -75.507141, age: 61),
    Florida: (longitude: -81.686783, age: 64), Georgia: (longitude: -
    83.643074, age: 74), Illinois: (longitude: -88.986137, age: 60),
    Indiana: (longitude: -86.258278, age: 49), Iowa: (longitude: -93.210526,
    age: 57), Kansas: (longitude: -96.726486, age: 60), Kentucky:
    (longitude: -84.670067, age: 50), Louisiana: (longitude: -91.867805,
    age: 50), Maine: (longitude: -69.381927, age: 68), Maryland: (longitude:
    -76.802101, age: 61), Massachusetts: (longitude: -71.530106, age: 60),
    Michigan: (longitude: -84.536095, age: 58), Minnesota: (longitude: -
    93.900192, age: 70), Mississippi: (longitude: -89.678696, age: 62),
    Missouri: (longitude: -92.288368, age: 43), Montana: (longitude: -
    110.454353, age: 51), Nebraska: (longitude: -98.268082, age: 52),
    Nevada: (longitude: -117.055374, age: 53), New Hampshire: (longitude: -
    71.563896, age: 42), New Jersey: (longitude: -74.521011, age: 54), New
    Mexico: (longitude: -106.248482, age: 57), New York: (longitude: -
    74.948051, age: 59), North Carolina: (longitude: -79.806419, age: 60),
    North Dakota: (longitude: -99.784012, age: 60), Ohio: (longitude: -
    82.764915, age: 65), Oklahoma: (longitude: -96.928917, age: 62),
    Pennsylvania: (longitude: -77.209755, age: 68), Rhode Island:
    (longitude: -71.51178, age: 46), South Carolina: (longitude: -80.945007,
    age: 70), South Dakota: (longitude: -99.438828, age: 64), Tennessee:
    (longitude: -86.692345, age: 58), Texas: (longitude: -97.563461, age:
    59), Vermont: (longitude: -72.710686, age: 58), Virginia: (longitude: -
    78.169968, age: 60), West Virginia: (longitude: -80.954453, age: 66),
    Wisconsin: (longitude: -89.616508, age: 49), Wyoming: (longitude: -
    107.30249, age: 55)]
```

```
Cluster 1: [Alaska: (longitude: -152.404419, age: 66), California:
    (longitude: -119.681564, age: 79), Hawaii: (longitude: -157.498337, age:
    60), Idaho: (longitude: -114.478828, age: 75), Oregon: (longitude: -
    122.070938, age: 56), Utah: (longitude: -111.862434, age: 70),
    Washington: (longitude: -121.490494, age: 66)]
```

Cluster 1 represents the extreme Western states, all geographically next to each other (if you consider Alaska and Hawaii next to the Pacific coast states). They all have relatively old governors and hence formed an interesting cluster. Do folks on the Pacific Rim like older governors? We cannot determine anything conclusive from these clusters beyond a correlation. Figure 6.3 illustrates the result. Squares are cluster 1, and circles are cluster 0.

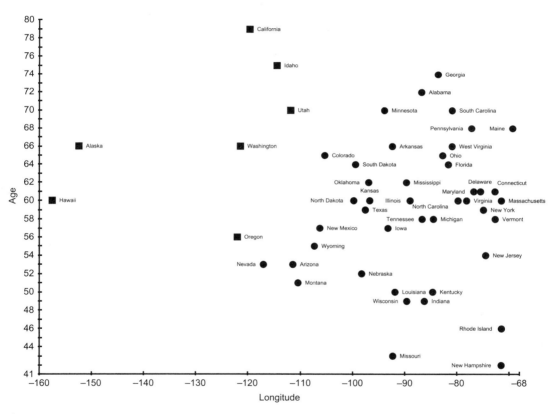

Figure 6.3 Data points in cluster 0 are designated by circles, and data points in cluster 1 are designated by squares.

TIP It cannot be emphasized enough that your results with k-means using random initialization of centroids will vary. Be sure to run k-means multiple times with any data set.

6.4   *Clustering Michael Jackson albums by length*

Michael Jackson released 10 solo studio albums. In the following example, we will cluster those albums by looking at two dimensions: album length (in minutes) and number of tracks. This example is a nice contrast with the preceding governors example because it is easy to see the clusters in the original data set without even running k-means. An example like this can be a good way of debugging an implementation of a clustering algorithm.

> **NOTE**   Both of the examples in this chapter make use of two-dimensional data points, but k-means can work with data points of any number of dimensions.

The example is presented here in its entirety as one code listing. If you look at the album data in the following code listing before even running the example, it is clear that Michael Jackson made longer albums toward the end of his career. So the two clusters of albums should probably be divided between earlier albums and later albums. *HIStory: Past, Present, and Future, Book I* is an outlier and can also logically end up in its own solo cluster. An *outlier* is a data point that lies outside the normal limits of a data set.

Listing 6.15   mj.py

```
from __future__ import annotations
from typing import List
from data_point import DataPoint
from kmeans import KMeans


class Album(DataPoint):
    def __init__(self, name: str, year: int, length: float, tracks: float) ->
    None:
        super().__init__([length, tracks])
        self.name = name
        self.year = year
        self.length = length
        self.tracks = tracks

    def __repr__(self) -> str:
        return f"{self.name}, {self.year}"


if __name__ == "__main__":
    albums: List[Album] = [Album("Got to Be There", 1972, 35.45, 10),
    Album("Ben", 1972, 31.31, 10),
                           Album("Music & Me", 1973, 32.09, 10),
    Album("Forever, Michael", 1975, 33.36, 10),
                           Album("Off the Wall", 1979, 42.28, 10),
    Album("Thriller", 1982, 42.19, 9),
                           Album("Bad", 1987, 48.16, 10), Album("Dangerous",
    1991, 77.03, 14),
                           Album("HIStory: Past, Present and Future, Book I",
    1995, 148.58, 30), Album("Invincible", 2001, 77.05, 16)]
    kmeans: KMeans[Album] = KMeans(2, albums)
```

```
clusters: List[KMeans.Cluster] = kmeans.run()
for index, cluster in enumerate(clusters):
    print(f"Cluster {index} Avg Length {cluster.centroid.dimensions[0]}
Avg Tracks {cluster.centroid.dimensions[1]}: {cluster.points}\n")
```

Note that the attributes name and year are only recorded for labeling purposes and are not included in the actual clustering. Here is an example output:

```
Converged after 1 iterations
Cluster 0 Avg Length -0.5458820039179509 Avg Tracks -0.5009878988684237: [Got
    to Be There, 1972, Ben, 1972, Music & Me, 1973, Forever, Michael, 1975,
    Off the Wall, 1979, Thriller, 1982, Bad, 1987]

Cluster 1 Avg Length 1.2737246758085523 Avg Tracks 1.1689717640263217:
    [Dangerous, 1991, HIStory: Past, Present and Future, Book I, 1995,
    Invincible, 2001]
```

The reported cluster averages are interesting. Note that the averages are z-scores. Cluster 1's three albums, Michael Jackson's final three albums, were about one standard deviation longer than the average of all ten of his solo albums.

6.5 *K-means clustering problems and extensions*

When k-means clustering is implemented using random starting points, it may completely miss useful points of division within the data. This often results in a lot of trial and error for the operator. Figuring out the right value for "k" (the number of clusters) is also difficult and error prone if the operator does not have good insight into how many groups of data should exist.

There are more sophisticated versions of k-means that can try to make educated guesses or do automatic trial and error regarding these problematic variables. One popular variant is k-means++, which attempts to solve the initialization problem by choosing centroids based on a probability distribution of distance to every point instead of pure randomness. An even better option for many applications is to choose good starting regions for each of the centroids based on information about the data that is known ahead of time—in other words, a version of k-means where the user of the algorithm chooses the initial centroids.

The runtime for k-means clustering is proportional to the number of data points, the number of clusters, and the number of dimensions of the data points. It can become unusable in its basic form when there are a high number of points that have a large number of dimensions. There are extensions that try to not do as much calculation between every point and every center by evaluating whether a point really has the potential to move to another cluster before doing the calculation. Another option for numerous-point or high-dimension data sets is to run just a sampling of the data points through k-means. This will approximate the clusters that the full k-means algorithm may find.

Outliers in a data set may result in strange results for k-means. If an initial centroid happens to fall near an outlier, it could form a cluster of one (as could potentially happen with the *HIStory* album in the Michael Jackson example). K-means may run better with outliers removed.

Finally, the mean is not always considered a good measure of the center. K-medians looks at the median of each dimension, and k-medoids uses an actual point in the data set as the middle of each cluster. There are statistical reasons beyond the scope of this book for choosing each of these centering methods, but common sense dictates that for a tricky problem it may be worth trying each of them and sampling the results. The implementations of each are not that different.

6.6   *Real-world applications*

Clustering is often the purview of data scientists and statistical analysts. It is used widely as a way to interpret data in a variety of fields. K-means clustering, in particular, is a useful technique when little is known about the structure of the data set.

In data analysis, clustering is an essential technique. Imagine a police department that wants to know where to put cops on patrol. Imagine a fast-food franchise that wants to figure out where its best customers are, to send promotions. Imagine a boat-rental operator that wants to minimize accidents by analyzing when they occur and who causes them. Now imagine how they could solve their problems using clustering.

Clustering helps with pattern recognition. A clustering algorithm may detect a pattern that the human eye misses. For instance, clustering is sometimes used in biology to identify groups of incongruous cells.

In image recognition, clustering helps to identify nonobvious features. Individual pixels can be treated as data points with their relationship to one another being defined by distance and color difference.

In political science, clustering is sometimes used to find voters to target. Can a political party find disenfranchised voters concentrated in a single district that they should focus their campaign dollars on? What issues are similar voters likely to be concerned about?

6.7   *Exercises*

1   Create a function that can import data from a CSV file into `DataPoints`.
2   Create a function using an external library like `matplotlib` that creates a color-coded scatter plot of the results of any run of `KMeans` on a two-dimensional data set.
3   Create a new initializer for `KMeans` that takes initial centroid positions instead of assigning them randomly.
4   Research and implement the k-means++ algorithm.

Fairly simple neural networks

When we hear about advances in artificial intelligence these days, in the late 2010s, they generally concern a particular subdiscipline known as *machine learning* (computers learning some new information without being explicitly told it). More often than not those advances are being driven by a particular machine-learning technique known as *neural networks*. Although invented decades ago, neural networks have been going through a kind of renaissance as improved hardware and newly discovered research-driven software techniques enable a new paradigm known as *deep learning.*

Deep learning has turned out to be a broadly applicable technique. It has been found useful in everything from hedge-fund algorithms to bioinformatics. Two deep-learning applications that consumers have become familiar with are image recognition and speech recognition. If you have ever asked your digital assistant what the weather is or had a photo program recognize your face, there was probably some deep learning going on.

Deep-learning techniques utilize the same building blocks as simpler neural networks. In this chapter we will explore those blocks by building a simple neural network. It will not be state of the art, but it will give you a basis for understanding deep learning (which is based on more complex neural networks than we will build). Most practitioners of machine learning do not build neural networks from scratch. Instead, they use popular, highly optimized, off-the-shelf frameworks that do the heavy lifting. Although this chapter will not help you learn how to use any specific framework, and the network we will build will not be useful for an actual application, it will help you understand how those frameworks work at a low level.

7.1 *Biological basis?*

The human brain is the most incredible computational device in existence. It cannot crunch numbers as fast as a microprocessor, but its ability to adapt to new situations, learn new skills, and be creative is unsurpassed by any known machine. Since the dawn of computers, scientists have been interested in modeling the brain's machinery. Each nerve cell in the brain is known as a *neuron*. Neurons in the brain are networked to one another via connections known as *synapses*. Electricity passes through synapses to power these networks of neurons—also known as *neural networks*.

> **NOTE** The preceding description of biological neurons is a gross oversimplification for analogy's sake. In fact, biological neurons have parts like axons, dendrites, and nuclei that you may remember from high-school biology. And synapses are actually gaps between neurons where neurotransmitters are secreted to enable those electrical signals to pass.

Although scientists have identified the parts and functions of neurons, the details of how biological neural networks form complex thought patterns are still not well understood. How do they process information? How do they form original thoughts? Most of our knowledge of how the brain works comes from looking at it on a macro level. Functional magnetic resonance imaging (fMRI) scans of the brain show where blood flows when a human is doing a particular activity or thinking a particular thought (illustrated in figure 7.1). This and other macro-techniques can lead to inferences about how the various parts are connected, but they do not explain the mysteries of how individual neurons aid in the development of new thoughts.

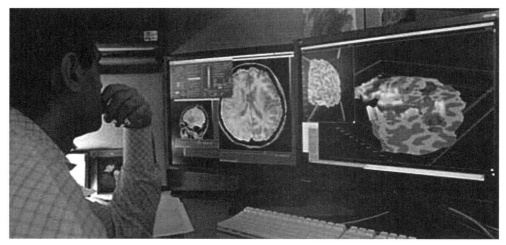

Public domain, U.S. National Institute for Mental Health

Figure 7.1   A researcher studies fMRI images of the brain. fMRI images do not tell us much about how individual neurons function or how neural networks are organized.

Teams of scientists are racing around the globe to unlock the brain's secrets, but consider this: The human brain has approximately 100,000,000,000 neurons, and each of them may have connections with as many as tens of thousands of other neurons. Even for a computer with billions of logic gates and terabytes of memory, a single human brain would be impossible to model using today's technology. Humans will still likely be the most advanced general-purpose learning entities for the foreseeable future.

> **NOTE** A general-purpose learning machine that is equivalent to human beings in abilities is the goal of so-called *strong AI* (also known as *artificial general intelligence*). At this point in history, it is still the stuff of science fiction. *Weak AI* is the type of AI you see every day: computers intelligently solving specific tasks they were preconfigured to accomplish.

If biological neural networks are not fully understood, then how has modeling them been an effective computational technique? Although digital neural networks, known as *artificial neural networks*, are inspired by biological neural networks, inspiration is where the similarities end. Modern artificial neural networks do not claim to work like their biological counterparts. In fact, that would be impossible, because we do not completely understand how biological neural networks work to begin with.

7.2 Artificial neural networks

In this section we will look at what is arguably the most common type of artificial neural network, a *feed-forward* network with *backpropagation*—the same type we will later be developing. *Feed-forward* means the signal is generally moving in one direction through the network. *Backpropagation* means we will determine errors at the end of each signal's traversal through the network and try to distribute fixes for those errors back through the network, especially affecting the neurons that were most responsible for them. There are many other types of artificial neural networks, and perhaps this chapter will pique your interest in exploring further.

7.2.1 Neurons

The smallest unit in an artificial neural network is a neuron. It holds a vector of weights, which are just floating-point numbers. A vector of inputs (also just floating-point numbers) is passed to the neuron. It combines those inputs with its weights using a dot product. It then runs an *activation function* on that product and spits the result out as its output. This action can be thought of as analogous to a real neuron firing.

An activation function is a transformer of the neuron's output. The activation function is almost always nonlinear, which allows neural networks to represent solutions to nonlinear problems. If there were no activation functions, the entire neural network would just be a linear transformation. Figure 7.2 shows a single neuron and its operation.

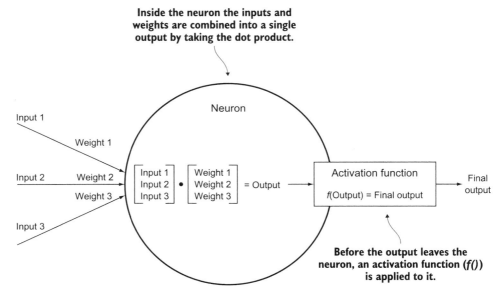

Figure 7.2   A single neuron combines its weights with input signals to produce an output signal that is modified by an activation function.

NOTE There are some math terms in this section that you may not have seen since a precalculus or linear algebra class. Explaining what vectors or dot products are is beyond the scope of this chapter, but you will likely get an intuition of what a neural network does by following along in this chapter, even if you do not understand all of the math. Later in the chapter there will be some calculus, including the use of derivatives and partial derivatives, but even if you do not understand all of the math, you should be able to follow the code. In fact, this chapter will not explain how to derive the formulas using calculus. Instead, it will focus on using the derivations.

7.2.2   *Layers*

In a typical feed-forward artificial neural network, neurons are organized in layers. Each layer consists of a certain number of neurons lined up in a row or column (depending on the diagram; the two are equivalent). In a feed-forward network, which is what we will be building, signals always pass in a single direction from one layer to the next. The neurons in each layer send their output signal to be used as input to the neurons in the next layer. Every neuron in each layer is connected to every neuron in the next layer.

The first layer is known as the *input layer*, and it receives its signals from some external entity. The last layer is known as the *output layer*, and its output typically must be interpreted by an external actor to get an intelligent result. The layers between the input and output layers are known as *hidden layers*. In simple neural networks like the

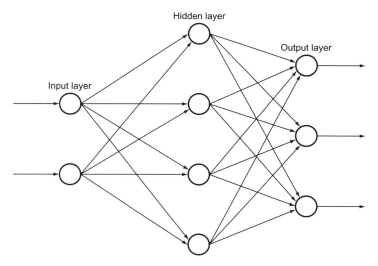

Figure 7.3   A simple neural network with one input layer of two neurons, one hidden layer of four neurons, and one output layer of three neurons. The number of neurons in each layer in this figure is arbitrary.

one we will be building in this chapter, there is just one hidden layer, but deep-learning networks have many. Figure 7.3 shows the layers working together in a simple network. Note how the outputs from one layer are used as the inputs to every neuron in the next layer.

These layers just manipulate floating-point numbers. The inputs to the input layer are floating-point numbers, and the outputs from the output layer are floating-point numbers.

Obviously, these numbers must represent something meaningful. Imagine that the network was designed to classify small black-and-white images of animals. Perhaps the input layer has 100 neurons representing the grayscale intensity of each pixel in a 10 x 10 pixel animal image, and the output layer has 5 neurons representing the likelihood that the image is of a mammal, reptile, amphibian, fish, or bird. The final classification could be determined by the output neuron with the highest floating-point output. If the output numbers were 0.24, 0.65, 0.70, 0.12, and 0.21, respectively, the image would be determined to be an amphibian.

7.2.3   *Backpropagation*

The last piece of the puzzle, and the inherently most complex part, is backpropagation. Backpropagation finds the error in a neural network's output and uses it to modify the weights of neurons. The neurons most responsible for the error are most heavily modified. But where does the error come from? How can we know the error? The error comes from a phase in the use of a neural network known as *training*.

TIP There are steps written out (in English) for several mathematical formulas in this section. Pseudo formulas (not using proper notation) are in the accompanying figures. This approach will make the formulas readable for those uninitiated in (or out of practice with) mathematical notation. If the more formal notation (and the derivation of the formulas) interests you, check out chapter 18 of Norvig and Russell's *Artificial Intelligence*.[1]

Before they can be used, most neural networks must be trained. We must know the right outputs for some inputs so that we can use the difference between expected outputs and actual outputs to find errors and modify weights. In other words, neural networks know nothing until they are told the right answers for a certain set of inputs, so that they can prepare themselves for other inputs. Backpropagation only occurs during training.

NOTE Because most neural networks must be trained, they are considered a type of *supervised* machine learning. Recall from chapter 6 that the k-means algorithm and other cluster algorithms are considered a form of *unsupervised* machine learning because once they are started, no outside intervention is required. There are other types of neural networks than the one described in this chapter that do not require pretraining and are considered a form of unsupervised learning.

The first step in backpropagation is to calculate the error between the neural network's output for some input and the expected output. This error is spread across all of the neurons in the output layer. (Each neuron has an expected output and its actual output.) The derivative of the output neuron's activation function is then applied to what was output by the neuron before its activation function was applied. (We cache its pre-activation function output.) This result is multiplied by the neuron's error to find its *delta*. This formula for finding the delta uses a partial derivative, and its calculus derivation is beyond the scope of this book, but we are basically figuring out how much of the error each output neuron was responsible for. See figure 7.4 for a diagram of this calculation.

  Deltas must then be calculated for every neuron in the hidden layer(s) in the network. We must determine how much each neuron was responsible for the incorrect output in the output layer. The deltas in the output layer are used to calculate the deltas in the preceding hidden layer. For each previous layer, the deltas are calculated by taking the dot product of the next layer's weights with respect to the particular neuron in question and the deltas already calculated in the next layer. This value is multiplied by the derivative of the activation function applied to a neuron's last output (cached before the activation function was applied) to get the neuron's delta. Again, this formula is derived using a partial derivative, which you can read about in more mathematically focused texts.

---

[1] Stuart Russell and Peter Norvig, *Artificial Intelligence: A Modern Approach*, 3rd edition (Pearson, 2010).

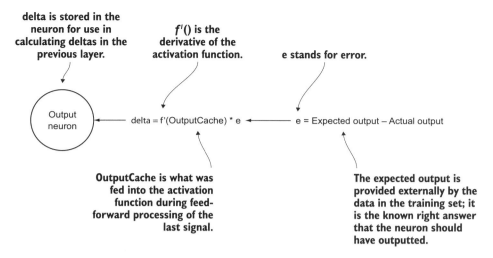

Figure 7.4   The mechanism by which an output neuron's delta is calculated during the backpropagation phase of training

Figure 7.5 shows the actual calculation of deltas for neurons in hidden layers. In a network with multiple hidden layers, neurons O1, O2, and O3 could be neurons in the next hidden layer instead of in the output layer.

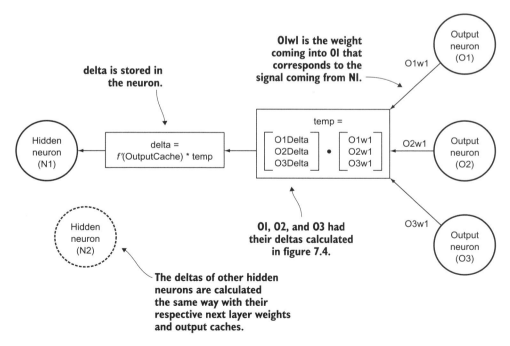

Figure 7.5   How a delta is calculated for a neuron in a hidden layer

Last, but most important, all of the weights for every neuron in the network must be updated by multiplying each individual weight's last input with the delta of the neuron and something called a *learning rate*, and adding that to the existing weight. This method of modifying the weight of a neuron is known as *gradient descent*. It is like climbing down a hill representing the error function of the neuron toward a point of minimal error. The delta represents the direction we want to climb, and the learning rate affects how fast we climb. It is hard to determine a good learning rate for an unknown problem without trial and error. Figure 7.6 shows how every weight in the hidden layer and output layer is updated.

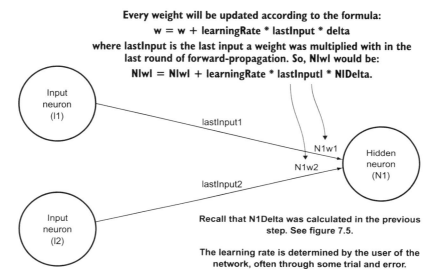

Every weight will be updated according to the formula:
w = w + learningRate * lastInput * delta
where lastInput is the last input a weight was multiplied with in the last round of forward-propagation. So, N1w1 would be:
N1w1 = N1w1 + learningRate * lastInput1 * N1Delta.

Input neuron (I1)

lastInput1

N1w1

N1w2

Hidden neuron (N1)

lastInput2

Input neuron (I2)

Recall that N1Delta was calculated in the previous step. See figure 7.5.

The learning rate is determined by the user of the network, often through some trial and error.

Figure 7.6   The weights of every hidden layer and output layer neuron are updated using the deltas calculated in the previous steps, the prior weights, the prior inputs, and a user-determined learning rate.

Once the weights are updated, the neural network is ready to be trained again with another input and expected output. This process repeats until the network is deemed well trained by the neural network's user. This can be determined by testing it against inputs with known correct outputs.

Backpropagation is complicated. Do not worry if you do not yet grasp all of the details. The explanation in this section may not be enough. Ideally, implementing backpropagation will take your understanding to the next level. As we implement our neural network and backpropagation, keep in mind this overarching theme: Backpropagation is a way of adjusting each individual weight in the network according to its responsibility for an incorrect output.

7.2.4 *The big picture*

We covered a lot of ground in this section. Even if the details do not yet make sense, it is important to keep the main themes in mind for a feed-forward network with back-propagation:

- Signals (floating-point numbers) move through neurons organized in layers in one direction. Every neuron in each layer is connected to every neuron in the next layer.
- Each neuron (except in the input layer) processes the signals it receives by combining them with weights (also floating-point numbers) and applying an activation function.
- During a process called training, network outputs are compared with expected outputs to calculate errors.
- Errors are backpropagated through the network (back toward where they came from) to modify weights so that they are more likely to create correct outputs.

There are more methods for training neural networks than the one explained here. There are also many other ways for signals to move within neural networks. The method explained here, and that we will be implementing, is just a particularly common form that serves as a decent introduction. Appendix B lists further resources for learning more about neural networks (including other types) and the math.

7.3 *Preliminaries*

Neural networks utilize mathematical mechanisms that require a lot of floating-point operations. Before we develop the actual structures of our simple neural network, we will need some mathematical primitives. These simple primitives are used extensively in the code that follows, so if you can find ways to accelerate them, it will really improve the performance of your neural network.

> **WARNING** The complexity of the code in this chapter is arguably greater than any other in the book. There is a lot of build-up, with actual results seen only at the very end. There are many resources about neural networks that help you build one in very few lines of code, but this example is aimed at exploring the machinery and how the different components work together in a readable and extensible fashion. That is our goal, even if the code is a little longer and more expressive.

7.3.1 *Dot product*

As you will recall, dot products are required both for the feed-forward phase and for the backpropagation phase. Luckily, a dot product is simple to implement using the Python built-in functions `zip()` and `sum()`. We will keep our preliminary functions in a util.py file.

```
Listing 7.1    util.py

from typing import List
from math import exp


# dot product of two vectors
def dot_product(xs: List[float], ys: List[float]) -> float:
    return sum(x * y for x, y in zip(xs, ys))
```

7.3.2   *The activation function*

Recall that the activation function transforms the output of a neuron before the signal passes to the next layer (see figure 7.2). The activation function has two purposes: It allows the neural network to represent solutions that are not just linear transformations (as long as the activation function itself is not just a linear transformation), and it can keep the output of each neuron within a certain range. An activation function should have a computable derivative so that it can be used for backpropagation.

Sigmoid functions are a popular set of activation functions. One particularly popular sigmoid function (often just referred to as "the sigmoid function") is illustrated in figure 7.7 (referred to in the figure as $S(x)$), along with its equation and derivative ($S'(x)$). The result of the sigmoid function will always be a value between 0 and 1. Having the value consistently be between 0 and 1 is useful for the network, as you will see. You will shortly see the formulas from the figure written out in code.

There are other activation functions, but we will use the sigmoid function. Here is a straightforward conversion of the formulas in figure 7.7 into code:

```
Listing 7.2    util.py continued

# the classic sigmoid activation function
def sigmoid(x: float) -> float:
    return 1.0 / (1.0 + exp(-x))


def derivative_sigmoid(x: float) -> float:
    sig: float = sigmoid(x)
    return sig * (1 - sig)
```

7.4   *Building the network*

We will create classes to model all three organizational units in the network: neurons, layers, and the network itself. For the sake of simplicity, we will start from the smallest (neurons), move to the central organizing component (layers), and build up to the largest (the whole network). As we go from smallest component to largest component, we will encapsulate the previous level. Neurons only know about themselves. Layers know about the neurons they contain and other layers. And the network knows about all of the layers.

> **NOTE**   There are many long lines of code in this chapter that do not neatly fit in the column limits of a printed book. I strongly recommend downloading the source code for this chapter from the book's source code repository and

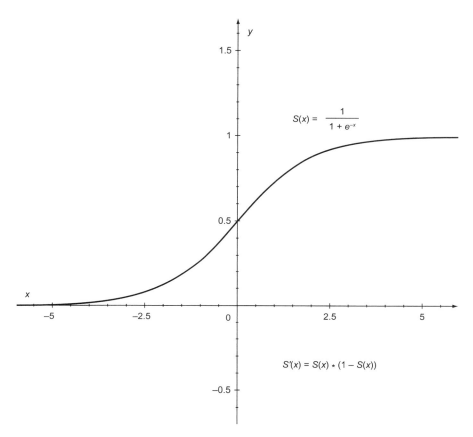

Figure 7.7   The sigmoid activation function (S(x)) will always return a value between 0 and 1. Note that its derivative is easy to compute as well (S'(x)).

following along on your computer screen as you read: https://github.com/ davecom/ClassicComputerScienceProblemsInPython.

7.4.1   *Implementing neurons*

Let's start with a neuron. An individual neuron will store many pieces of state, including its weights, its delta, its learning rate, a cache of its last output, and its activation function, along with the derivative of that activation function. Some of these elements could be more efficiently stored up a level (in the future Layer class), but they are included in the following Neuron class for illustrative purposes.

Listing 7.3   neuron.py

```
from typing import List, Callable
from util import dot_product


class Neuron:
```

```
def __init__(self, weights: List[float], learning_rate: float,
  activation_function: Callable[[float], float], derivative_activation_
  function: Callable[[float], float]) -> None:
     self.weights: List[float] = weights
     self.activation_function: Callable[[float], float] = activation_
  function
     self.derivative_activation_function: Callable[[float], float] =
  derivative_activation_function
     self.learning_rate: float = learning_rate
     self.output_cache: float = 0.0
     self.delta: float = 0.0

def output(self, inputs: List[float]) -> float:
     self.output_cache = dot_product(inputs, self.weights)
     return self.activation_function(self.output_cache)
```

Most of these parameters are initialized in the __init__() method. Because delta and output_cache are not known when a Neuron is first created, they are just initialized to 0. All of the neuron's variables are mutable. In the life of the neuron (as we will be using it) their values may never change, but there is still a reason to make them mutable: flexibility. If this Neuron class were to be used with other types of neural networks, it is possible that some of these values might change on the fly. There are neural networks that change the learning rate as the solution approaches and that automatically try different activation functions. Here, we are trying to keep the Neuron class maximally flexible for other neural network applications.

The only other method, other than __init__(), is output(). output() takes the input signals (inputs) coming to the neuron and applies the formula discussed earlier in the chapter (see figure 7.2). The input signals are combined with the weights via a dot product, and this is cached in output_cache. Recall from the section on backpropagation that this value, obtained before the activation function is applied, is used to calculate delta. Finally, before the signal is sent on to the next layer (by being returned from output()), the activation function is applied to it.

That is it! An individual neuron in this network is fairly simple. It cannot do much beyond take an input signal, transform it, and send it off to be processed further. It maintains several elements of state that are used by the other classes.

7.4.2   *Implementing layers*

A layer in our network will need to maintain three pieces of state: its neurons, the layer that preceded it, and an output cache. The output cache is similar to that of a neuron, but up one level. It caches the outputs (after activation functions are applied) of every neuron in the layer.

At creation time, a layer's main responsibility is to initialize its neurons. Our Layer class's __init__() method therefore needs to know how many neurons it should be initializing, what their activation functions should be, and what their learning rates should be. In this simple network, every neuron in a layer has the same activation function and learning rate.

Listing 7.4 layer.py

```
from __future__ import annotations
from typing import List, Callable, Optional
from random import random
from neuron import Neuron
from util import dot_product


class Layer:
    def __init__(self, previous_layer: Optional[Layer], num_neurons: int,
      learning_rate: float, activation_function: Callable[[float], float],
      derivative_activation_function: Callable[[float], float]) -> None:
        self.previous_layer: Optional[Layer] = previous_layer
        self.neurons: List[Neuron] = []
        # the following could all be one large list comprehension
        for i in range(num_neurons):
            if previous_layer is None:
                random_weights: List[float] = []
            else:
                random_weights = [random() for _ in range(len(previous_
      layer.neurons))]
            neuron: Neuron = Neuron(random_weights, learning_rate,
      activation_function, derivative_activation_function)
            self.neurons.append(neuron)
        self.output_cache: List[float] = [0.0 for _ in range(num_neurons)]
```

As signals are fed forward through the network, the Layer must process them through
every neuron. (Remember that every neuron in a layer receives the signals from every
neuron in the previous layer.) outputs() does just that. outputs() also returns the
result of processing them (to be passed by the network to the next layer) and caches
the output. If there is no previous layer, that indicates the layer is an input layer, and it
just passes the signals forward to the next layer.

Listing 7.5 layer.py continued

```
def outputs(self, inputs: List[float]) -> List[float]:
    if self.previous_layer is None:
        self.output_cache = inputs
    else:
        self.output_cache = [n.output(inputs) for n in self.neurons]
    return self.output_cache
```

There are two distinct types of deltas to calculate in backpropagation: deltas for neurons
in the output layer and deltas for neurons in hidden layers. The formulas are described
in figures 7.4 and 7.5, and the following two methods are rote translations of those formulas. These methods will later be called by the network during backpropagation.

Listing 7.6 layer.py continued

```
# should only be called on output layer
def calculate_deltas_for_output_layer(self, expected: List[float]) -> None:
    for n in range(len(self.neurons)):
```

```
        self.neurons[n].delta = self.neurons[n].derivative_activation_
        function(self.neurons[n].output_cache) * (expected[n] - self.output_
        cache[n])

    # should not be called on output layer
    def calculate_deltas_for_hidden_layer(self, next_layer: Layer) -> None:
        for index, neuron in enumerate(self.neurons):
            next_weights: List[float] = [n.weights[index] for n in next_
        layer.neurons]
            next_deltas: List[float] = [n.delta for n in next_layer.neurons]
            sum_weights_and_deltas: float = dot_product(next_weights, next_
        deltas)
            neuron.delta = neuron.derivative_activation_function(neuron.output_
        cache) * sum_weights_and_deltas
```

7.4.3 Implementing the network

The network itself has only one piece of state: the layers that it manages. The `Network` class is responsible for initializing its constituent layers.

The `__init__()` method takes an `int` list describing the structure of the network. For example, the list `[2, 4, 3]` describes a network with 2 neurons in its input layer, 4 neurons in its hidden layer, and 3 neurons in its output layer. In this simple network, we will assume that all layers in the network will make use of the same activation function for their neurons and the same learning rate.

Listing 7.7   network.py

```
from __future__ import annotations
from typing import List, Callable, TypeVar, Tuple
from functools import reduce
from layer import Layer
from util import sigmoid, derivative_sigmoid

T = TypeVar('T') # output type of interpretation of neural network


class Network:
    def __init__(self, layer_structure: List[int], learning_rate: float,
        activation_function: Callable[[float], float] = sigmoid, derivative_
        activation_function: Callable[[float], float] = derivative_sigmoid) ->
        None:
        if len(layer_structure) < 3:
            raise ValueError("Error: Should be at least 3 layers (1 input, 1
        hidden, 1 output)")
        self.layers: List[Layer] = []
        # input layer
        input_layer: Layer = Layer(None, layer_structure[0], learning_rate,
        activation_function, derivative_activation_function)
        self.layers.append(input_layer)
        # hidden layers and output layer
        for previous, num_neurons in enumerate(layer_structure[1::]):
            next_layer = Layer(self.layers[previous], num_neurons, learning_
        rate, activation_function, derivative_activation_function)
            self.layers.append(next_layer)
```

The outputs of the neural network are the result of signals running through all of its layers. Note how compactly `reduce()` is used in `outputs()` to pass signals from one layer to the next repeatedly through the whole network.

Listing 7.8 network.py continued

```
# Pushes input data to the first layer, then output from the first
# as input to the second, second to the third, etc.
def outputs(self, input: List[float]) -> List[float]:
    return reduce(lambda inputs, layer: layer.outputs(inputs), self.layers,
      input)
```

The `backpropagate()` method is responsible for computing deltas for every neuron in the network. It uses the `Layer` methods `calculate_deltas_for_output_layer()` and `calculate_deltas_for_hidden_layer()` in sequence. (Recall that in backpropagation, deltas are calculated backward.) It passes the expected values of output for a given set of inputs to `calculate_deltas_for_output_layer()`. That method uses the expected values to find the error used for delta calculation.

Listing 7.9 network.py continued

```
# Figure out each neuron's changes based on the errors of the output
# versus the expected outcome
def backpropagate(self, expected: List[float]) -> None:
    # calculate delta for output layer neurons
    last_layer: int = len(self.layers) - 1
    self.layers[last_layer].calculate_deltas_for_output_layer(expected)
    # calculate delta for hidden layers in reverse order
    for l in range(last_layer - 1, 0, -1):
        self.layers[l].calculate_deltas_for_hidden_layer(self.layers[l + 1])
```

`backpropagate()` is responsible for calculating all deltas, but it does not actually modify any of the network's weights. `update_weights()` must be called after `backpropagate()` because weight modification depends on deltas. This method follows directly from the formula in figure 7.6.

Listing 7.10 network.py continued

```
# backpropagate() doesn't actually change any weights
# this function uses the deltas calculated in backpropagate() to
# actually make changes to the weights
def update_weights(self) -> None:
    for layer in self.layers[1:]: # skip input layer
        for neuron in layer.neurons:
            for w in range(len(neuron.weights)):
                neuron.weights[w] = neuron.weights[w] + (neuron.learning_rate
      * (layer.previous_layer.output_cache[w]) * neuron.delta)
```

Neuron weights are modified at the end of each round of training. Training sets (inputs coupled with expected outputs) must be provided to the network. The `train()` method takes a list of lists of inputs and a list of lists of expected outputs.

It runs each input through the network and then updates its weights by calling backpropagate() with the expected output (and update_weights() after that). Try adding code here to print out the error rate as the network goes through a training set to see how the network gradually decreases its error rate as it rolls down the hill in gradient descent.

Listing 7.11 network.py continued

```python
# train() uses the results of outputs() run over many inputs and compared
# against expecteds to feed backpropagate() and update_weights()
def train(self, inputs: List[List[float]], expecteds: List[List[float]]) ->
    None:
    for location, xs in enumerate(inputs):
        ys: List[float] = expecteds[location]
        outs: List[float] = self.outputs(xs)
        self.backpropagate(ys)
        self.update_weights()
```

Finally, after a network is trained, we need to test it. validate() takes inputs and expected outputs (not unlike train()), but uses them to calculate an accuracy percentage rather than perform training. It is assumed that the network is already trained. validate() also takes a function, interpret_output(), that is used for interpreting the output of the neural network to compare it to the expected output. (Perhaps the expected output is a string like "Amphibian" instead of a set of floating-point numbers.) interpret_output() must take the floating-point numbers it gets as output from the network and convert them into something comparable to the expected outputs. It is a custom function specific to a data set. validate() returns the number of correct classifications, the total number of samples tested, and the percentage of correct classifications.

Listing 7.12 network.py continued

```python
# for generalized results that require classification
# this function will return the correct number of trials
# and the percentage correct out of the total
def validate(self, inputs: List[List[float]], expecteds: List[T], interpret_
    output: Callable[[List[float]], T]) -> Tuple[int, int, float]:
    correct: int = 0
    for input, expected in zip(inputs, expecteds):
        result: T = interpret_output(self.outputs(input))
        if result == expected:
            correct += 1
    percentage: float = correct / len(inputs)
    return correct, len(inputs), percentage
```

The neural network is done! It is ready to be tested with some actual problems. Although the architecture we built is general-purpose enough to be used for a variety of problems, we will concentrate on a popular kind of problem: classification.

7.5   *Classification problems*

In chapter 6 we categorized a data set with k-means clustering, using no preconceived notions about where each individual piece of data belonged. In clustering, we know we want to find categories of data, but we do not know ahead of time what those categories are. In a classification problem, we are also trying to categorize a data set, but there are preset categories. For example, if we were trying to classify a set of pictures of animals, we might decide ahead of time on categories like mammal, reptile, amphibian, fish, and bird.

There are many machine-learning techniques that can be used for classification problems. Perhaps you have heard of support vector machines, decision trees, or naive Bayes classifiers. (There are others, too.) Recently, neural networks have become widely deployed in the classification space. They are more computationally intensive than some of the other classification algorithms, but their ability to classify seemingly arbitrary kinds of data makes them a powerful technique. Neural network classifiers are behind much of the interesting image classification that powers modern photo software.

Why is there renewed interest in using neural networks for classification problems? Hardware has become fast enough that the extra computation involved, compared to other algorithms, makes the benefits worthwhile.

7.5.1   *Normalizing data*

The data sets that we want to work with generally require some "cleaning" before they are input into our algorithms. Cleaning may involve removing extraneous characters, deleting duplicates, fixing errors, and other menial tasks. The aspect of cleaning we will need to perform for the two data sets we are working with is normalization. In chapter 6 we did this via the zscore_normalize() method in the KMeans class. Normalization is about taking attributes recorded on different scales and converting them to a common scale.

Every neuron in our network outputs values between 0 and 1 due to the sigmoid activation function. It sounds logical that a scale between 0 and 1 would make sense for the attributes in our input data set as well. Converting a scale from some range to a range between 0 and 1 is not challenging. For any value, V, in a particular attribute range with maximum, max, and minimum, min, the formula is just newV = (oldV - min) / (max - min). This operation is known as *feature scaling*. Here is a Python implementation to add to util.py.

Listing 7.13   util.py continued

```
# assume all rows are of equal length
# and feature scale each column to be in the range 0 - 1
def normalize_by_feature_scaling(dataset: List[List[float]]) -> None:
    for col_num in range(len(dataset[0])):
        column: List[float] = [row[col_num] for row in dataset]
        maximum = max(column)
```

```
        minimum = min(column)
        for row_num in range(len(dataset)):
            dataset[row_num][col_num] = (dataset[row_num][col_num] -
minimum) / (maximum - minimum)
```

Look at the `dataset` parameter. It is a reference to a list of lists that will be modified in place. In other words, `normalize_by_feature_scaling()` does not receive a copy of the data set. It receives a reference to the original data set. This is a situation where we want to make changes to a value rather than receive back a transformed copy.

Note also that our program assumes that data sets are two-dimensional lists of `floats`.

7.5.2   *The classic iris data set*

Just as there are classic computer science problems, there are classic data sets in machine learning. These data sets are used to validate new techniques and compare them to existing ones. They also serve as good starting points for people learning machine learning for the first time. Perhaps the most famous is the iris data set. Originally collected in the 1930s, the data set consists of 150 samples of iris plants (pretty flowers), split amongst three different species (50 of each). Each plant is measured on four different attributes: sepal length, sepal width, petal length, and petal width.

It is worth noting that a neural network does not care what the various attributes represent. Its model for training makes no distinction between sepal length and petal length in terms of importance. If such a distinction should be made, it is up to the user of the neural network to make appropriate adjustments.

The source code repository that accompanies this book contains a comma-separated values (*CSV*) file that features the iris data set.[2] The iris data set is from the University of California's UCI Machine Learning Repository: M. Lichman, UCI Machine Learning Repository (Irvine, CA: University of California, School of Information and Computer Science, 2013), http://archive.ics.uci.edu/ml. A CSV file is just a text file with values separated by commas. It is a common interchange format for tabular data, including spreadsheets.

Here are a few lines from iris.csv:

```
5.1,3.5,1.4,0.2,Iris-setosa
4.9,3.0,1.4,0.2,Iris-setosa
4.7,3.2,1.3,0.2,Iris-setosa
4.6,3.1,1.5,0.2,Iris-setosa
5.0,3.6,1.4,0.2,Iris-setosa
```

Each line represents one data point. The four numbers represent the four attributes (sepal length, sepal width, petal length, and petal width), which, again, are arbitrary to us in terms of what they actually represent. The name at the end of each line represents the particular iris species. All five lines are for the same species because this

---

[2]   The repository is available from GitHub at https://github.com/davecom/ClassicComputerScienceProblems InPython.

sample was taken from the top of the file, and the three species are clumped together, with fifty lines each.

To read the CSV file from disk, we will use a few functions from the Python standard library. The `csv` module will help us read the data in a structured way. The built-in `open()` function creates a file object that is passed to `csv.reader()`. Beyond those few lines, the rest of the following code listing just rearranges the data from the CSV file to prepare it to be consumed by our network for training and validation.

Listing 7.14 iris_test.py

```python
import csv
from typing import List
from util import normalize_by_feature_scaling
from network import Network
from random import shuffle

if __name__ == "__main__":
    iris_parameters: List[List[float]] = []
    iris_classifications: List[List[float]] = []
    iris_species: List[str] = []
    with open('iris.csv', mode='r') as iris_file:
        irises: List = list(csv.reader(iris_file))
        shuffle(irises) # get our lines of data in random order
        for iris in irises:
            parameters: List[float] = [float(n) for n in iris[0:4]]
            iris_parameters.append(parameters)
            species: str = iris[4]
            if species == "Iris-setosa":
                iris_classifications.append([1.0, 0.0, 0.0])
            elif species == "Iris-versicolor":
                iris_classifications.append([0.0, 1.0, 0.0])
            else:
                iris_classifications.append([0.0, 0.0, 1.0])
            iris_species.append(species)
    normalize_by_feature_scaling(iris_parameters)
```

`iris_parameters` represents the collection of four attributes per sample that we are using to classify each iris. `iris_classifications` is the actual classification of each sample. Our neural network will have three output neurons, with each representing one possible species. For instance, a final set of outputs of [0.9, 0.3, 0.1] will represent a classification of iris-setosa, because the first neuron represents that species, and it is the largest number.

For training, we already know the right answers, so each iris has a premarked answer. For a flower that should be iris-setosa, the entry in `iris_classifications` will be [1.0, 0.0, 0.0]. These values will be used to calculate the error after each training step. `iris_species` corresponds directly to what each flower should be classified as in English. An iris-setosa will be marked as "Iris-setosa" in the data set.

WARNING The lack of error-checking code makes this code fairly dangerous. It is not suitable as is for production, but it is fine for testing.

Let's define the neural network itself.

Listing 7.15   iris_test.py continued

```
iris_network: Network = Network([4, 6, 3], 0.3)
```

The `layer_structure` argument specifies a network with three layers (one input layer, one hidden layer, and one output layer) with `[4, 6, 3]`. The input layer has four neurons, the hidden layer has six neurons, and the output layer has three neurons. The four neurons in the input layer map directly to the four parameters that are used to classify each specimen. The three neurons in the output layer map directly to the three different species that we are trying to classify each input within. The hidden layer's six neurons are more the result of trial and error than some formula. The same is true of `learning_rate`. These two values (the number of neurons in the hidden layer and the learning rate) can be experimented with if the accuracy of the network is suboptimal.

Listing 7.16   iris_test.py continued

```python
def iris_interpret_output(output: List[float]) -> str:
    if max(output) == output[0]:
        return "Iris-setosa"
    elif max(output) == output[1]:
        return "Iris-versicolor"
    else:
        return "Iris-virginica"
```

`iris_interpret_output()` is a utility function that will be passed to the network's `validate()` method to help identify correct classifications.

The network is finally ready to be trained.

Listing 7.17   iris_test.py continued

```python
# train over the first 140 irises in the data set 50 times
iris_trainers: List[List[float]] = iris_parameters[0:140]
iris_trainers_corrects: List[List[float]] = iris_classifications[0:140]
for _ in range(50):
    iris_network.train(iris_trainers, iris_trainers_corrects)
```

We train on the first 140 irises out of the 150 in the data set. Recall that the lines read from the CSV file were shuffled. This ensures that every time we run the program, we will be training on a different subset of the data set. Note that we train over the 140 irises 50 times. Modifying this value will have a large effect on how long it takes your neural network to train. Generally, the more training, the more accurately the neural network will perform. The final test will be to verify the correct classification of the final 10 irises from the data set.

Listing 7.18   iris_test.py continued

```
# test over the last 10 of the irises in the data set
iris_testers: List[List[float]] = iris_parameters[140:150]
iris_testers_corrects: List[str] = iris_species[140:150]
iris_results = iris_network.validate(iris_testers, iris_testers_corrects,
    iris_interpret_output)
print(f"{iris_results[0]} correct of {iris_results[1]} = {iris_results[2] *
    100}%")
```

All of the work leads up to this final question: Out of 10 randomly chosen irises from the data set, how many can our neural network correctly classify? Because there is randomness in the starting weights of each neuron, different runs may give you different results. You can try tweaking the learning rate, the number of hidden neurons, and the number of training iterations to make your network more accurate.

Ultimately, you should see a result like this:

```
9 correct of 10 = 90.0%
```

7.5.3   *Classifying wine*

We are going to test our neural network with another data set, one based on the chemical analysis of wine cultivars from Italy.[3] There are 178 samples in the data set. The machinery of working with it will be much the same as with the iris data set, but the layout of the CSV file is slightly different. Here is a sample:

```
1,14.23,1.71,2.43,15.6,127,2.8,3.06,.28,2.29,5.64,1.04,3.92,1065
1,13.2,1.78,2.14,11.2,100,2.65,2.76,.26,1.28,4.38,1.05,3.4,1050
1,13.16,2.36,2.67,18.6,101,2.8,3.24,.3,2.81,5.68,1.03,3.17,1185
1,14.37,1.95,2.5,16.8,113,3.85,3.49,.24,2.18,7.8,.86,3.45,1480
1,13.24,2.59,2.87,21,118,2.8,2.69,.39,1.82,4.32,1.04,2.93,735
```

The first value on each line will always be an integer from 1 to 3 representing one of three cultivars that the sample may be a kind of. But notice how many more parameters there are for classification. In the iris data set, there were just four. In this wine data set, there are 13.

Our neural network model will scale just fine. We simply need to increase the number of input neurons. wine_test.py is analogous to iris_test.py, but there are some minor changes to account for the different layouts of the respective files.

Listing 7.19   wine_test.py

```
import csv
from typing import List
from util import normalize_by_feature_scaling
from network import Network
from random import shuffle
```

---

[3]   M. Lichman, UCI Machine Learning Repository (Irvine, CA: University of California, School of Information and Computer Science, 2013), http://archive.ics.uci.edu/ml.

```
if __name__ == "__main__":
    wine_parameters: List[List[float]] = []
    wine_classifications: List[List[float]] = []
    wine_species: List[int] = []
    with open('wine.csv', mode='r') as wine_file:
        wines: List = list(csv.reader(wine_file, quoting=csv.QUOTE_
    NONNUMERIC))
        shuffle(wines) # get our lines of data in random order
        for wine in wines:
            parameters: List[float] = [float(n) for n in wine[1:14]]
            wine_parameters.append(parameters)
            species: int = int(wine[0])
            if species == 1:
                wine_classifications.append([1.0, 0.0, 0.0])
            elif species == 2:
                wine_classifications.append([0.0, 1.0, 0.0])
            else:
                wine_classifications.append([0.0, 0.0, 1.0])
            wine_species.append(species)
    normalize_by_feature_scaling(wine_parameters)
```

The layer configuration for the wine-classification network needs 13 input neurons, as was already mentioned (one for each parameter). It also needs three output neurons. (There are three cultivars of wine, just as there were three species of iris.) Interestingly, the network works well with fewer neurons in the hidden layer than in the input layer. One possible intuitive explanation is that some of the input parameters are not actually helpful for classification, and it is useful to cut them out during processing. This is not, in fact, exactly how having fewer neurons in the hidden layer works, but it is an interesting intuitive idea.

Listing 7.20   wine_test.py continued

```
wine_network: Network = Network([13, 7, 3], 0.9)
```

Once again, it can be interesting to experiment with a different number of hidden-layer neurons or a different learning rate.

Listing 7.21   wine_test.py continued

```
def wine_interpret_output(output: List[float]) -> int:
    if max(output) == output[0]:
        return 1
    elif max(output) == output[1]:
        return 2
    else:
        return 3
```

wine_interpret_output() is analogous to iris_interpret_output(). Because we do not have names for the wine cultivars, we are just working with the integer assignment in the original data set.

Listing 7.22 wine_test.py continued

```
# train over the first 150 wines 10 times
wine_trainers: List[List[float]] = wine_parameters[0:150]
wine_trainers_corrects: List[List[float]] = wine_classifications[0:150]
for _ in range(10):
    wine_network.train(wine_trainers, wine_trainers_corrects)
```

We will train over the first 150 samples in the data set, leaving the last 28 for validation. We will train 10 times over the samples, significantly less than the 50 for the iris data set. For whatever reason (perhaps innate qualities of the data set or tuning of parameters like the learning rate and number of hidden neurons), this data set requires less training to achieve significant accuracy than the iris data set.

Listing 7.23 wine_test.py continued

```
# test over the last 28 of the wines in the data set
wine_testers: List[List[float]] = wine_parameters[150:178]
wine_testers_corrects: List[int] = wine_species[150:178]
wine_results = wine_network.validate(wine_testers, wine_testers_corrects,
    wine_interpret_output)
print(f"{wine_results[0]} correct of {wine_results[1]} = {wine_results[2] *
    100}%")
```

With a little luck, your neural network should be able to classify the 28 samples quite accurately.

```
27 correct of 28 = 96.42857142857143%
```

7.6 *Speeding up neural networks*

Neural networks require a lot of vector/matrix math. Essentially, this means taking a list of numbers and doing an operation on all of them at once. Libraries for optimized, performant vector/matrix math are increasingly important as machine learning continues to permeate our society. Many of these libraries take advantage of GPUs, because GPUs are optimized for this role. (Vectors/matrices are at the heart of computer graphics.) An older library specification you may have heard of is BLAS (Basic Linear Algebra Subprograms). A BLAS implementation underlies the popular Python numerical library NumPy.

Beyond the GPU, CPUs have extensions that can speed up vector/matrix processing. NumPy includes functions that make use of *single instruction, multiple data* (SIMD) instructions. SIMD instructions are special microprocessor instructions that allow multiple pieces of data to be processed at once. They are sometimes known as *vector instructions*.

Different microprocessors include different SIMD instructions. For example, the SIMD extension to the G4 (a PowerPC architecture processor found in early '00s Macs) was known as AltiVec. ARM microprocessors, like those found in iPhones, have an extension known as NEON. And modern Intel microprocessors include SIMD extensions known as MMX, SSE, SSE2, and SSE3. Luckily, you do not need to know the differences. A library like NumPy will automatically choose the right instructions for computing efficiently on the underlying architecture that your program is running on.

It is no surprise, then, that real-world neural network libraries (unlike our toy library in this chapter) use NumPy arrays as their base data structure instead of Python standard library lists. But they go even further. Popular Python neural network libraries like TensorFlow and PyTorch not only make use of SIMD instructions, but also make extensive use of GPU computing. Because GPUs are explicitly designed for fast vector computations, this accelerates neural networks by an order of magnitude compared with running on a CPU alone.

Let's be clear: *You would never want to naively implement a neural network for production using just the Python standard library as we did in this chapter.* Instead, you should use a well optimized, SIMD- and GPU-enabled library like TensorFlow. The only exceptions would be a neural network library designed for education or one that had to run on an embedded device without SIMD instructions or a GPU.

7.7   *Neural network problems and extensions*

Neural networks are all the rage right now, thanks to advances in deep learning, but they have some significant shortcomings. The biggest problem is that a neural network solution to a problem is something of a black box. Even when neural networks work well, they do not give the user much insight into how they solve the problem. For instance, the iris data set classifier we worked on in this chapter does not clearly show how much each of the four parameters in the input affects the output. Was sepal length more important than sepal width for classifying each sample?

It is possible that careful analysis of the final weights for the trained network could provide some insight, but such analysis is nontrivial and does not provide the kind of insight that, say, linear regression does in terms of the meaning of each variable in the function being modeled. In other words, a neural network may solve a problem, but it does not explain how the problem is solved.

Another problem with neural networks is that to become accurate, they often require very large data sets. Imagine an image classifier for outdoor landscapes. It may need to classify thousands of different types of images (forests, valleys, mountains, streams, steppes, and so on). It will potentially need millions of training images. Not only are such large data sets hard to come by, but also, for some applications they may be completely non-existent. It tends to be large corporations and governments that have the data-warehousing and technical facilities for collecting and storing such massive data sets.

Finally, neural networks are computationally expensive. As you probably noticed, just training on the iris data set can bring your Python interpreter to its knees. Pure Python is not a computationally performant environment (without C-backed libraries like NumPy at least), but on any computational platform where neural networks are used, it is the sheer number of calculations that have to be performed in training the network, more than anything else, that takes so much time. Many tricks abound to make neural networks more performant (like using SIMD instructions or GPUs), but ultimately, training a neural network requires a lot of floating-point operations.

One nice caveat is that training is much more computationally expensive than actually using the network. Some applications do not require ongoing training. In those instances, a trained network can just be dropped into an application to solve a problem. For example, the first version of Apple's Core ML framework does not even support training. It only supports helping app developers run pretrained neural network models in their apps. An app developer creating a photo app can download a freely licensed image-classification model, drop it into Core ML, and start using performant machine learning in an app instantly.

In this chapter, we only worked with a single type of neural network: a feed-forward network with backpropagation. As has been mentioned, many other kinds of neural networks exist. Convolutional neural networks are also feed-forward, but they have multiple different types of hidden layers, different mechanisms for distributing weights, and other interesting properties that make them especially well designed for image classification. In recurrent neural networks, signals do not just travel in one direction. They allow feedback loops and have proven useful for continuous input applications like handwriting recognition and voice recognition.

A simple extension to our neural network that would make it more performant would be the inclusion of bias neurons. A bias neuron is like a dummy neuron in a layer that allows the next layer's output to represent more functions by providing a constant input (still modified by a weight) into it. Even simple neural networks used for real-world problems usually contain bias neurons. If you add bias neurons to our existing network, you will likely find that it requires less training to achieve a similar level of accuracy.

7.8 Real-world applications

Although they were first imagined in the middle of the 20th century, artificial neural networks did not become commonplace until the last decade. Their widespread application was held back by a lack of sufficiently performant hardware. Today, artificial neural networks have become the most explosive growth area in machine learning because they work!

Artificial neural networks have enabled some of the most exciting user-facing computing applications in decades. These include practical voice recognition (practical in terms of sufficient accuracy), image recognition, and handwriting recognition. Voice recognition is present in typing aids like Dragon Naturally Speaking and digital assistants like Siri, Alexa, and Cortana. A specific example of image recognition is Facebook's automatic tagging of people in a photo using facial recognition. In recent versions of iOS, you can search works within your notes, even if they are handwritten, by employing handwriting recognition.

An older recognition technology that can be powered by neural networks is OCR (optical character recognition). OCR is used every time you scan a document and it comes back as selectable text instead of an image. OCR enables toll booths to read license plates and envelopes to be quickly sorted by the postal service.

In this chapter you have seen neural networks used successfully for classification problems. Similar applications that neural networks work well in are recommendation systems. Think of Netflix suggesting a movie you might like to watch or Amazon suggesting a book you might want to read. There are other machine learning techniques that work well for recommendation systems, too (Amazon and Netflix do not necessarily use neural networks for these purposes; the details of their systems are likely proprietary), so neural networks should only be selected after all options have been explored.

Neural networks can be used in any situation where an unknown function needs to be approximated. This makes them useful for prediction. Neural networks can be employed to predict the outcome of a sporting event, election, or the stock market (and they are). Of course, their accuracy is a product of how well they are trained, and that has to do with how large a data set relevant to the unknown-outcome event is available, how well the parameters of the neural network are tuned, and how many iterations of training are run. With prediction, like most neural network applications, one of the hardest parts is deciding upon the structure of the network itself, which is often ultimately determined by trial and error.

7.9   *Exercises*

1   Use the neural network framework developed in this chapter to classify items in another data set.

2   Create a generic function, `parse_CSV()`, with flexible-enough parameters that it could replace both of the CSV parsing examples in this chapter.

3   Try running the examples with a different activation function. (Remember to also find its derivative.) How does the change in activation function affect the accuracy of the network? Does it require more or less training?

4   Take the problems in this chapter and re-create their solutions using a popular neural network framework like TensorFlow or PyTorch.

5   Rewrite the `Network`, `Layer`, and `Neuron` classes using NumPy to accelerate the execution of the neural network developed in this chapter.

Adversarial search

8

A two-player, zero-sum, perfect information game is one in which both opponents have all of the information about the state of the game available to them, and any gain in advantage for one is a loss of advantage for the other. Such games include tic-tac-toe, Connect Four, checkers, and chess. In this chapter we will study how to create an artificial opponent that can play such games with great skill. In fact, the techniques discussed in this chapter, coupled with modern computing power, can create artificial opponents that play simple games of this class perfectly and that can play complex games beyond the ability of any human opponent.

8.1 *Basic board game components*

As with most of our more complex problems in this book, we will try to make our solution as generic as possible. In the case of adversarial search, that means making our search algorithms non-game-specific. Let's start by defining some simple base classes that define all of the state our search algorithms will need. Later, we can subclass those base classes for the specific games we are implementing (tic-tac-toe and Connect Four) and feed the subclasses into the search algorithms to make them "play" the games. Here are those base classes:

Listing 8.1   board.py

```
from __future__ import annotations
from typing import NewType, List
from abc import ABC, abstractmethod

Move = NewType('Move', int)


class Piece:
```

153

```
    @property
    def opposite(self) -> Piece:
        raise NotImplementedError("Should be implemented by subclasses.")


class Board(ABC):
    @property
    @abstractmethod
    def turn(self) -> Piece:
        ...

    @abstractmethod
    def move(self, location: Move) -> Board:
        ...

    @property
    @abstractmethod
    def legal_moves(self) -> List[Move]:
        ...

    @property
    @abstractmethod
    def is_win(self) -> bool:
        ...

    @property
    def is_draw(self) -> bool:
        return (not self.is_win) and (len(self.legal_moves) == 0)

    @abstractmethod
    def evaluate(self, player: Piece) -> float:
        ...
```

The `Move` type will represent a move in a game. It is, at heart, just an integer. In games like tic-tac-toe and Connect Four, an integer can represent a move by indicating a square or column where a piece should be placed. `Piece` is a base class for a piece on the board in a game. It will also double as our turn indicator. This is why the `opposite` property is needed. We need to know whose turn follows a given turn.

> **TIP** Because tic-tac-toe and Connect Four only have one kind of piece, the `Piece` class can double as a turn indicator in this chapter. For a more complex game, like chess, that has different kinds of pieces, turns can be indicated by an integer or a Boolean. Alternatively, just the "color" attribute of a more complex `Piece` type could be used to indicate turn.

The `Board` abstract base class is the actual maintainer of state. For any given game that our search algorithms will compute, we need to be able to answer four questions:

- Whose turn is it?
- What legal moves can be played in the current position?
- Is the game won?
- Is the game drawn?

That last question, about draws, is actually a combination of the previous two questions for many games. If the game is not won but there are no legal moves, then it is a draw. This is why our abstract base class, `Game`, can already have a concrete implementation of the `is_draw` property. In addition, there are a couple of actions we need to be able to take:

- Make a move to go from the current position to a new position.
- Evaluate the position to see which player has an advantage.

Each of the methods and properties in `Board` is a proxy for one of the preceding questions or actions. The `Board` class could also be called Position in game parlance, but we will use that nomenclature for something more specific in each of our subclasses.

8.2   Tic-tac-toe

Tic-tac-toe is a simple game, but it can be used to illustrate the same minimax algorithm that can be applied in advanced strategy games like Connect Four, checkers, and chess. We will build a tic-tac-toe AI that plays perfectly using minimax.

> **NOTE**   This section assumes that you are familiar with the game tic-tac-toe and its standard rules. If not, a quick search on the web should get you up to speed.

8.2.1   Managing tic-tac-toe state

Let's develop some structures to keep track of the state of a tic-tac-toe game as it progresses.

First, we need a way of representing each square on the tic-tac-toe board. We will use an enum called `TTTPiece`, a subclass of `Piece`. A tic-tac-toe piece can be X, O, or empty (represented by E in the enum).

Listing 8.2   tictactoe.py

```python
from __future__ import annotations
from typing import List
from enum import Enum
from board import Piece, Board, Move


class TTTPiece(Piece, Enum):
    X = "X"
    O = "O"
    E = " " # stand-in for empty

    @property
    def opposite(self) -> TTTPiece:
        if self == TTTPiece.X:
            return TTTPiece.O
        elif self == TTTPiece.O:
            return TTTPiece.X
        else:
            return TTTPiece.E

def __str__(self) -> str:
    return self.value
```

The class `TTTPiece` has a property, `opposite`, that returns another `TTTPiece`. This will be useful for flipping from one player's turn to the other player's turn after a tic-tac-toe move. To represent moves, we will just use an integer that corresponds to a square on the board where a piece is placed. As you recall, `Move` was defined as an integer in board.py.

A tic-tac-toe board has nine positions organized in three rows and three columns. For simplicity, these nine positions can be represented using a one-dimensional list. Which squares receive which numeric designation (a.k.a., index in the array) is arbitrary, but we will follow the scheme outlined in figure 8.1.

0	1	2
3	4	5
6	7	8

Figure 8.1   The one-dimensional list indices that correspond to each square in the tic-tac-toe board

The main holder of state will be the class `TTTBoard`. `TTTBoard` keeps track of two different pieces of state: the position (represented by the aforementioned one-dimensional list) and the player whose turn it is.

Listing 8.3   **tictactoe.py continued**

```
class TTTBoard(Board):
    def __init__(self, position: List[TTTPiece] = [TTTPiece.E] * 9, turn:
    TTTPiece = TTTPiece.X) -> None:
        self.position: List[TTTPiece] = position
        self._turn: TTTPiece = turn

    @property
    def turn(self) -> Piece:
        return self._turn
```

A default board is one where no moves have yet been made (an empty board). The constructor for `Board` has default parameters that initialize such a position, with X to move (the usual first player in tic-tac-toe). You may wonder why the `_turn` instance variable and `turn` property exist. This was a trick to ensure that all `Board` subclasses will keep track of whose turn it is. There is no clear and obvious way in Python to specify in an abstract base class that subclasses must include a particular instance variable, but there is such a mechanism for properties.

`TTTBoard` is an informally immutable data structure; `TTTBoards` should not be modified. Instead, every time a move needs to be played, a new `TTTBoard` with the position changed to accommodate the move will be generated. This will later be helpful in our search algorithm. When the search branches, we will not inadvertently change the position of a board from which potential moves are still being analyzed.

Listing 8.4   **tictactoe.py continued**

```
def move(self, location: Move) -> Board:
    temp_position: List[TTTPiece] = self.position.copy()
    temp_position[location] = self._turn
    return TTTBoard(temp_position, self._turn.opposite)
```

A legal move in tic-tac-toe is any empty square. The following property, `legal_moves`, uses a list comprehension to generate potential moves for a given position.

```python
@property
def legal_moves(self) -> List[Move]:
    return [Move(l) for l in range(len(self.position)) if self.position[l] ==
    TTTPiece.E]
```

The indices that the list comprehension acts on are `int` indexes into the position list. Conveniently (and purposely), a `Move` is also defined as a type of `int`, allowing this definition of `legal_moves` to be so succinct.

There are many ways to scan the rows, columns, and diagonals of a tic-tac-toe board to check for wins. The following implementation of the property `is_win` does so with a hard-coded, seemingly endless amalgamation of `and`, `or`, and `==`. It is not the prettiest code, but it does the job in a straightforward manner.

```python
@property
def is_win(self) -> bool:
    # three row, three column, and then two diagonal checks
    return self.position[0] == self.position[1] and self.position[0] ==
    self.position[2] and self.position[0] != TTTPiece.E or \
    self.position[3] == self.position[4] and self.position[3] ==
    self.position[5] and self.position[3] != TTTPiece.E or \
    self.position[6] == self.position[7] and self.position[6] ==
    self.position[8] and self.position[6] != TTTPiece.E or \
    self.position[0] == self.position[3] and self.position[0] ==
    self.position[6] and self.position[0] != TTTPiece.E or \
    self.position[1] == self.position[4] and self.position[1] ==
    self.position[7] and self.position[1] != TTTPiece.E or \
    self.position[2] == self.position[5] and self.position[2] ==
    self.position[8] and self.position[2] != TTTPiece.E or \
    self.position[0] == self.position[4] and self.position[0] ==
    self.position[8] and self.position[0] != TTTPiece.E or \
    self.position[2] == self.position[4] and self.position[2] ==
    self.position[6] and self.position[2] != TTTPiece.E
```

If all of a row's, column's, or diagonal's squares are not empty, and they contain the same piece, the game has been won.

A game is drawn if it is not won and there are no more legal moves left; that property was already covered by the `Board` abstract base class. Finally, we need a way of evaluating a particular position and pretty-printing the board.

```python
    def evaluate(self, player: Piece) -> float:
        if self.is_win and self.turn == player:
            return -1
        elif self.is_win and self.turn != player:
```

```
            return 1
        else:
            return 0

    def __repr__(self) -> str:
        return f"""{self.position[0]}|{self.position[1]}|{self.position[2]}
-----
{self.position[3]}|{self.position[4]}|{self.position[5]}
-----
{self.position[6]}|{self.position[7]}|{self.position[8]}"""
```

For most games, an evaluation of a position needs to be an approximation, because we cannot search the game to the very end to find out with certainty who wins or loses depending on what moves are played. But tic-tac-toe has a small enough search space that we can search from any position to the very end. Therefore, the evaluate() method can simply return one number if the player wins, a worse number for a draw, and an even worse number for a loss.

8.2.2 *Minimax*

Minimax is a classic algorithm for finding the best move in a two-player, zero-sum game with perfect information, like tic-tac-toe, checkers, or chess. It has been extended and modified for other types of games as well. Minimax is typically implemented using a recursive function in which each player is designated either the maximizing player or the minimizing player.

The maximizing player aims to find the move that will lead to maximal gains. However, the maximizing player must account for moves by the minimizing player. After each attempt to maximize the gains of the maximizing player, minimax is called recursively to find the opponent's reply that minimizes the maximizing player's gains. This continues back and forth (maximizing, minimizing, maximizing, and so on) until a base case in the recursive function is reached. The base case is a terminal position (a win or a draw) or a maximal search depth.

Minimax will return an evaluation of the starting position for the maximizing player. For the evaluate() method of the TTTBoard class, if the best possible play by both sides will result in a win for the maximizing player, a score of 1 will be returned. If the best play will result in a loss, -1 is returned. A 0 is returned if the best play is a draw.

These numbers are returned when a base case is reached. They then bubble up through all of the recursive calls that led to the base case. For each recursive call to maximize, the best evaluations one level further down bubble up. For each recursive call to minimize, the worst evaluations one level further down bubble up. In this way, a decision tree is built. Figure 8.2 illustrates such a tree that facilitates bubbling up for a game with two moves left.

For games that have too deep a search space to reach a terminal position (such as checkers and chess), minimax is stopped after a certain depth (the number of moves deep to search, sometimes called *ply*). Then the evaluation function kicks in, using heuristics to score the state of the game. The better the game is for the originating

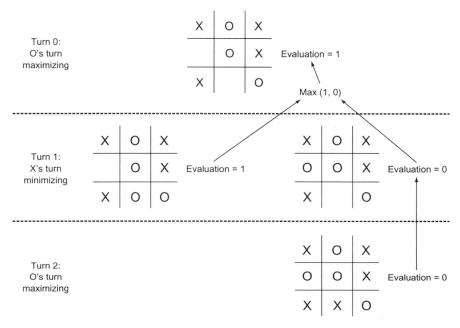

Figure 8.2 A minimax decision tree for a tic-tac-toe game with two moves left. To maximize the likelihood of winning, the initial player, O, will choose to play O in the bottom center. Arrows indicate the positions from which a decision is made.

player, the higher the score that is awarded. We will come back to this concept with Connect Four, which has a much larger search space than tic-tac-toe.

Here is minimax() in its entirety:

Listing 8.8 minimax.py

```python
from __future__ import annotations
from board import Piece, Board, Move

# Find the best possible outcome for original player
def minimax(board: Board, maximizing: bool, original_player: Piece, max_
    depth: int = 8) -> float:
    # Base case - terminal position or maximum depth reached
    if board.is_win or board.is_draw or max_depth == 0:
        return board.evaluate(original_player)

    # Recursive case - maximize your gains or minimize the opponent's gains
    if maximizing:
        best_eval: float = float("-inf") # arbitrarily low starting point
        for move in board.legal_moves:
            result: float = minimax(board.move(move), False, original_player,
    max_depth - 1)
            best_eval = max(result, best_eval)
        return best_eval
    else: # minimizing
```

```
        worst_eval: float = float("inf")
        for move in board.legal_moves:
            result = minimax(board.move(move), True, original_player, max_
    depth - 1)
            worst_eval = min(result, worst_eval)
        return worst_eval
```

In each recursive call, we need to keep track of the board position, whether we are maximizing or minimizing, and who we are trying to evaluate the position for (original_player). The first few lines of minimax() deal with the base case: a terminal node (a win, loss, or draw) or the maximum depth being reached. The rest of the function is the recursive cases.

One recursive case is maximization. In this situation, we are looking for a move that yields the highest possible evaluation. The other recursive case is minimization, where we are looking for the move that results in the lowest possible evaluation. Either way, the two cases alternate until we reach a terminal state or the maximum depth (base case).

Unfortunately, we cannot use our implementation of minimax() as is to find the best move for a given position. It returns an evaluation (a float value). It does not tell us what best first move led to that evaluation.

Instead, we will create a helper function, find_best_move(), that loops through calls to minimax() for each legal move in a position to find the move that evaluates to the highest value. You can think of find_best_move() as the first maximizing call to minimax(), but with us keeping track of those initial moves.

Listing 8.9   minimax.py continued

```
# Find the best possible move in the current position
# looking up to max_depth ahead
def find_best_move(board: Board, max_depth: int = 8) -> Move:
    best_eval: float = float("-inf")
    best_move: Move = Move(-1)
    for move in board.legal_moves:
        result: float = minimax(board.move(move), False, board.turn, max_
    depth)
        if result > best_eval:
            best_eval = result
            best_move = move
    return best_move
```

We now have everything ready to find the best possible move for any tic-tac-toe position.

8.2.3   *Testing minimax with tic-tac-toe*

Tic-tac-toe is such a simple game that it's easy for us, as humans, to figure out the definite correct move in a given position. This makes it possible to easily develop unit tests. In the following code snippet, we will challenge our minimax algorithm to find the correct next move in three different tic-tac-toe positions. The first is easy and only requires it to think to the next move for a win. The second requires a block; the AI must stop its opponent from scoring a victory. The last is a little bit more challenging and requires the AI to think two moves into the future.

Listing 8.10 tictactoe_tests.py

```python
import unittest
from typing import List
from minimax import find_best_move
from tictactoe import TTTPiece, TTTBoard
from board import Move


class TTTMinimaxTestCase(unittest.TestCase):
    def test_easy_position(self):
        # win in 1 move
        to_win_easy_position: List[TTTPiece] = [TTTPiece.X, TTTPiece.O,
        TTTPiece.X,
                                                TTTPiece.X, TTTPiece.E,
        TTTPiece.O,
                                                TTTPiece.E, TTTPiece.E,
        TTTPiece.O]
        test_board1: TTTBoard = TTTBoard(to_win_easy_position, TTTPiece.X)
        answer1: Move = find_best_move(test_board1)
        self.assertEqual(answer1, 6)

    def test_block_position(self):
        # must block O's win
        to_block_position: List[TTTPiece] = [TTTPiece.X, TTTPiece.E,
        TTTPiece.E,
                                             TTTPiece.E, TTTPiece.E,
        TTTPiece.O,
                                             TTTPiece.E, TTTPiece.X,
        TTTPiece.O]
        test_board2: TTTBoard = TTTBoard(to_block_position, TTTPiece.X)
        answer2: Move = find_best_move(test_board2)
        self.assertEqual(answer2, 2)


    def test_hard_position(self):
        # find the best move to win 2 moves
        to_win_hard_position: List[TTTPiece] = [TTTPiece.X, TTTPiece.E,
        TTTPiece.E,
                                                TTTPiece.E, TTTPiece.E,
        TTTPiece.O,
                                                TTTPiece.O, TTTPiece.X,
        TTTPiece.E]
        test_board3: TTTBoard = TTTBoard(to_win_hard_position, TTTPiece.X)
        answer3: Move = find_best_move(test_board3)
        self.assertEqual(answer3, 1)

if __name__ == '__main__':
    unittest.main()
```

All three of the tests should pass when you run tictactoe_tests.py.

TIP   It does not take much code to implement minimax, and it will work for many more games than just tic-tac-toe. If you plan to implement minimax for another game, it is important to set yourself up for success by creating data structures that work well for the way minimax is designed, like the `Board` class. A common mistake for students learning minimax is to use a modifiable data structure that gets changed by a recursive call to minimax and then cannot be rewound to its original state for additional calls.

8.2.4   *Developing a tic-tac-toe AI*

With all of these ingredients in place, it is trivial to take the next step and develop a full artificial opponent that can play an entire game of tic-tac-toe. Instead of evaluating a test position, the AI will just evaluate the position generated by each opponent's move. In the following short code snippet, the tic-tac-toe AI plays against a human opponent who goes first:

Listing 8.11   tictactoe_ai.py

```python
from minimax import find_best_move
from tictactoe import TTTBoard
from board import Move, Board

board: Board = TTTBoard()


def get_player_move() -> Move:
    player_move: Move = Move(-1)
    while player_move not in board.legal_moves:
        play: int = int(input("Enter a legal square (0-8):"))
        player_move = Move(play)
    return player_move


if __name__ == "__main__":
    # main game loop
    while True:
        human_move: Move = get_player_move()
        board = board.move(human_move)
        if board.is_win:
            print("Human wins!")
            break
        elif board.is_draw:
            print("Draw!")
            break
        computer_move: Move = find_best_move(board)
        print(f"Computer move is {computer_move}")
        board = board.move(computer_move)
        print(board)
        if board.is_win:
            print("Computer wins!")
            break
        elif board.is_draw:
            print("Draw!")
            break
```

Because the default `max_depth` of `find_best_move()` is 8, this tic-tac-toe AI will always see to the very end of the game. (The maximum number of moves in tic-tac-toe is nine, and the AI goes second.) Therefore, it should play perfectly every time. A perfect game is one in which both opponents play the best possible move every turn. The result of a perfect game of tic-tac-toe is a draw. With this in mind, you should never be able to beat the tic-tac-toe AI. If you play your best, it will be a draw. If you make a mistake, the AI will win. Try it out yourself. You should not be able to beat it

8.3   Connect Four

In Connect Four,[2] two players alternate dropping different-colored pieces in a seven-column, six-row vertical grid. Pieces fall from the top of the grid to the bottom until they hit the bottom or another piece. In essence, the player's only decision each turn is which of the seven columns to drop a piece into. The player may not drop it into a full column. The first player that has four pieces of their color next to one another with no breaks in a row, column, or diagonal wins. If no player achieves this, and the grid is completely filled, the game is a draw.

8.3.1   Connect Four game machinery

Connect Four, in many ways, is similar to tic-tac-toe. Both games are played on a grid and require the player to line up pieces to win. But because the Connect Four grid is larger and has many more ways to win, evaluating each position is significantly more complex.

   Some of the following code will look very familiar, but the data structures and the evaluation method are quite different from tic-tac-toe. Both games are implemented as subclasses of the same base `Piece` and `Board` classes you saw at the beginning of the chapter, making `minimax()` usable for both games.

Listing 8.12   connectfour.py

```
from __future__ import annotations
from typing import List, Optional, Tuple
from enum import Enum
from board import Piece, Board, Move

class C4Piece(Piece, Enum):
    B = "B"
    R = "R"
    E = " " # stand-in for empty

    @property
    def opposite(self) -> C4Piece:
        if self == C4Piece.B:
            return C4Piece.R
        elif self == C4Piece.R:
            return C4Piece.B
```

---

[2]   Connect Four is a trademark of Hasbro, Inc. It is used here only in a descriptive and positive manner.

```
    else:
        return C4Piece.E

def __str__(self) -> str:
    return self.value
```

The C4Piece class is almost identical to the TTTPiece class.

Next, we have a function for generating all of the potential winning segments in a certain-size Connect Four grid:

Listing 8.13   connectfour.py continued

```python
def generate_segments(num_columns: int, num_rows: int, segment_length: int) -
    > List[List[Tuple[int, int]]]:
    segments: List[List[Tuple[int, int]]] = []
    # generate the vertical segments
    for c in range(num_columns):
        for r in range(num_rows - segment_length + 1):
            segment: List[Tuple[int, int]] = []
            for t in range(segment_length):
                segment.append((c, r + t))
            segments.append(segment)

    # generate the horizontal segments
    for c in range(num_columns - segment_length + 1):
        for r in range(num_rows):
            segment = []
            for t in range(segment_length):
                segment.append((c + t, r))
            segments.append(segment)

    # generate the bottom left to top right diagonal segments
    for c in range(num_columns - segment_length + 1):
        for r in range(num_rows - segment_length + 1):
            segment = []
            for t in range(segment_length):
                segment.append((c + t, r + t))
            segments.append(segment)

    # generate the top left to bottom right diagonal segments
    for c in range(num_columns - segment_length + 1):
        for r in range(segment_length - 1, num_rows):
            segment = []
            for t in range(segment_length):
                segment.append((c + t, r - t))
            segments.append(segment)
    return segments
```

This function returns a list of lists of grid locations (tuples of column/row combinations). Each list in the list contains four grid locations. We call each of these lists of four grid locations a *segment*. If any segment from the board is all the same color, that color has won the game.

Being able to quickly search all of the segments on the board is useful for both checking whether a game is over (someone has won) and for evaluating a position.

Hence, you will notice in the next code snippet that we cache the segments for a given size board as a class variable called SEGMENTS in the C4Board class.

Listing 8.14   connectfour.py continued

```
class C4Board(Board):
    NUM_ROWS: int = 6
    NUM_COLUMNS: int = 7
    SEGMENT_LENGTH: int = 4
    SEGMENTS: List[List[Tuple[int, int]]] = generate_segments(NUM_COLUMNS,
     NUM_ROWS, SEGMENT_LENGTH)
```

The C4Board class has an internal class called Column. This class is not strictly necessary because we could use a one-dimensional list to represent the grid as we did for tic-tac-toe or a two-dimensional list just as well. And using the Column class probably slightly decreases performance as opposed to either of those solutions. But thinking about the Connect Four board as a group of seven columns is conceptually powerful and makes writing the rest of the C4Board class slightly easier.

Listing 8.15   connectfour.py continued

```
class Column:
    def __init__(self) -> None:
        self._container: List[C4Piece] = []

    @property
    def full(self) -> bool:
        return len(self._container) == C4Board.NUM_ROWS

    def push(self, item: C4Piece) -> None:
        if self.full:
            raise OverflowError("Trying to push piece to full column")
        self._container.append(item)

    def __getitem__(self, index: int) -> C4Piece:
        if index > len(self._container) - 1:
            return C4Piece.E
        return self._container[index]

    def __repr__(self) -> str:
        return repr(self._container)

    def copy(self) -> C4Board.Column:
        temp: C4Board.Column = C4Board.Column()
        temp._container = self._container.copy()
        return temp
```

The Column class is very similar to the Stack class we used in earlier chapters. This makes sense, because conceptually during play, a Connect Four column is a stack that can be pushed to but never popped. But unlike our earlier stacks, a column in Connect Four has an absolute limit of six items. Also interesting is the __getitem__() special method that allows a Column instance to be subscripted by index. This enables a list of columns to be treated like a two-dimensional list. Note that even if the backing _container does not have an item at some particular row, __getitem__() will still return an empty piece.

The next four methods are relatively similar to their tic-tac-toe equivalents.

Listing 8.16   connectfour.py continued

```python
def __init__(self, position: Optional[List[C4Board.Column]] = None, turn:
    C4Piece = C4Piece.B) -> None:
    if position is None:
        self.position: List[C4Board.Column] = [C4Board.Column() for _ in
    range(C4Board.NUM_COLUMNS)]
    else:
        self.position = position
    self._turn: C4Piece = turn

@property
def turn(self) -> Piece:
    return self._turn

def move(self, location: Move) -> Board:
    temp_position: List[C4Board.Column] = self.position.copy()
    for c in range(C4Board.NUM_COLUMNS):
        temp_position[c] = self.position[c].copy()
    temp_position[location].push(self._turn)
    return C4Board(temp_position, self._turn.opposite)

@property
def legal_moves(self) -> List[Move]:
    return [Move(c) for c in range(C4Board.NUM_COLUMNS) if not
    self.position[c].full]
```

A helper method, _count_segment(), returns the number of black and red pieces in a particular segment. It is followed by the win-checking method, is_win(), which looks at all of the segments in the board and determines a win by using _count_segment() to see if any segments have four of the same color.

Listing 8.17   connectfour.py continued

```python
# Returns the count of black and red pieces in a segment
def _count_segment(self, segment: List[Tuple[int, int]]) -> Tuple[int, int]:
    black_count: int = 0
    red_count: int = 0
    for column, row in segment:
        if self.position[column][row] == C4Piece.B:
            black_count += 1
        elif self.position[column][row] == C4Piece.R:
            red_count += 1
    return black_count, red_count

@property
def is_win(self) -> bool:
    for segment in C4Board.SEGMENTS:
        black_count, red_count = self._count_segment(segment)
        if black_count == 4 or red_count == 4:
            return True
    return False
```

Like `TTTBoard`, `C4Board` can use the abstract base class `Board`'s `is_draw` property without modification.

Finally, to evaluate a position, we will evaluate all of its representative segments, one segment at a time, and sum those evaluations to return a result. A segment that has both red and black pieces will be considered worthless. A segment that has two of the same color and two empties will be considered a score of 1. A segment with three of the same color will be scored 100. Finally, a segment with four of the same color (a win) is scored 1,000,000. If the segment is the opponent's segment, we will negate its score. `_evaluate_segment()` is a helper method that evaluates a single segment using the preceding formula. The composite score of all segments using `_evaluate_segment()` is generated by `evaluate()`.

Listing 8.18 connectfour.py continued

```python
def _evaluate_segment(self, segment: List[Tuple[int, int]], player: Piece) ->
        float:
    black_count, red_count = self._count_segment(segment)
    if red_count > 0 and black_count > 0:
        return 0 # mixed segments are neutral
    count: int = max(red_count, black_count)
    score: float = 0
    if count == 2:
        score = 1
    elif count == 3:
        score = 100
    elif count == 4:
        score = 1000000
    color: C4Piece = C4Piece.B
    if red_count > black_count:
        color = C4Piece.R
    if color != player:
        return -score
    return score

def evaluate(self, player: Piece) -> float:
    total: float = 0
    for segment in C4Board.SEGMENTS:
        total += self._evaluate_segment(segment, player)
    return total

def __repr__(self) -> str:
    display: str = ""
    for r in reversed(range(C4Board.NUM_ROWS)):
        display += "|"
        for c in range(C4Board.NUM_COLUMNS):
            display += f"{self.position[c][r]}" + "|"
        display += "\n"
    return display
```

8.3.2   *A Connect Four AI*

Amazingly, the same `minimax()` and `find_best_move()` functions we developed for tic-tac-toe can be used unchanged with our Connect Four implementation. In the following code snippet, there are only a couple of changes from the code for our tic-tac-toe AI. The big difference is that `max_depth` is now set to 3. That enables the computer's thinking time per move to be reasonable. In other words, our Connect Four AI looks at (evaluates) positions up to three moves in the future.

Listing 8.19   connectfour_ai.py

```python
from minimax import find_best_move
from connectfour import C4Board
from board import Move, Board

board: Board = C4Board()


def get_player_move() -> Move:
    player_move: Move = Move(-1)
    while player_move not in board.legal_moves:
        play: int = int(input("Enter a legal column (0-6):"))
        player_move = Move(play)
    return player_move


if __name__ == "__main__":
    # main game loop
    while True:
        human_move: Move = get_player_move()
        board = board.move(human_move)
        if board.is_win:
            print("Human wins!")
            break
        elif board.is_draw:
            print("Draw!")
            break
        computer_move: Move = find_best_move(board, 3)
        print(f"Computer move is {computer_move}")
        board = board.move(computer_move)
        print(board)
        if board.is_win:
            print("Computer wins!")
            break
        elif board.is_draw:
            print("Draw!")
            break
```

Try playing the Connect Four AI. You will notice that it takes a few seconds to generate each move, unlike the tic-tac-toe AI. It will probably still beat you unless you're carefully thinking about your moves. It at least will not make any completely obvious mistakes. We can improve its play by increasing the depth that it searches, but each computer move will take exponentially longer to compute.

TIP   Did you know Connect Four has been "solved" by computer scientists? To solve a game means to know the best move to play in any position. The best first move in Connect Four is to place your piece in the center column.

8.3.3   *Improving minimax with alpha-beta pruning*

Minimax works well, but we are not getting a very deep search at present. There is a small extension to minimax, known as *alpha-beta pruning*, that can improve search depth by excluding positions in the search that will not result in improvements over positions already searched. This magic is accomplished by keeping track of two values between recursive minimax calls: alpha and beta. *Alpha* represents the evaluation of the best maximizing move found up to this point in the search tree, and *beta* represents the evaluation of the best minimizing move found so far for the opponent. If beta is ever less than or equal to alpha, it's not worth further exploring this branch of the search, because a better or equivalent move has already been found than what will be found farther down this branch. This heuristic decreases the search space significantly.

Here is `alphabeta()` as just described. It should be put into our existing minimax.py file.

Listing 8.20   minimax.py continued

```python
def alphabeta(board: Board, maximizing: bool, original_player: Piece, max_
        depth: int = 8, alpha: float = float("-inf"), beta: float =
        float("inf")) -> float:
    # Base case - terminal position or maximum depth reached
    if board.is_win or board.is_draw or max_depth == 0:
        return board.evaluate(original_player)

    # Recursive case - maximize your gains or minimize the opponent's gains
    if maximizing:
        for move in board.legal_moves:
            result: float = alphabeta(board.move(move), False, original_
    player, max_depth - 1, alpha, beta)
            alpha = max(result, alpha)
            if beta <= alpha:
                break
        return alpha
    else:  # minimizing
        for move in board.legal_moves:
            result = alphabeta(board.move(move), True, original_player, max_
    depth - 1, alpha, beta)
            beta = min(result, beta)
            if beta <= alpha:
                break
        return beta
```

Now you can make two very small changes to take advantage of our new function. Change `find_best_move()` in minimax.py to use `alphabeta()` instead of `minimax()`, and change the search depth in connectfour_ai.py to 5 from 3. With these changes, your average Connect Four player will not be able to beat our AI. On my computer, using `minimax()` at a depth of 5, our Connect Four AI takes about 3 minutes per move, whereas using `alphabeta()` at the same depth takes about 30 seconds per move. That's one sixth of the time! That is quite an incredible improvement.

8.4   Minimax improvements beyond alpha-beta pruning

The algorithms presented in this chapter have been deeply studied, and many improvements have been found over the years. Some of those improvements are game-specific, such as "bitboards" in chess decreasing the time it takes to generate legal moves, but most are general techniques that can be utilized for any game.

One common technique is iterative deepening. In iterative deepening, first the search function is run to a maximum depth of 1. Then it is run to a maximum depth of 2. Then it is run to a maximum depth of 3, and so on. When a specified time limit is reached, the search is stopped. The result from the last completed depth is returned.

The examples in this chapter were hardcoded to a certain depth. This is okay if the game is played without a game clock and time limits or if we do not care how long the computer takes to think. Iterative deepening enables an AI to take a fixed amount of time to find its next move instead of a fixed amount of search depth with a variable amount of time to complete it.

Another potential improvement is quiescence search. In this technique, the minimax search tree will be further expanded along routes that cause large changes in position (captures in chess, for instance), rather than routes that have relatively "quiet" positions. In this way, ideally the search will not waste computing time on boring positions that are unlikely to gain the player a significant advantage.

The two best ways to improve upon minimax search is to search to a greater depth in the allotted amount of time or improve upon the evaluation function used to assess a position. Searching more positions in the same amount of time requires spending less time on each position. This can come from finding code efficiencies or using faster hardware, but it can also come at the expense of the latter improvement technique—improving the evaluation of each position. Using more parameters or heuristics to evaluate a position may take more time, but it can ultimately lead to a better engine that needs less search depth to find a good move.

Some evaluation functions used for minimax search with alpha-beta pruning in chess have dozens of heuristics. Genetic algorithms have even been used to tune these heuristics. How much should the capture of a knight be worth in a game of chess? Should it be worth as much as a bishop? These heuristics can be the secret sauce that separates a great chess engine from one that is just good.

8.5   Real-world applications

Minimax, combined with further extensions like alpha-beta pruning, is the basis of most modern chess engines. It has been applied to a wide variety of strategy games with great success. In fact, most of the board-game artificial opponents that you play on your computer probably use some form of minimax.

Minimax (with its extensions, like alpha-beta pruning) has been so effective in chess that it led to the famous 1997 defeat of the human chess world champion, Gary Kasparov, by Deep Blue, a chess-playing computer made by IBM. The match was a highly anticipated and game-changing event. Chess was seen as a domain of the highest intellectual caliber. The fact that a computer could exceed human ability in chess meant, to some, that artificial intelligence should be taken seriously.

Two decades later, the vast majority of chess engines still are based on minimax. Today's minimax-based chess engines far exceed the strength of the world's best human chess players. New machine-learning techniques are starting to challenge pure minimax-based (with extensions) chess engines, but they have yet to definitively prove their superiority in chess.

The higher the branching factor for a game, the less effective minimax will be. The branching factor is the average number of potential moves in a position for some game. This is why recent advances in computer play of the board game Go have required exploration of other domains, like machine learning. A machine-learning-based Go AI has now defeated the best human Go player. The branching factor (and therefore the search space) for Go is simply overwhelming for minimax-based algorithms that attempt to generate trees containing future positions. But Go is the exception rather than the rule. Most traditional board games (checkers, chess, Connect Four, Scrabble, and the like) have search spaces small enough that minimax-based techniques can work well.

If you are implementing a new board-game artificial opponent or even an AI for a turn-based purely computer-oriented game, minimax is probably the first algorithm you should reach for. Minimax can also be used for economic and political simulations, as well as experiments in game theory. Alpha-beta pruning should work with any form of minimax.

8.6 *Exercises*

1 Add unit tests to tic-tac-toe to ensure that the properties `legal_moves`, `is_win`, and `is_draw` work correctly.

2 Create minimax unit tests for Connect Four.

3 The code in tictactoe_ai.py and connectfour_ai.py is almost identical. Refactor it into two methods that can be used for either game.

4 Change connectfour_ai.py to have the computer play against itself. Does the first player or the second player win? Is it the same player every time?

5 Can you find a way (through profiling the existing code or otherwise) to optimize the evaluation method in connectfour.py to enable a higher search depth in the same amount of time?

6 Use the `alphabeta()` function developed in this chapter together with a Python library for legal chess move generation and maintenance of chess game state to develop a chess AI.

Miscellaneous problems

Throughout this book we have covered a myriad of problem-solving techniques relevant to modern software development tasks. To study each technique, we have explored famous computer science problems. But not every famous problem fits the mold of the prior chapters. This chapter is a gathering point for famous problems that did not quite fit into any other chapter. Think of these problems as a bonus: more interesting problems with less scaffolding around them.

9.1 The knapsack problem

The knapsack problem is an optimization problem that takes a common computational need—finding the best use of limited resources given a finite set of usage options—and spins it into a fun story. A thief enters a home with the intent to steal. He has a knapsack, and he is limited in what he can steal by the capacity of the knapsack. How does he figure out what to put into the knapsack? The problem is illustrated in figure 9.1.

If the thief could take any amount of any item, he could simply divide each item's value by its weight to figure out the most valuable items for the available capacity. But to make the scenario more realistic, let's say that the thief cannot take half of an item (such as 2.5 televisions). Instead, we will come up with a way to solve the 0/1 variant of the problem, so-called because it enforces another rule: The thief may only take one or none of each item.

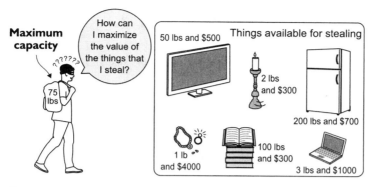

Figure 9.1 **The burglar must decide what items to steal because the capacity of the knapsack is limited.**

First, let's define a `NamedTuple` to hold our items.

Listing 9.1 knapsack.py

```python
from typing import NamedTuple, List


class Item(NamedTuple):
    name: str
    weight: int
    value: float
```

If we tried to solve this problem using a brute-force approach, we would look at every combination of items available to be put in the knapsack. For the mathematically inclined, this is known as a *powerset*, and a powerset of a set (in our case, the set of items) has 2^N different possible subsets, where N is the number of items. Therefore, we would need to analyze 2^N combinations ($O(2^N)$). This is okay for a small number of items, but it is untenable for a large number. Any approach that solves a problem using an exponential number of steps is an approach we want to avoid.

Instead, we will use a technique known as *dynamic programming*, which is similar in concept to memoization (chapter 1). Instead of solving a problem outright with a brute-force approach, in dynamic programming one solves subproblems that make up the larger problem, stores those results, and utilizes those stored results to solve the larger problem. As long as the capacity of the knapsack is considered in discrete steps, the problem can be solved with dynamic programming.

For instance, to solve the problem for a knapsack with a 3-pound capacity and three items, we can first solve the problem for a 1-pound capacity and one possible item, 2-pound capacity and one possible item, and 3-pound capacity and one possible item. We can then use the results of that solution to solve the problem for 1-pound capacity and two possible items, 2-pound capacity and two possible items, and 3-pound capacity and two possible items. Finally, we can solve for all three possible items.

All along the way we will fill in a table that tells us the best possible solution for each combination of items and capacity. Our function will first fill in the table and then figure out the solution based on the table.[1]

Listing 9.2   knapsack.py continued

```python
def knapsack(items: List[Item], max_capacity: int) -> List[Item]:
    # build up dynamic programming table
    table: List[List[float]] = [[0.0 for _ in range(max_capacity + 1)] for _
    in range(len(items) + 1)]
    for i, item in enumerate(items):
        for capacity in range(1, max_capacity + 1):
            previous_items_value: float = table[i][capacity]
            if capacity >= item.weight: # item fits in knapsack
                value_freeing_weight_for_item: float = table[i][capacity -
    item.weight]
                # only take if more valuable than previous item
                table[i + 1][capacity] = max(value_freeing_weight_for_item +
    item.value, previous_items_value)
            else: # no room for this item
                table[i + 1][capacity] = previous_items_value
    # figure out solution from table
    solution: List[Item] = []
    capacity = max_capacity
    for i in range(len(items), 0, -1): # work backwards
        # was this item used?
        if table[i - 1][capacity] != table[i][capacity]:
            solution.append(items[i - 1])
            # if the item was used, remove its weight
            capacity -= items[i - 1].weight
    return solution
```

The inner loop of the first part of this function will execute $N * C$ times, where N is the number of items and C is the maximum capacity of the knapsack. Therefore, the algorithm performs in $O(N * C)$ time, a significant improvement over the brute-force approach for a large number of items. For instance, for the 11 items that follow, a brute-force algorithm would need to examine 2^11 or 2,048 combinations. The preceding dynamic programming function will execute 825 times, because the maximum capacity of the knapsack in question is 75 arbitrary units (11 * 75). This difference would grow exponentially with more items.

Let's look at the solution in action.

---

[1] I studied several resources to write this solution, the most authoritative of which was *Algorithms* (Addison-Wesley, 1988), 2nd edition, by Robert Sedgewick (p. 596). I looked at several examples of the 0/1 knapsack problem on Rosetta Code, most notably the Python dynamic programming solution (http://mng.bz/kx8C), which this function is largely a port of, back from the Swift version of the book. (It went from Python to Swift and back to Python again.)

Listing 9.3 knapsack.py continued

```python
if __name__ == "__main__":
    items: List[Item] = [Item("television", 50, 500),
                         Item("candlesticks", 2, 300),
                         Item("stereo", 35, 400),
                         Item("laptop", 3, 1000),
                         Item("food", 15, 50),
                         Item("clothing", 20, 800),
                         Item("jewelry", 1, 4000),
                         Item("books", 100, 300),
                         Item("printer", 18, 30),
                         Item("refrigerator", 200, 700),
                         Item("painting", 10, 1000)]
    print(knapsack(items, 75))
```

If you inspect the results printed to the console, you will see that the optimal items to take are the painting, jewelry, clothing, laptop, stereo, and candlesticks. Here's some sample output showing the most valuable items for the thief to steal, given the limited-capacity knapsack:

```
[Item(name='painting', weight=10, value=1000), Item(name='jewelry', weight=1,
    value=4000), Item(name='clothing', weight=20, value=800),
    Item(name='laptop', weight=3, value=1000), Item(name='stereo',
    weight=35, value=400), Item(name='candlesticks', weight=2, value=300)]
```

To get a better idea of how this all works, let's look at some of the particulars of the function:

```python
for i, item in enumerate(items):
    for capacity in range(1, max_capacity + 1):
```

For each possible number of items, we loop through all of the capacities in a linear fashion, up to the maximum capacity of the knapsack. Notice that I say "each possible number of items" instead of each item. When i equals 2, it does not just represent item 2. It represents the possible combinations of the first two items for every explored capacity. item is the next item that we are considering stealing:

```python
previous_items_value: float = table[i][capacity]
if capacity >= item.weight: # item fits in knapsack
```

previous_items_value is the value of the last combination of items at the current capacity being explored. For each possible combination of items, we consider whether adding in the latest "new" item is even possible.

If the item weighs more than the knapsack capacity we are considering, we simply copy over the value for the last combination of items that we considered for the capacity in question:

```python
else: # no room for this item
    table[i + 1][capacity] = previous_items_value
```

Otherwise, we consider whether adding in the "new" item will result in a higher value than the last combination of items at that capacity that we considered. We do this by adding the value of the item to the value already computed in the table for the previous combination of items at a capacity equal to the item's weight, subtracted from the current capacity we are considering. If this value is higher than the last combination of items at the current capacity, we insert it; otherwise, we insert the last value:

```
value_freeing_weight_for_item: float = table[i][capacity - item.weight]
# only take if more valuable than previous item
table[i + 1][capacity] = max(value_freeing_weight_for_item + item.value,
    previous_items_value)
```

That concludes building up the table. To actually find which items are in the solution, though, we need to work backward from the highest capacity and the final explored combination of items:

```
for i in range(len(items), 0, -1): # work backwards
    # was this item used?
    if table[i - 1][capacity] != table[i][capacity]:
```

We start from the end and loop through our table from right to left, checking whether there was a change in the value inserted into the table at each stop. If there was, that means we added the new item that was considered in a particular combination because the combination was more valuable than the prior one. Therefore, we add that item to the solution. Also, capacity is decreased by the weight of the item, which can be thought of as moving up the table:

```
solution.append(items[i - 1])
# if the item was used, remove its weight
capacity -= items[i - 1].weight
```

> **NOTE** Throughout both the build-up of the table and the solution search, you may have noticed some manipulation of iterators and table size by 1. This is done for convenience from a programmatic perspective. Think about how the problem is built from the bottom up. When the problem begins, we are dealing with a zero-capacity knapsack. If you work your way up from the bottom in a table, it will become clear why we need the extra row and column.

Are you still confused? Table 9.1 is the table the knapsack() function builds. It would be quite a large table for the preceding problem, so instead, let's look at a table for a knapsack with 3-pound capacity and three items: matches (1 pound), flashlight (2 pounds), and book (1 pound). Assume those items are valued at $5, $10, and $15, respectively.

Table 9.1   An example of a knapsack problem of three items

	0 lb.	1 lb.	2 lb.	3 lb.
Matches (1 lb., $5)	0	5	5	5
Flashlight (2 lbs., $10)	0	5	10	15
Book (1 lb., $15)	0	15	20	25

As you look across the table from left to right, the weight is increasing (how much you are trying to fit in the knapsack). As you look down the table from top to bottom, the number of items you are attempting to fit is increasing. On the first row, you are only trying to fit the matches. On the second row, you fit the most valuable combination of the matches and the flashlight that the knapsack can hold. On the third row, you fit the most valuable combination of all three items.

As an exercise to facilitate your understanding, try filling in a blank version of this table yourself, using the algorithm described in the `knapsack()` function with these same three items. Then use the algorithm at the end of the function to read back the right items from the table. This table corresponds to the `table` variable in the function.

9.2 The Traveling Salesman Problem

The Traveling Salesman Problem is one of the most classic and talked-about problems in all of computing. A salesman must visit all of the cities on a map exactly once, returning to his start city at the end of the journey. There is a direct connection from every city to every other city, and the salesman may visit the cities in any order. What is the shortest path for the salesman?

The problem can be thought of as a graph problem (chapter 4), with the cities being the vertices and the connections between them being the edges. Your first instinct might be to find the minimum spanning tree, as described in chapter 4. Unfortunately, the solution to the Traveling Salesman Problem is not so simple. The minimum spanning tree is the shortest way to connect all of the cities, but it does not provide the shortest path for visiting all of them exactly once.

Although the problem, as posed, appears fairly simple, there is no algorithm that can solve it quickly for an arbitrary number of cities. What do I mean by "quickly"? I mean that the problem is what is known as *NP hard*. An NP-hard (non-deterministic polynomial hard) problem is a problem for which no polynomial time algorithm exists. (The time it takes is a polynomial function of the size of the input.) As the number of cities that the salesman needs to visit increases, the difficulty of solving the problem grows exceptionally quickly. It is much harder to solve the problem for 20 cities than 10. It is impossible (to the best of current knowledge), in a reasonable amount of time, to solve the problem perfectly (optimally) for millions of cities.

> **NOTE** The naive approach to the Traveling Salesman Problem is O($n!$). Why this is the case is discussed in section 9.2.2. We suggest reading section 9.2.1 before reading 9.2.2, though, because the implementation of a naive solution to the problem will make its complexity obvious.

9.2.1 The naive approach

The naive approach to the problem is simply to try every possible combination of cities. Attempting the naive approach will illustrate the difficulty of the problem and this approach's unsuitability for brute-force attempts at larger scales.

OUR SAMPLE DATA

In our version of the Traveling Salesman Problem, the salesman is interested in visiting five of the major cities of Vermont. We will not specify a starting (and therefore ending) city. Figure 9.2 illustrates the five cities and the driving distances between them. Note that there is a distance listed for the route between every pair of cities.

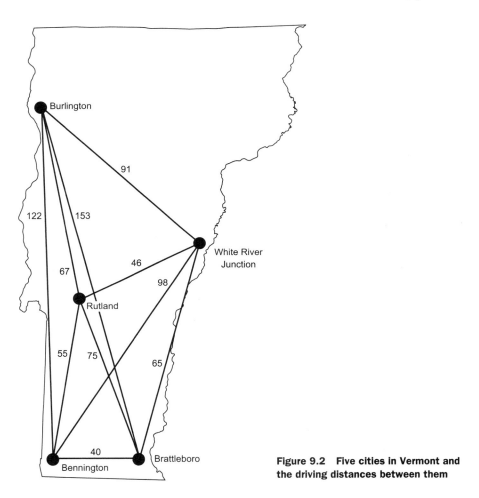

Figure 9.2   Five cities in Vermont and the driving distances between them

Perhaps you have seen driving distances in table form before. In a driving-distance table, one can easily look up the distance between any two cities. Table 9.2 lists the driving distances for the five cities in the problem.

Table 9.2 Driving distances between cities in Vermont

	Rutland	Burlington	White River Junction	Bennington	Brattleboro
Rutland	0	67	46	55	75
Burlington	67	0	91	122	153
White River Junction	46	91	0	98	65
Bennington	55	122	98	0	40
Brattleboro	75	153	65	40	0

We will need to codify both the cities and the distances between them for our problem. To make the distances between cities easy to look up, we will use a dictionary of dictionaries, with the outer set of keys representing the first of a pair and the inner set of keys representing the second. This will be the type Dict[str, Dict[str, int]], and it will allow lookups like vt_distances["Rutland"]["Burlington"], which should return 67.

Listing 9.4 tsp.py

```python
from typing import Dict, List, Iterable, Tuple
from itertools import permutations

vt_distances: Dict[str, Dict[str, int]] = {
    "Rutland":
        {"Burlington": 67,
         "White River Junction": 46,
         "Bennington": 55,
         "Brattleboro": 75},
    "Burlington":
        {"Rutland": 67,
         "White River Junction": 91,
         "Bennington": 122,
         "Brattleboro": 153},
    "White River Junction":
        {"Rutland": 46,
         "Burlington": 91,
         "Bennington": 98,
         "Brattleboro": 65},
    "Bennington":
        {"Rutland": 55,
         "Burlington": 122,
         "White River Junction": 98,
         "Brattleboro": 40},
    "Brattleboro":
        {"Rutland": 75,
         "Burlington": 153,
         "White River Junction": 65,
         "Bennington": 40}
}
```

FINDING ALL PERMUTATIONS

The naive approach to solving the Traveling Salesman Problem requires generating every possible permutation of the cities. There are many permutation-generation algorithms; they are simple enough to ideate that you could almost certainly come up with one on your own.

One common approach is backtracking. You first saw backtracking in chapter 3 in the context of solving a constraint-satisfaction problem. In constraint-satisfaction problem solving, backtracking is used after a partial solution is found that does not satisfy the problem's constraints. In such a case, you revert to an earlier state and continue the search along a different path than that which led to the incorrect partial solution.

To find all of the permutations of the items in a list (say, our cities), you could also use backtracking. After making a swap between elements to go down a path of further permutations, you can backtrack to the state before the swap was made so that a different swap can be made in order to go down a different path.

Luckily, there is no need to reinvent the wheel by writing a permutation-generation algorithm, because the Python standard library has a `permutations()` function in its `itertools` module. In the following code snippet, we generate all of the permutations of the Vermont cities that our travelling salesman would need to visit. Because there are five cities, this is 5! (5 factorial), or 120 permutations.

Listing 9.5   tsp.py continued

```
vt_cities: Iterable[str] = vt_distances.keys()
city_permutations: Iterable[Tuple[str, ...]] = permutations(vt_cities)
```

BRUTE-FORCE SEARCH

We can now generate all of the permutations of the city list, but this is not quite the same as a Traveling Salesman Problem path. Recall that in the Traveling Salesman Problem, the salesman must return, at the end, to the same city that he started in. We can easily add the first city in a permutation to the end of a permutation using a list comprehension.

Listing 9.6   tsp.py continued

```
tsp_paths: List[Tuple[str, ...]] = [c + (c[0],) for c in city_permutations]
```

We are now ready to try testing the paths we have permuted. A brute-force search approach painstakingly looks at every path in a list of paths and uses the distance between two cities lookup table (`vt_distances`) to calculate each path's total distance. It prints both the shortest path and that path's total distance.

Listing 9.7   tsp.py continued

```
if __name__ == "__main__":
    best_path: Tuple[str, ...]
    min_distance: int = 99999999999 # arbitrarily high number
    for path in tsp_paths:
```

```
distance: int = 0
last: str = path[0]
for next in path[1:]:
    distance += vt_distances[last][next]
    last = next
if distance < min_distance:
    min_distance = distance
    best_path = path
print(f"The shortest path is {best_path} in {min_distance} miles.")
```

We finally can brute-force the cities of Vermont, finding the shortest path to reach all five. The output should look something like the following, and the best path is illustrated in figure 9.3.

```
The shortest path is ('Rutland', 'Burlington', 'White River Junction',
    'Brattleboro', 'Bennington', 'Rutland') in 318 miles.
```

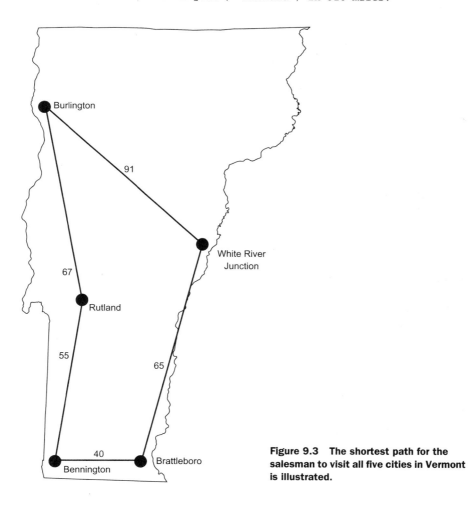

Figure 9.3 The shortest path for the salesman to visit all five cities in Vermont is illustrated.

9.2.2   *Taking it to the next level*

There is no easy answer to the Traveling Salesman Problem. Our naive approach quickly becomes infeasible. The number of permutations generated is n factorial ($n!$), where n is the number of cities in the problem. If we were to include just one more city (six instead of five), the number of evaluated paths would grow by a factor of six. Then it would be seven times harder to solve the problem for just one more city after that. This is not a scalable approach!

In the real world, the naive approach to the Traveling Salesman Problem is seldom used. Most algorithms for instances of the problem with a large number of cities are approximations. They try to solve the problem for a near-optimal solution. The near-optimal solution may be within a small known band of the perfect solution. (For example, perhaps they will be no more than 5% less efficient.)

Two techniques that have already appeared in this book have been used to attempt the Traveling Salesman Problem on large data sets. Dynamic programming, which we used in the knapsack problem earlier in this chapter, is one approach. Another is genetic algorithms, as described in chapter 5. Many journal articles have been published attributing genetic algorithms to near-optimal solutions for the traveling salesman with large numbers of cities.

9.3   *Phone number mnemonics*

Before there were smartphones with built-in address books, telephones included letters on each of the keys on their number pads. The reason for these letters was to provide easy mnemonics by which to remember phone numbers. In the United States, typically the 1 key would have no letters, 2 would have ABC, 3 DEF, 4 GHI, 5 JKL, 6 MNO, 7 PQRS, 8 TUV, 9 WXYZ, and 0 no letters. For example, 1-800-MY-APPLE corresponds to the phone number 1-800-69-27753. Once in a while you will still find these mnemonics in advertisements, so the numbers on the keypad have made their way into modern smartphone apps, as evidenced by figure 9.4.

How does one come up with a new mnemonic for a phone number? In the 1990s there was popular shareware to help with the effort. These pieces of software would generate every permutation of a phone number's letters and then look through a dictionary to find words that were contained in the permutations. They would then show the permutations

Figure 9.4   The Phone app in iOS retains the letters on keys that its telephone forebears contained.

with the most complete words to the user. We will do the first half of the problem. The dictionary lookup will be left as an exercise.

In the last problem, when we looked at permutation generation, we used the `permutations()` function to generate the potential paths for the Traveling Salesman Problem. However, as was mentioned, there are many different ways to generate permutations. For this problem in particular, instead of swapping two positions in an existing permutation to generate a new one, we will generate each permutation from the ground up. We will do this by looking at the potential letters that match each numeral in the phone number and continually add more options to the end as we go to each successive numeral. This is a kind of Cartesian product, and once again, the Python standard library's `itertools` module has us covered.

First, we will define a mapping of numerals to potential letters.

Listing 9.8 tsp.py continued

```python
from typing import Dict, Tuple, Iterable, List
from itertools import product

phone_mapping: Dict[str, Tuple[str, ...]] = {"1": ("1",),
                                             "2": ("a", "b", "c"),
                                             "3": ("d", "e", "f"),
                                             "4": ("g", "h", "i"),
                                             "5": ("j", "k", "l"),
                                             "6": ("m", "n", "o"),
                                             "7": ("p", "q", "r", "s"),
                                             "8": ("t", "u", "v"),
                                             "9": ("w", "x", "y", "z"),
                                             "0": ("0",)}
```

The next function combines all of those possibilities for each numeral into a list of possible mnemonics for a given phone number. It does this by creating a list of tuples of potential letters for each digit in the phone number and then combining them through the Cartesian product function `product()` from `itertools`. Note the use of the unpack (`*`) operator to use the tuples in `letter_tuples` as the arguments for `product()`.

Listing 9.9 tsp.py continued

```python
def possible_mnemonics(phone_number: str) -> Iterable[Tuple[str, ...]]:
    letter_tuples: List[Tuple[str, ...]] = []
    for digit in phone_number:
        letter_tuples.append(phone_mapping.get(digit, (digit,)))
    return product(*letter_tuples)
```

Now we can find all of the possible mnemonics for a phone number.

Listing 9.10 tsp.py continued

```python
if __name__ == "__main__":
    phone_number: str = input("Enter a phone number:")
    print("Here are the potential mnemonics:")
```

```
for mnemonic in possible_mnemonics(phone_number):
    print("".join(mnemonic))
```

It turns out that the phone number 1440787 can also be written as 1GH0STS. That is easier to remember.

9.4   *Real-world applications*

Dynamic programming, as used with the knapsack problem, is a widely applicable technique that can make seemingly intractable problems solvable by breaking them into constituent smaller problems and building up a solution from those parts. The knapsack problem itself is related to other optimization problems where a finite amount of resources (the capacity of the knapsack) must be allocated amongst a finite but exhaustive set of options (the items to steal). Imagine a college that needs to allocate its athletic budget. It does not have enough money to fund every team, and it has some expectation of how much alumni donations each team will bring in. It can run a knapsack-like problem to optimize the budget's allocation. Problems like this are common in the real world.

The Traveling Salesman Problem is an everyday occurrence for shipping and distribution companies like UPS and FedEx. Package delivery companies want their drivers to travel the shortest routes possible. Not only does this make the drivers' jobs more pleasant, but it also saves fuel and maintenance costs. We all travel for work or for pleasure, and finding optimal routes when visiting many destinations can save resources. But the Traveling Salesman Problem is not just for routing travel; it comes up in almost any routing scenario that requires singular visits to nodes. Although a minimum spanning tree (chapter 4) may minimize the amount of wire needed to connect a neighborhood, it does not tell us the optimal amount of wire if every house must be forward-connected to just one other house as part of a giant circuit that returns to its origination. The Traveling Salesman Problem does.

Permutation-generation techniques like the ones used in the naive approach to the Traveling Salesman Problem and the phone number mnemonics problem are useful for testing all sorts of brute-force algorithms. For instance, if you were trying to crack a short password, you could generate every possible permutation of the characters that could potentially be in the password. Practitioners of such large-scale permutation-generation tasks would be wise to use an especially efficient permutation-generation algorithm like Heap's algorithm.[2]

9.5   *Exercises*

1 Reprogram the naive approach to the Traveling Salesman Problem, using the graph framework from chapter 4.
2 Implement a genetic algorithm, as described in chapter 5, to solve the Traveling Salesman Problem. Start with the simple data set of Vermont cities described in

[2] Robert Sedgewick, "Permutation Generation Methods" (Princeton University), http://mng.bz/87Te.

this chapter. Can you get the genetic algorithm to arrive at the optimal solution in a short amount of time? Then attempt the problem with an increasingly large number of cities. How well does the genetic algorithm hold up? You can find a large number of data sets specifically made for the Traveling Salesman Problem by searching the web. Develop a testing framework for checking the efficiency of your method.

3 Use a dictionary with the phone number mnemonics program and return only permutations that contain valid dictionary words.

appendix A
Glossary

This appendix defines a selection of key terms from throughout the book.

activation function   A function that transforms the output of a *neuron* in an *artificial neural network*, generally to render it capable of handling nonlinear transformations or to ensure its output value is clamped within some range (chapter 7).

acyclic   A *graph* with no *cycles* (chapter 4).

admissible heuristic   A *heuristic* for the A* search algorithm that never overestimates the cost to reach the goal (chapter 2).

artificial neural network   A simulation of a biological *neural network* using computational tools to solve problems not easily reduced into forms amenable to traditional algorithmic approaches. Note that the operation of an *artificial neural network* generally strays significantly from its biological counterpart (chapter 7).

auto-memoization   A version of *memoization* implemented at the language level, in which the results of function calls without side effects are stored for lookup upon further identical calls (chapter 1).

backpropagation   A technique used for *training neural network* weights according to a set of inputs with known-correct outputs. Partial derivatives are used to calculate each weight's "responsibility" for the error between actual results and expected results. These *deltas* are used to update the weights for future runs (chapter 7).

backtracking   Returning to an earlier decision point (to go a different direction than was last pursued) after hitting a wall in a search problem (chapter 3).

bit string   A data structure that stores a sequence of 1s and 0s represented using a single bit of memory for each. This is sometimes referred to as a *bit vector* or *bit array* (chapter 1).

centroid   The center point in a *cluster*. Typically, each dimension of this point is the mean of the rest of the points in that dimension (chapter 6).

chromosome   In a genetic algorithm, each individual in the *population* is referred to as a *chromosome* (chapter 5).

cluster   See *clustering* (chapter 6).

clustering   An *unsupervised learning* technique that divides a data set into groups of related points, known as *clusters* (chapter 6).

codon   A combination of three *nucleotides* that form an amino acid (chapter 2).

compression   Encoding data (changing its form) to require less space (chapter 1).

connected   A graph property that indicates there is a *path* from any *vertex* to any other *vertex* (chapter 4).

constraint   A requirement that must be fulfilled in order for a constraint-satisfaction problem to be solved (chapter 3).

crossover   In a genetic algorithm, combining individuals from the *population* to create offspring that are a mixture of the parents and that will be a part of the next *generation* (chapter 5).

CSV   A text interchange format in which rows of data sets have their values separated by commas, and the rows themselves are generally separated by newline characters. *CSV* stands for *comma-separated values*. CSV is a common export format from spreadsheets and databases (chapter 7).

cycle   A *path* in a *graph* that visits the same *vertex* twice without *backtracking* (chapter 4).

decompression   Reversing the process of *compression*, returning the data to its original form (chapter 1).

deep learning   Something of a buzzword, deep learning can refer to any of several techniques that use advanced machine-learning algorithms to analyze big data. Most commonly, deep learning refers to using multilayer *artificial neural networks* to solve problems using large data sets (chapter 7).

delta   A value that is representative of a gap between the expected value of a weight in a *neural network* and its actual value. The expected value is determined through the use of *training* data and *backpropagation* (chapter 7).

digraph   See *directed graph* (chapter 4).

directed graph   Also known as a *digraph*, a directed graph is a *graph* in which *edges* may only be traversed in one direction (chapter 4).

domain   The possible values of a *variable* in a constraint-satisfaction problem (chapter 3).

dynamic programming   Instead of solving a large problem outright using a brute-force approach, in dynamic programming the problem is broken up into smaller subproblems that are each more manageable (chapter 9).

edge   A connection between two *vertices* (nodes) in a *graph* (chapter 4).

exclusive or   See *XOR* (chapter 1).

feed-forward   A type of *neural network* in which signals propagate in one direction (chapter 7).

fitness function   A function that evaluates the effectiveness of a potential solution to a problem (chapter 5).

generation   One round in the evaluation of a genetic algorithm; also used to refer to the *population* of individuals active in a round (chapter 5).

genetic programming   Programs that modify themselves using the *selection, crossover,* and *mutation* operators to find solutions to programming problems that are non-obvious (chapter 5).

gradient descent   The method of modifying an *artificial neural network*'s weights using the *deltas* calculated during *backpropagation* and the *learning rate* (chapter 7).

graph   An abstract mathematical construct that is used for modeling a real-world problem by dividing the problem into a set of *connected* nodes. The nodes are known as *vertices*, and the connections are known as *edges* (chapter 4).

greedy algorithm   An algorithm that always selects the best immediate choice at any decision point, hopeful that it will lead to the globally optimal solution (chapter 4).

heuristic   An intuition about the way to solve a problem that points in the right direction (chapter 2).

hidden layer   Any layers between the *input layer* and the *output layer* in a *feed-forward artificial neural network* (chapter 7).

infinite loop   A loop that does not terminate (chapter 1).

infinite recursion   A set of recursive calls that does not terminate but instead continues to make additional recursive calls. Analogous to an *infinite loop*. Usually caused by the lack of a base case (chapter 1).

input layer   The first layer of a *feed-forward artificial neural network* that receives its input from some kind of external entity (chapter 7).

learning rate   A value, usually a constant, used to adjust the rate at which weights are modified in an *artificial neural network*, based on calculated *deltas* (chapter 7).

memoization   A technique in which the results of computational tasks are stored for later retrieval from memory, saving additional computation time to re-create the same results (chapter 1).

minimum spanning tree   A *spanning tree* that connects all vertices using the minimum total weight of *edges* (chapter 4).

mutate   In a genetic algorithm, randomly changing some property of an individual before it is included in the next *generation* (chapter 5).

natural selection   The evolutionary process by which well-adapted organisms succeed and poorly adapted organisms fail. Given a limited set of resources in the environment, the organisms best suited to leverage those resources will survive and propagate. Over several *generations*, this leads to helpful traits being propagated amongst a *population*, hence being naturally selected by the constraints of the environment (chapter 5).

neural network   A network of multiple *neurons* that act in concert to process information. *Neurons* are often thought about as being organized in layers (chapter 7).

neuron   An individual nerve cell, such as those in the human brain (chapter 7).

normalization   The process of making different types of data comparable (chapter 6).

NP-hard   A problem that belongs to a class of problems for which there is no known polynomial time algorithm to solve (chapter 9).

nucleotide   One instance of one of the four bases of DNA: adenine (A), cytosine (C), guanine (G), and thymine (T) (chapter 2).

output layer   The last layer in a *feed-forward artificial neural network* that is used for determining the result of the network for a given input and problem (chapter 7).

path   A set of *edges* that connects two vertices in a *graph* (chapter 4).

ply   A turn (often thought of as a move) in a two-player game (chapter 8).

population   In a genetic algorithm, the population is the collection of individuals (each representing a potential solution to the problem) competing to solve the problem (chapter 5).

priority queue   A data structure that pops items based on a "priority" ordering. For instance, a priority queue may be used with a collection of emergency calls in order to respond to the highest-priority calls first (chapter 2).

queue   An abstract data structure that enforces the ordering FIFO (First-In-First-Out). A queue implementation provides at least the operations push and pop for adding and removing elements, respectively (chapter 2).

recursive function   A function that calls itself (chapter 1).

selection   The process of selecting individuals in a *generation* of a genetic algorithm for reproduction to create individuals for the next *generation* (chapter 5).

sigmoid function   One of a set of popular *activation functions* used in *artificial neural networks*. The eponymous sigmoid function always returns a value between 0 and 1. It is also useful for ensuring that results beyond just linear transformations can be represented by the network (chapter 7).

SIMD instructions   Microprocessor instructions optimized for doing calculations using vectors, also sometimes known as vector instructions. *SIMD* stands for *single instruction, multiple data* (chapter 7).

spanning tree   A *tree* that connects every *vertex* in a *graph* (chapter 4).

stack   An abstract data structure that enforces the Last-In-First-Out (LIFO) ordering. A stack implementation provides at least the operations push and pop for adding and removing elements, respectively (chapter 2).

supervised learning   Any machine-learning technique in which the algorithm is somehow guided toward correct results using outside resources (chapter 7).

synapses   Gaps between *neurons* in which neurotransmitters are released to allow for the conduction of electrical current. In layman's terms, these are the connections between *neurons* (chapter 7).

training   A phase in which an *artificial neural network* has its weights adjusted by using *backpropagation* with known-correct outputs for some given inputs (chapter 7).

tree   A *graph* that has only one *path* between any two vertices. A tree is *acyclic* (chapter 4).

unsupervised learning   Any machine-learning technique that does not use foreknowledge to reach its conclusions—in other words, a technique that is not guided but instead runs on its own (chapter 6).

variable   In the context of a constraint-satisfaction problem, a variable is some parameter that must be solved for as part of the problem's solution. The possible values of the variable are its *domain*. The requirements for a solution are one or more *constraints* (chapter 3).

vertex   A single node in a *graph* (chapter 4).

XOR   A logical bitwise operation that returns `true` when either of its operands is true but not when both are true or neither is true. The abbreviation stands for *exclusive or*. In Python, the ^ operator is used for XOR (chapter 1).

z-score   The number of standard deviations a data point is away from the mean of a data set (chapter 6).

appendix B
More resources

Where should you go next? This book covered a wide swath of topics, and this appendix will connect you with great resources that will help you explore them further.

B.1 Python

As was stated in the introduction, *Classic Computer Science Problems in Python* assumes you have at least an intermediate knowledge of the Python language. Here, I list two Python books that I personally have used and recommend to take your Python knowledge to the next level. These titles are not appropriate for Python beginners (instead, check out *The Quick Python Book* by Naomi Ceder [Manning, 2018] for that), but rather can turn intermediate Python users into advanced Python users.

- Luciano Ramalho, *Fluent Python: Clear, Concise, and Effective Programming* (O'Reilly, 2015)
  - One of the only popular Python language books that doesn't straddle the line between beginner and intermediate/advanced; this book is clearly aimed at intermediate/advanced programmers
  - Covers a large swath of advanced Python topics
  - Teaches best practices; this is the book that will teach you to write "Pythonic" code
  - Contains numerous code examples for every topic and explains the inner workings of the Python standard library
  - Can be a bit verbose in parts, but you can easily skip those bits
- David Beazley and Brian K. Jones, *Python Cookbook*, 3rd edition (O'Reilly, 2013)
  - Teaches common everyday programming tasks by example
  - Some of the tasks go well beyond beginners' tasks.
  - Makes strong use of the Python standard library

– A little dated (doesn't include the latest standard library tools) due to its five-year-old release date; I hope a fourth edition will come out soon

B.2 *Algorithms and data structures*

To quote this book's introduction, "This is not a data structures and algorithms textbook." There is little use of big-O notation in this book, and there are no mathematical proofs. This is more of a hands-on tutorial to important programming techniques, and there is value in having a real textbook too. Not only will it provide you with a more formal explanation of why certain techniques work, but it will also serve as a useful reference. Online resources are great, but sometimes it is good to have information that has been meticulously vetted by academics and publishers.

- Thomas Cormen, Charles Leiserson, Ronald Rivest, and Clifford Stein, *Introduction to Algorithms*, 3rd edition (MIT Press, 2009), https://mitpress.mit.edu/books/introduction-algorithms-third-edition.
  - This is one of the most-cited texts in computer science—so definitive that it is often just referred to by the initials of its authors: CLRS
  - Comprehensive and rigorous in its coverage
  - Its teaching style is sometimes seen as less approachable than other texts, but it is still an excellent reference.
  - Pseudocode is provided for most algorithms.
  - A fourth edition is being developed, and because this book is expensive, it may be worth looking into when the fourth edition is due to be released.
- Robert Sedgewick and Kevin Wayne, *Algorithms*, 4th edition (Addison-Wesley Professional, 2011), http://algs4.cs.princeton.edu/home/.
  - An approachable yet comprehensive introduction to algorithms and data structures
  - Well organized with full examples of all algorithms in Java
  - Popular in college algorithms classes
- Steven Skiena, *The Algorithm Design Manual*, 2nd edition (Springer, 2011), http://www.algorist.com.
  - Different in its approach from other textbooks in this discipline
  - Offers less code but more descriptive discussion of appropriate uses of each algorithm
  - Offers a "choose your own adventure"-like guide to a wide range of algorithms
- Aditya Bhargava, *Grokking Algorithms* (Manning, 2016), https://www.manning.com/books/grokking-algorithms.
  - A graphical approach to teaching basic algorithms, with cute cartoons to boot
  - Not a reference textbook, but instead a guide to learning some basic selected topics for the first time

B.3   *Artificial intelligence*

Artificial intelligence is changing our world. In this book you not only were introduced to some traditional artificial intelligence search techniques like A* and minimax, but also to techniques from its exciting subdiscipline, machine learning, like k-means and neural networks. Learning more about artificial intelligence is not only interesting, but also will ensure you are prepared for the next wave of computing.

- Stuart Russell and Peter Norvig, *Artificial Intelligence: A Modern Approach*, 3rd edition (Pearson, 2009), http://aima.cs.berkeley.edu.
  - The definitive textbook on AI, often used in college courses
  - Wide in its breadth
  - Excellent source code repositories (implemented versions of the pseudocode in the book) available online
- Stephen Lucci and Danny Kopec, *Artificial Intelligence in the 21st Century*, 2nd edition (Mercury Learning and Information, 2015), http://mng.bz/1N46.
  - An approachable text for those looking for a more down-to-earth and colorful guide than Russell and Norvig
  - Interesting vignettes on practitioners and many references to real-world applications
- Andrew Ng, "Machine Learning" course (Stanford University), https://www.coursera.org/learn/machine-learning/.
  - A free online course that covers many of the fundamental algorithms in machine learning
  - Taught by a world-renowned expert
  - Often referenced as a great starting point in the field by practitioners

B.4   *Functional programming*

Python can be programmed in a functional style, but it wasn't really designed for that. Delving into the reaches of functional programming is possible in Python itself, but it can also be helpful to work in a purely functional language and then take some of the ideas you learn from that experience back to Python.

- Harold Abelson and Gerald Jay Sussman with Julie Sussman, *Structure and Interpretation of Computer Programs* (MIT Press, 1996), https://mitpress.mit.edu/sicp/.
  - A classic introduction to functional programming often used in introductory computer science college classes
  - Teaches in Scheme, an easy-to-pick-up, purely functional language
  - Available online for free
- Aslam Khan, *Grokking Functional Programming* (Manning, 2018), https://www.manning.com/books/grokking-functional-programming.
  - A graphical and friendly introduction to functional programming

- David Mertz, *Functional Programming in Python* (O'Reilly, 2015), https://www.oreilly.com/programming/free/functional-programming-python.csp.
  - Gives a basic introduction to some functional programming utilities in the Python standard library
  - Free
  - Only 37 pages long—not very comprehensive, but instead a kickstart

B.5   *Open source projects useful for machine learning*

There are several useful third-party Python libraries optimized for high-performance machine learning. A couple of these projects were mentioned in chapter 7. These projects offer more features and utility than you can probably develop yourself. For serious machine learning or big data applications, you should use these libraries (or their equivalents).

- NumPy, http://www.numpy.org.
  - The de facto standard Python numeric library
  - Implemented largely in C for fast performance
  - Underlies many Python machine-learning libraries, including TensorFlow and scikit-learn
- TensorFlow, https://www.tensorflow.org.
  - One of the most popular Python libraries for working with neural networks
- pandas, https://pandas.pydata.org.
  - Popular library for importing data sets into Python and manipulating them
- scikit-learn, http://scikit-learn.org/stable/.
  - Well-tested and feature-full versions of several of the machine-learning algorithms taught in this book (and many, many more)

appendix C
A brief introduction to type hints

Python introduced type hints (or type annotations) as an official part of the language through PEP 484 and Python version 3.5. Since then, type hints have become more common throughout many Python codebases, and the language has added more robust support for them. Type hints are used in every source code listing in this book. In this short appendix, I aim to introduce type hints, explain why they are useful, explain some of their problems, and link you to more in-depth resources about them.

> **WARNING** This appendix is not meant to be comprehensive. Instead, it's a brief kickstart. Please see the official Python documentation for details: https://docs.python.org/3/library/typing.html.

C.1   What are type hints?

Type hints are a way of annotating the expected types of variables, function parameters, and function return types in Python. In other words, they are a way that a programmer can indicate the type that is expected in a certain part of a Python program. Most Python programs are written without type hints. In fact, before reading this book, even if you are an intermediate Python programmer, it is very possible that you have never seen a Python program with type hints.

Because Python does not require the programmer to specify the type of a variable, the only way to figure out the type of a variable without type hints is through inspection (literally reading the source code up to that point or running it and printing the type) or documentation. This is problematic because it makes Python code harder to read (although some would say the opposite, and we will get to that later in this appendix). Another issue is that because Python is very flexible, it allows the programmer to use the same variable to refer to multiple types of

195

objects, which can lead to errors. Type hints can help prevent this style of programming and alleviate these errors.

Now that Python has type hints, we call it a *gradually typed* language—meaning that
you can use type annotations when you want to, but they are not required. In this
short introduction I hope to convince you (despite perhaps your resistance to how
they fundamentally change the look of the language) that having type hints available
is a good thing—a good thing that you should take advantage of in your code.

C.2   *What do type hints look like?*

Type hints are added to the line of code where a variable or a function is declared.
A colon (:) is used to indicate the start of a type hint for a variable or a function
parameter, and an arrow (->) is used to indicate the start of a type hint for a function
return type. For example, take the following line of Python code:

```
def repeat(item, times):
```

Without reading the function definition, can you tell what this function is supposed to
do? Is it supposed to print out a string a certain number of times? Is it supposed to do
something else? Of course, one could read the function definition to figure out what
it's supposed to do, but that would take more time. The author of this function has
also, unfortunately, not provided any documentation. Let's try it again with type hints:

```
def repeat(item: Any, times: int) -> List[Any]:
```

That's a lot clearer. Just looking at the type hints, it would appear that this function
takes an `item` of `Any` type and returns a `List` filled with `times` number of that item. Of
course, documentation would still help make this function more understandable, but
at least the user of this library now knows what kind of values to supply it and what
kind of value it can be expected to return.

Suppose the library that this function is supposed to be used with only works with
floating-point numbers, and this function was meant to be used as a setup for lists to be
used in other functions. We can easily change the type hints to indicate the floating-
point constraint:

```
def repeat(item: float, times: int) -> List[float]:
```

Now it's clear that `item` must be a `float`, and the returned list will be filled with
`floats`. Well, the word *must* is rather strong. Type hints, as of Python 3.7, have no bear-
ing on the execution of a Python program. They truly are just hints rather than musts.
At runtime, a Python program can completely ignore its type hints and break any of its
supposed constraints. However, type-checker tooling can evaluate the type hints in a
program during development and tell the programmer if there are any illegitimate
calls to a function. A call of `repeat("hello", 30)` can be caught before it enters production (because `"hello"` is not a `float`).

Let's look at one more example. This time, we will examine a type hint for a variable declaration:

```
myStrs: List[str] = repeat(4.2, 2)
```

That type hint does not make sense. It says that `myStrs` is expected to be a list of strings. But we know from the previous type hint that `repeat()` returns a list of floats. Again, because Python, as of version 3.7, does not verify type hints for correctness during execution, this mistaken type hint will have no effect on the running of the program. However, a type checker could catch this programmer error or misconception about the right type before it became a disaster

C.3 *Why are type hints useful?*

Now that you know what type hints are, you may be wondering why all of this trouble is worth it. After all, you have also learned that type hints are ignored by Python at runtime. Why would one spend all this time adding type annotations to the code when the Python interpreter couldn't care less? As has already been touched upon, type hints are a good idea for two primary reasons: They self-document the code, and they allow a type checker to verify the correctness of a program prior to execution.

In most programming languages with static typing (like Java or Haskell), required type declarations make it very clear what parameters a function (or method) expects and what type it will return. This alleviates some of the documentation burden on the programmer. For instance, it is completely unnecessary to specify what the following Java method expects as parameters or return type:

```
/* Eats the world, returning the amount of money generated as refuse. */
public float eatWorld(World w, Software s) { … }
```

Contrast this with the required documentation for the equivalent method written in traditional Python, without type hints:

```
# Eat the world
# Parameters:
# w - the World to eat
# s - the Software to eat the World with
# Returns:
# The amount of money generated by eating the world as a float
def eat_world(w, s):
```

By allowing us to self-document our code, type hints make Python documentation as succinct as statically typed languages:

```
# Eat the world, returning the amount of money generated as refuse.
def eat_world(w: World, s: Software) -> float:
```

Take it to an extreme. Imagine you inherit a codebase that has no comments whatsoever. Will a commentless codebase be easier to make sense of with type hints or without type hints? The type hints will save you from having to dig into the actual code of a commentless function to understand what types to pass it as parameters and what type to expect it to return.

Remember, a type hint is essentially a way of stating what type is expected at some point in a program. Yet Python does nothing to verify this expectation. That's where a type checker comes in. A type checker can take a file of Python source code filled with type hints and verify if they actually will hold when the program is run.

There are multiple different type checkers for Python type hints. For example, the popular Python IDE PyCharm has a type checker built in. If you edit a program in PyCharm with type hints, it will automatically point out type errors. This will help you catch your mistakes before you even finish writing a function.

The leading Python type checker, as I write this book, is mypy. The mypy project is led by Guido van Rossum, the same person who originally created Python itself. Does that leave any doubt in your mind that type hints could potentially have a very prominent role in the future of Python? After you install mypy, using it is as simple as running `mypy example.py`, where `example.py` is the name of the file you want to type check. mypy will spit out to the console all of the type errors in your program or nothing if there are no errors.

There may be other ways type hints will be useful in the future. Right now, type hints have no impact on the performance of a running Python program. (To reiterate one last time, they are ignored at runtime.) But it is possible that future versions of Python will use the type information from type hints to perform optimizations. In such a world, perhaps you will be able to speed up the execution of your Python program by simply adding type hints. This is pure speculation, of course. I know of no plans to implement type hint-based optimizations in Python.

C.4   *What are the downsides of type hints?*

There are three potential downsides of using type hints:

- Code with type hints takes longer to write than code without type hints.
- Type hints can arguably lead to a decrease of readability in some cases.
- Type hints are still not fully baked, and implementing some typing constraints with Python's current implementations can be confusing.

Code with type hints takes longer to write for two reasons: It's simply more typing (literally more keys hit on the keyboard), and you have to reason more about your code. Reasoning about your code is almost always a good thing, but doing extra reasoning will slow you down. However, you will hopefully make up for that lost time by catching errors with a type checker before your program even runs. The time spent debugging errors that could be caught by a type checker is probably greater than the time spent reasoning about types at composition time for any complex codebase.

Some people find Python code with type hints less readable than Python code without them. The two reasons for this are probably unfamiliarity and verbosity. Any syntax you are not familiar with is going to be less readable than a syntax you are familiar with. Type hints really do change the look of Python programs, making them potentially unfamiliar at first. This can only be alleviated by writing and reading more Python code with type hints. The second issue, verbosity, is more fundamental. Python is famous for its concise syntax. Often the same program in Python is significantly shorter than its equivalent in another language. Python code with type hints is not as compact. It cannot be as quickly scanned by the naked eye; there's just a lot more there. The tradeoff is that the understanding of the code can be greater following the first read, even if that read takes longer. With type hints, you immediately see all of the expected types, which is a leg up over having to scan the code itself to understand the types or having to read the documentation.

Finally, type hints are still in flux. They have definitely improved since they were first introduced in Python 3.5, but there are still edge cases in which type hints do not work well. An example of this is in chapter 2. The `Protocol` type, usually an important part of a type system, is not yet in the Python standard library's typing module, so it was necessary in chapter 2 to include the third-party `typing_extensions` module. There are plans to include `Protocol` in a future version of the official Python standard library, but the fact that it's not included is a testament to the fact that these are still early days for type hints in Python. Throughout the writing of this book, I ran into several such edge cases that were confusing to solve, given the existing primitives available in the standard library. Because type hints are not required in Python, it is okay at this stage to just ignore them in areas where they would be inconvenient to use. You can still get some benefit by using type hints halfway.

C.5 *Getting more information*

Every chapter of this book is filled with examples of type hints, but it is not a tutorial on using type hints. The best place to get started with type hints is Python's official documentation for the typing module (https://docs.python.org/3/library/typing.html). That documentation explains not only all of the different built-in types that are available, but also how to use them for several advanced scenarios, beyond the scope of this brief introduction.

The other type hint resource that you should really check out is the mypy project (http://mypy-lang.org). mypy is the leading Python type checker. In other words, it is the piece of software that you will use to actually verify the validity of your type hints. Beyond installing it and using it, you should also check out mypy's documentation (https://mypy.readthedocs.io/). The documentation is rich and explains how to use type hints in some scenarios that the standard library's documentation does not. For instance, one particularly confusing area is generics. The mypy generics documentation is a good starting point. Another nice resource is the "type hints cheat sheet" put out by mypy (https://mypy.readthedocs.io/en/stable/cheat_sheet_py3.html).

index